CONGRESS, PARLIAMENT AND DEFENCE

Also by Andrew Cox

ADVERSARY POLITICS AND LAND

POLITICS, POLICY AND THE EUROPEAN RECESSION (*editor*)

THE POLITICS OF URBAN CHANGE

POWER IN CAPITALIST SOCIETY

CONGRESS, PARLIAMENT AND DEFENCE

The Impact of Legislative Reform on Defence Accountability in Britain and America

Andrew Cox
Senior Lecturer in Politics
University of Hull

and

Stephen Kirby
Lecturer in Politics
University of Hull

M
MACMILLAN

First published 1986
Published by
THE MACMILLAN PRESS LTD
Houndmills, Basingstoke, Hampshire RG21 2XS
and London
Companies and representatives
throughout the world

Typeset by Vine & Gorfin Ltd, Exmouth, Devon

Printed in Hong Kong

Cox, Andrew
Congress, Parliament and defence: the impact of legislative reform on defence accountability in Britain and America.
1. Great Britain. *Parliament* 2. Great Britain -National security 3. Great Britain—Military policy 4. United States, *Congress* 5. United States—National security 6. United States—Military policy
I. Title II. Kirby, Stephen
327.41 US647
ISBN 0-333-30927-8

Contents

List of Figures

Fig. 1.2 is from J. Ronald Fox, *Arming America: How the U.S. Buys Weapons* (Boston: Division of Research, Harvard Business School, 1974) p. 39 (adapted from Lt. Col. David I. Cleland and, First Lt. William R. King, 'The Defense Market System'. *Defence Industry Bulletin* (Jan. 1968) p. 7; Figs 2.3 and 2.4 are from David Heald, *Public Expenditure: Its Defence and Reform* (London: Martin Robertson, 1983) pp. 24, 25; Fig. 4.1 is from *Long Range Planning* (Nov. 1970) p. 21; and Figs 4.2 and 4.3 are from Malcolm Chalmers, *The Cost of Britain's Defence* (Peace Studies Paper, No. 10, University of Bradford, 1984) pp. 55, 56.

List of Tables

Table 2.1 is from *Economic Trends, Annual Supplement, 1985* (HMSO) p. 8; Tables 4.1 and 4.3 are from Malcolm Chalmers, *The Cost of Britain's Defence* (Peace Studies Paper, No. 10, University of Bradford, 1984) pp. 72 and 74; and Table 8.2 is from L. Freedman, 'Britain's Contributions to NATO', *International Affairs*, Vol. 54 (Jan. 1978) p. 38.

Preface

As usual with the preparation of any book the authors incur an enormous number of debts to those who have given their time and knowledge to assist in the research effort undertaken. We would like, therefore, to thank all those-legislators, Civil Servants, servicemen, defence committee staff members, academics and defence contractors – who have assisted us in Britain and America. A particular vote of thanks must, however, go to John Bourn and Peter Nailor for their efforts in enabling us to understand the complexities of the system of defence accountability in Britain and America. We also give a vote of thanks of the (British) Economic and Social Research Council for providing financial assistance to enable us to undertake extensive research work on both sides of the Atlantic. Finally we would like to express our thanks to Enid and Pat for their efforts in the preparation of the typescript. The ideas and arguments presented here are, however, our own and neither the ESRC nor anyone mentioned here is responsible for them.

ANDREW COX and STEPHEN KIRBY

Introduction: Defence Accountability and the Public Interest

Britain in the mid-1980s has been exposed to a number of highly embarrassing revelations concerning the defence and security establishments and its own citizens. Under the Thatcher administration there have been a whole series of contentious issues which have questioned the traditional assumption that Parliament is able to control and make accountable the activities of the defence and national security services. Perhaps the most obvious of these has been the Belgrano or Ponting case. In this case a senior civil servant in the Ministry of Defence chose to leak information to a Member of Parliament about the sinking of an Argentinian cruiser during the Falklands War. The civil servant's defence was that the executive and the Services were using the cloak of national security to defend their own personal and party political reputations from embarrassment. This, Clive Ponting argued, was not in the 'national interest' and, therefore, he had a duty to provide information to Parliament which did not jeopardise national security to ensure accountability of the defence establishment. At his subsequent trial in early 1985 Clive Ponting's view was upheld by jury despite the fact that the judge in the case argued that Ponting was guilty of breaking the official secrets act.

This is not the only case of a similar nature. Preceding this was the case of a Ministry of Defence secretary – one Sara Tisdale – who was imprisoned for six months for leaking information on the arrival of Cruise missiles in Britain, which the Ministry of Defence wanted to keep secret. In January 1985 a low ranking civil servant, named Clive Williams, was jailed for a similar period for receiving £1500 from the Observer newspaper for information on waste and cost over-runs in the procurement of naval equipment which was not readily available in Parliament.

Taken with the banning of trade union activity at GCHQ (Britain's intelligence surveillance centre) many on the left of British politics have seen these discrete examples as evidence of a growing lack of accountability in the field of defence. This is seen to be so because it is unusual in Britain to have so many individuals indicted for leaking defence information on the grounds that Parliamentary democracy and civil liberties are being undermined. Indeed this was the basis also on which a former MI5 agent – Cathy Massiter – made a number of revelations in early 1985 about the unlawful interception of mail and phone-tapping of perfectly legally constituted trade unions and pressure groups – such as Friends of the Earth, the Campaign for Nuclear Disarmament and the National Council for Civil Liberties.

While 1984 and 1985 have witnessed an apparent plethora of revelations of this kind in Britain such findings are not unique on the other side of the Atlantic. One can see from the evidence as presented during the Watergate scandal that the use by the executive branch of covert surveillance agencies – like the CIA – to burgle, intercept mail, tap wires and indulge in dirty tricks was taken to a fine art under the Nixon administration. More worrying, perhaps, for those who see this as an attack on civil liberties is not the fact that Nixon indulged in such practices to excess, and used the blanket cover or 'national security' to hide his misdemeanours, but the fact that the previous administrations had also used similar techniques – if not to the same degree or with the personally damaging effects as Richard Nixon. Revelations by former CIA agents like Philip Agee in the 1970s indicate that the accountabilty of the Security Services in the United States are, and have been, open to serious question.[1] Furthermore, as the 1985 court case of General Westmorland – one of the key military figures in the Vietnam war – reveals, the defence establishment itself has not been reticent in lying to Congress or doctoring figures to ensure enhanced expenditure and a maintenance of legislative commitment.

All of these developments are worrying to those concerned with the defence of civil liberties and the protection of parliamentary democracy. They are not, however, the only problems associated with the accountabilty of the defence establishment. While these issues and scandals have made the headlines in the media they can be seen as only the 'tip of an iceberg'. What then is the true nature of the problem? President Eisenhower in his final address spoke of the growth of a 'military–industrial complex' developing in America. Eisenhower argued that whether consciously or unwittingly a collusive relationship had developed between the defence establishment and large corporations in America. He feared that the financial and lobbying power of this complex might usurp the power of the legislature and the executive branch and ensure that public expenditure and defence policy priorities would be shaped exclusively by it.[2]

This theme of growing dominance of national policy and priorities by the defence establishments was taken up in the 1960s and early 1970s by liberals in America. Writers like J. K. Galbraith and Senator William Proxmire, who experienced the massive increase in defence expenditure during thenVietnam war argued that neither Congress nor the President and the executive branch were in a position either to control defence spending or wrest control of foreign and defence policy from the military–industrial complex.[3]

In Britain similar fears have been expressed by those on the left of the political spectrum. While the scale of a 'military–industrial complex' as witnessed in the United States has not been evident in Britain it has been argued that Britain has maintained foreign and defence policy commitments and expenditure levels way beyond the levels which the post-war economy has been able to sustain. This is not to deny that since the 1950s British defence commitments have been subject to continuous review and cumulative cuts. Rather it is to argue that while Britain has reduced its defence establishment it has still managed to spend more than any other of its NATO partners (excluding the United States of course) as a percentage of GNP on defence. The point critics make here is that this has been achieved despite the fact that Britain's economic performance has been one of the worst of the NATO allies.

Thus, while one cannot argue that Britain has a 'military–industrial complex' of the size of the United States there is an opinion in Parliament and the country that Britain's defence expenditure and commitments have been much higher than the nation can afford. Furthermore, as the experience of numerous cost and time over-runs in weapon systems procurement (from the TSR-2 in the 1960s to Tornado in the 1970s and the Trident nuclear weapon system in the 1980s) indicate, there is a sense that the legislature and the public have not always been able to scrutinise defence policy adequately.

Clearly, while defence policy and spending is a unique field of legislative scrutiny, because of its attachment to difficult issues associated with national security, there has been disquiet in Britain and the United States about the ability of the legislature to oversee defence spending and policy-making. Thus, while the security scandals outlined earlier are the most glaring examples of this disquiet it is the continuous post-war inability of legislatures to scrutinise and oversee a relatively high level of post-war defence expenditure which has occasioned most alarm. This is most glaringly revealed not by the Ponting or Watergate revelations but by the continous tendency for weapons procurement to escalate well beyond intended initial costs; by the failure of the legislature to query executive policy priorities or discover the information to allow a rational and dispassionate conclusion to be drawn; and, by the inability of the legislative to impose its own guidelines on expenditure totals for the various services or the defence budget as a whole.

In the remainder of this book we set out the findings of a research exercise which was conducted in Britain and America in the late 1970s and early 1980s. The aim of this exercise was to assess whether it is possible for the legislature to reform itself in order that it might be better able to scrutinise and control defence policy-making and expenditure in the public interest. The 1970s were of particular importance in this regard because in both legislatures – Congress and Parliament – a majority for institutional reform was created. While this majority was not aimed specifically at the oversight of defence alone, the need to enhance legislative scrutiny of defence was a salient issue for a significant number of the MPs and Congressmen and Senators involved.

As we shall see the impact of reform was not all that it might have been. While the new committee structures have enhanced the role of Congress and Parliament in finding out more about what is happening in defence, they have not led to the creation of a controlling or fully-fledged oversight role for defence accountabilty. Ther are a number of reasons for this of which the most important appear to be the shroud which the phase 'national security' can throw over an inquisitive legislature and the unwillingness of legislators to create an effective legisative role.

To state these broad conclusions here is, however, to run ahead of the evidence. The inability of reforms to transform either Congress or Parliament's defence role is explained in what follows. In the first two chapters we outline some of the problems of making defence accountable and the historical background to the reform movement in Congress and Parliament. Having outlined the high hopes envisaged for the new committee structures in the 1970s an analysis is made of three broad issues in each country. The three issues are defence expenditure levels, procurement policy and manpower policy. By analysing the way Congress and Parliament dealt with each of these issues prior to and in the wake of the 1970s reforms we are able to indicate the reasons why defence accountabilty is so difficult to achieve. In our final chapter we outline the broad reasons why reform has failed to achieve all that was intended of it. We also briefly outline why a further reform in Britain in the period after 1979 was bound to fail and, finally, we offer some tentative suggestions as to how reforms which would enhance defence accountability without fundamentally jeopardising national security might be achieved.

NOTES

1. Philip Agee, *Inside the Company: CIA Diary* (Middlesex, Harmondsworth, Penguin, 1975).
2. Quoted in William Proxmire, *Report from Wasteland* (New York: Praeger, 1970) p. 8.
3. J. K. Galbraith, *How to Control the Military* (London: NCLC Publishing Society, 1971).

Part I
The General Issues of Reform

1 Congress, Parliament and Defence Accountability

In essence accountabilty is the obligation on those who have been delegated to carry out public functions to reveal, to explain and to account financially for their actions and decisions.[1] In the field of defence the principal decisions are those about the proper allocation of resources for defence as against other public spending programmes; and, decisions about the proper allocation and management of resources within the defence programme. These decisions may be held accountable in at least three different ways. At the level of *policy accountability*, governments are required to offer justifications and explanations for the priority given to defence within the overall programme of public expenditure. *Programme accountability* is concerned with demonstrating that defence programmes are achieving the objective set for them. *Financial accountability* is concerned with checking the legality and probity of exenditure for defence, as well as providing procedures for checking that monies are spent economically and without waste. In its most extended form, financial accountability also involves checks that monies are spent efficiently and that optimum use is made of resources.[2]

The nature of the executive–legislative relationship is one of the major factors which determines how these forms of accountability can be exercised effectively.

In Britain (as we shall see in Chapter 2) Parliament's position *vis-à-vis* the executive denies it an effective strategic role which would enable it to hold the executive accountable at the policy level. Parliament is able to address the priorities established among public spending programmes in only a formal way and, at best, the British government has a duty 'to offer a political justification of its proposals to the House of Commons and to confirm this by mobilising its supporters in their defence'.[3] In the United States, the potential for accountability is wider than this because Congress, without a system of strong party discipline, is able independently to establish priorities for public spending. This gives it a strategic role in respect of the executive and encourages both the President and the Secretary of Defense to provide more detailed justification of defence policy. This is necessary in order to win the necessary congressional approval for their proposals.

The executive–legislative relationship is, however, only one factor which shapes the potential for accountability; the other is the strength of the procedures that the executive and its departments use to manage and account for the funds that are voted for public programmes including defence. It has been accepted by the Comptroller General in the United States[4] and by many academics in the United Kingdom[5] that the primary responsibility for accountability lies not with the legislature, but with the executive departments and ultimately with the head of government. It must be emphasised that no legislative procedure or legislative committee can *make* the executive accountable. The same is true of those auditing agencies, like the General Accounting Office (GAO) in the United States and the Audit and Exchequer Department (A&ED) in the United Kingdom, that assist the congressional and parliamentary committees. Legislators, the committees they man, the procedures they operate and the agencies upon which they rely cannot operate as a substitute for an accountable executive.

Quite clearly the constitutions of the United States and the United Kingdom lay responsibility for the formulation of defence policy, and recommendations about the allocation of resources to fulfil it, on their respective executives.[6] It is at this level that the major responsibility for policy accountability rests. A similar point may be made about programme accountability. The evaluation of the effectiveness of a programme in meeting its stated objectives is an essential part of efficient departmental management[7] and cannot be conducted by the legislature or any of its agencies. Of particular importance in programme management is the regulation and control of contractural arrangements between defence suppliers and defence departments, but here again primary responsibility lies with the Department.[8] Defence accounting in Britain is audited by the A&ED on behalf of the House of Commons, and the accounting methods used by the Department of Defence (DOD) are reviewed and authorised by the GAO, which also audits the defence accounts. In both Britain and America, however, the auditing function is essentially retrospective, and the probity and effectiveness of financial management is a major responsibility of the departments.

The potential for holding an executive department accountable is a product of the procedures that exist within them for considering priorities, for managing programmes and for accounting for monies. Without the exercise of responsible political judgement, efficient departmental management and systematic accounting, the executive would be unable to render an account of its activities and decisions to the legislature no matter how frequently legislators demanded that it should, and no matter how extensive and proficient the agencies that assist them. It is the combination of executive procedures for accountability and the executive–legislative relationship that determines the potential for accountability in the United States and the United Kingdom.

However, the degree to which that potential may be realised by Congress and Parliament rests upon other factors. Changes in legislative committee structures and in legislative procedures are important and will be considered at length in later chapters. Of considerable importance, however, are the size, power and competence of the agencies that assist Congress and Parliament in their oversight and audit role, as too are the independent resources of information and expertise that are available to congressional and parliamentary committees concerned with defence. The final factor that will condition the extent to which the potential for accountability in defence is realised is the nature of the defence activity itself which raises special problems such as the high priority placed upon secrecy, the difficulties that arise from working at the forefront of high-technology and the unusual conditions that prevail in the defence market. This chapter examines the extent to which the realisation of the potential for accountability in the United States and the United Kingdom is facilitated or hindered by the agencies that assist and have assisted Congress and Parliament, by the resources of information and expertise available to Congress and Parliament when dealing with defence, and by the special problems of defence itself.

PARLIAMENTARY AUDIT

Traditionally in Britain the Ministry of Defence (MOD) and the Government were held accountable in defence issues by Parliamentary audit. Since 1866 Parliament relied upon the Comptroller and Auditor General (C&AG) and his staff to assist in exercising most facets of financial accountability and, to a growing extent in recent years, also to exercise programme accountability. The statutory basis for the C&AGs role has excluded any consideration by him of policy issues, and there has been almost no demand from Parliament that he should.[9]

The statutory bases of the C&AGs authority are the Exchequer and Audit Department Acts of 1866 and 1921, which enact provisions that were intended to prevent government abuse in public expenditure rather than to allow the evaluation of the performance of central government departments. Despite considerable pressure from Commons committees, and from those called to give evidence before them,[10] successive governments have regarded as unnecessary a change in the legislative authority of the C&AG.[11] It is true however that the 1866 and 1921 Acts do not specify the scope of the audit to be carried out by the C&AG, and that, with the encouragement of the PAC, three principal forms of audit are now conducted by the Comptroller and his staff in the E&AD.

The traditional and still most frequently conducted audit concerns finance and the regularity of payments. The financial audit is one in which the C&AG checks the efficiency of accounting and financial control exercised by deparments and checks that financial transactions are properly authorised and accounted for. The 'regulatory' audit verifies that expenditure has been incurred on approved services and in accordance with statutory and other authority. From the beginning of this century, but increasingly in recent years,[12] the C&AG has also conducted value for money (VFM) audits by examining the economy and efficiency of departmental expenditures to bring to light waste, or extravagant spending. In this sort of audit, the C&AG has also been able to identify both the failure of departments to maximise receipts and the existence of financial arrangements that are detrimental to the exchequer. Most recently, and only in 'appropriate cases', the C&AG has extended value for money auditing to consider the effectiveness of departmental management, by assessing whether programmes or projects undertaken to meet established goals have in fact met them.[13]

These forms of audit provided the C&AG with the capacity and the expertise to conduct enquiries that could assist the Commons in calling the executive and the MOD to account at the financial and programme levels. There are several factors, however, that constrain the value and scope of that assistance. The first is that the C&AG is an office holder of the Crown and not a servant of the House of Commons; his role is simply to conduct audits 'on behalf of the

House of Commons'.[14] Members of Parliament traditionally complained that this allowed undue influence to be exerted by the executive over the C&AG and his department especially since the Civil Service Department has control over E&AD staff numbers and gradings. This point is not without force, and Sir Douglas Henley, noted in a letter of evidence to the PAC that

> Within E&AD, the increasing attention to economy and efficiency in the use of public money was paralled by a very restrictive attitude to its own use of resources. Its staff numbers (440 in 1950 rising to 580 in 1970) were not increased in any way commensurate with the growth of public spending and its audit responsibilities[15]

A management review of the A&ED in the 1978–79 session, conducted with the assistance of the Treasury and the Civil Service Department, confirmed that there was serious understaffing in the department and that numbers, which had reached 680 by March 1980, should be increased by 5% per year for five years, but that this could only be done with the 'Government's co-operation'.[16]

It is clear from the Comptroller's evidence that his department was unable to operate on an extensive scale, and this is confirmed by the fact that only 47 enquiries were conducted into defence issues between 1965 and 1978.[17] This fact relates and tends to compound another problem that arises from the status of the C&AG. As a servant of the Crown, he is able to exercise discretion about the studies and enquiries that his department undertakes. Frequent requests from Parliament that the C&AG should conduct enquiries at the request of any House of Commons select committee have been refused by the government on the grounds that such direction would limit the independence of the C&AG's office.[18] However, it is the existence of that independence which has concerned Parliament. Among the 47 defence reports conducted from 1965 to 1978, no more than a dozen concerned major defence projects, [19] whereas 'stores and their accounting deficiencies were examined repeatedly'[20] and covered such issues as cronograph watches, surpluses of army boots and navy catering frauds. These issues are no doubt important, but command only a fraction of the annual MOD budget compared to major equipment projects. The infrequency of major project studies by the A&ED no doubt reflects the lack of staff and resources already noted, and the relative paucity of major projects that the MOD had underway at any one time, although many such projects have gone unstudied. However, the inability of Parliament to decide how the C&AG's resources are deployed undermines its capacity to call the executive and the MOD to account in any specific or precise way.

Yet this lack of specificity accords with the views of past and present governments which have argued that the role of the C&AG could only be viewed in the context 'of the general framework of Parliamentary accountability which is based on the principal that Parliament grants the supply to the Crown and holds the Ministers of Her Majesty's Administration accountable for the use made of it.'[21] This policy has beeen promoted despite the fact that Parliament's lack of a srategic role and the frequency of disciplined government majorities in the Commons have rendered 'the formal framework of Parliamentary accountability' vacuous. Successive governments have also refused to give value-for-money and efficiency auditing any statutory basis by insisting upon the adequacy of the 1866 and 1921 acts. There has been a similar insistance that financial and regulatory audit should remain the foundation of the C&AG's work as a whole, even though it is recognised that 'it is difficult nowadays to relate them and their underlying assumptions directly to the way in which government manages and accounts for public spending or to the work of a modern national audit office'.[22]

The manner in which modern governments manage and account for defence spending not only relates poorly to the statutory basis and the assumptions of the C&AG, but it is also beyond the C&AG's authority to improve it even when problems have been identified. The 1866 Act enables the C&AG to look at deficiencies in departmental accounting systems, but the Treasury has the final say in the form that departmental accounting and management systems will take.[23] All departments follow a common vote accounting guide issued by the Treasury, even though it has remained relatively unchanged over many years.[24] Yet the PAC has noted that these systems frequently do not provide the minister with 'the information he reasonably needs in order to control the public expenditure for which he is responsible. This means that the form of public expenditure is often not sufficiently tested to see whether the same result could be obtained for less money or indeed better results for the same money'.[25] Such conclusions would appear corroborated by the major project studies which the C&AG did carry out in the field of defence and which revealed that every project over-ran its original estimates, and that no responsibility could ever be allocated for faulty design, late delivery or even for an abandoned project.[26] In its report on the General Management of the Executive Branch in America, the Hoover Commission established as early as 1949 the general principle that without responsibility there can be no accountability,[27] yet every one of the C&AG's reports on major defence projects and the PAC's enquiries based upon them have failed to meet that principle.

The C&AG's reports have had even less impact upon Parliament's ability to hold the executive accountable than even these shortcomings would suggest. The main reason is that the C&AG reports to the PAC alone and makes no recommendations or criticisms in its reports. The PAC with only 15 members is clearly limited in its ability to follow up on the Comptroller's reports, and even though its work is highly respected in Parliament its reports over 13 years were debated by a grand total of 98 MPs.[28] In addition, the C&AG is unable to conduct enquiries for other select committees on the grounds that he is debarred from considering the merits of particular policy objectives which are the concern of these other select committees, and that to assist them would also 'put at risk traditionally non-partisan character of examination by the PAC of matters raised in the C&AG's reports'.[29] Even when E&AD staff were seconded to other select committees, such as the Defence and External Affairs subcommittee of the Select Committee on Expenditure in the 1970s, it was argued that they: 'do not act as auditors, are not responsible to (the C&AG), and do not have the rights of access to departmental books and and papers'.[30] This means that the work of the C&AG, which is vital to the execution of financial and programme accountability, is confined to a single committee the *modus operandi* of which has been characterised by a study of politically non-controversial issues and whose members are recognised as non-expert and moderate.[31] When reporting on major defence projects, this committee could neither comment on the necessity for such technology, nor allocate responsibility when it was mismanaged or failed.[32] Other committees, principally SCOE in the 1970s, were vitally concerned with the issues of programme accountability that arose from these studies, yet were unable to tap even the limited resources of the C&AG and his department.

CONGRESSIONAL AUDIT

In sharp distinction to the more than 100 year old statutory basis of the C&AG's office, the statutory authority of the American

Comptroller General and the General Accounting Office has been revised frequently, and there are now some hundreds of statutory provisions authorising and requiring action by the GAO.[33] The Budget and Accounting Act of 1921 remains the foundation of the GAO's authority, and has relevance to all the functions that are carried out today, but 'much of what would have been only permissible earlier . . . now has been made mandatory, explicit, and emphatic – particularly in the assessment of efficiency, economy and the effectiveness of program operation'.[34] The Accounting and Auditing Act of 1950 makes the head of each executive agency responsible for establishing an accounting system that conforms to the principles and standards prescribed by the Comptroller General. The Legislative Reorganisation Act of 1970 reinforces the Comptroller's powers to review and analyse the results of the Government's programmes and activities, and empowered him to do so upon his own initiative, by order of either House of Congress or by the order of any committee in respect of a programme under its jurisdiction. Title VII of the Congressional Budget and Impounded Control Act of 1974 strengthens the GAO's evaluation role and Title VIII places the GAO under a specific obligation to help Congress and its committees improve their fiscal, budgetary and programme related information.[35]

In order to discharge these obligations, the GAO audits and evaluates the operation of nearly all Federal agencies and their programmes, assists congressional committees in developing methods and legislative requirements for evaluation, and also assists them in analysing and assessing the reports evaluation studies produced by the agencies.[36] In addition to this the GAO has advised several congressional committees about proposed sunset and sunrise legislation intended to improve congressional budget oversight and, if such legislation is enacted, it anticipates taking on several new audit and evaluation services for Congress.[37]

This body of legislation establishes the GAO as an arm of and makes it responsible to Congress. The GAO is charged with responding to congressional demands and also, since 1974, with using its own initiative 'to identify and specify the needs of the committees and members of Congress for fiscal, budgetary and program related information'.[38] The growing amount of legislation that contains *specific* requirements for GAO audit and evaluation work demonstrates the importance that Congress and Congressmen attach to it. This is reinforced by the number of requests that are made for reports in addition to the auditing work of the GAO. In the fiscal year ending 30 September 1979, the GAO submitted 285 reports to Congress, 298 to congressional committees, and 101 to individual members of Congress, as well as 299 to Federal agency officials.[39] In the same year the Comptroller General and his principal assistants testified on 188 occasions to congressional committees and 85 GAO staff were assigned to assist the staffs of 19 congressional committees and sub-committees.

The services provided by the GAO are very wide and the most important include:

1. Prescribing for Federal agencies' accounting principles and standards, approval of agencies' accounting systems and designs, and general assistance to agencies in improving their financial management systems.
2. Examination of agencies' financial management, systems and statements.
3. Review of agencies' internal audits.
4. Audit of contracts.
5. Audit of agencies' management efficiency and economy.
6. Audit and detailed analysis of programs at program sites in any geographical area.
7. Comprehensive management audits.
8. Audits which require full access to an agency's records.
9. Providing binding legal decisions (Comptroller General Decisions).
10. Settle and adjudicate claims and demands by or against the United States.
11. Audits and studies to determine compliance with statutes.
12. Statutory review of programmes.[40]

Clearly this range of activity allows the GAO to assist Congress in holding the executive and its agencies accountable at the policy, programme and financial levels. A recent study by a House of Representatives Select Committee indicated as much when it said of the scope of the GAO audit that the 'GAO simply seems to assume that the word "audit" will be accepted as broad enough to cover whatever it may decide to study', and that 'there seems to be very few respects of agency operation or administration into which the GAO will not venture'.[41] However, the Comptroller General has shown a clear understanding of the proper limits to which he and the GAO may go, and has shown restraint in respect of the assistance that can offered at the level of policy accountability. The GAO Audit Manual notes that the office is not intended to be a 'think tank' for Congress on pressing problems, nor should 'it assess overall national program priorities or budget funding requirements'.[42] In 1969 the Comptroller General also persuaded Senators Mondale and Case to withdraw a clause from their amendment to the Defense Procurement Authorization Bill which would have required the GAO specifically to weigh defence policy issues. The Comptroller argued that independent judgement on matters such as military strategy, threat assessment, and foreign policy was beyond the competence of his office.[43] Nevertheless, the GAO Audit Manual says that methods to improve the work of Federal programmes are within GAO's competence and that it should 'assist in the process of program choice',[44] and that in defence issues, that it should provide 'the data needed for Congress to macro-manage the military budgets so that priority programs can be retained'.[45] In this way the GAO has been able to give Congress valuable assistance in holding the executive accountable at the policy level, including defence policy.

In the field of programme accountability the GAO has developed great expertise, and since its reorganisation in 1972 has given much more emphasis to programme evaluation. In September 1974 the Office of Program Analysis was established within GAO, and it was later transformed into the Program Analysis Division (PAD). It has led the work of the GAO in providing evaluation guidelines and methodology, programme and budget information for congressional use, economic analysis of alternative programme approaches, and policy science. Many of its methods have been applied to the management systems and procurement decisions of the DOD by other divisions of the GAO. This is especially the case with the Procurement and Systems Analysis Division (PSAD) which monitors the executive's entire procurement and research and development programmes. Most of the Division's work is concentrated in the DOD, NASA, the defence related work of the Department of Energy and the Federal Supply Service of the General Services Administration.

Elmer B. Statts, the Comptroller General throughout the 1970s, has said that programme accountability is achieved when 'through oversight, responsible political leaders (i) *learn* about executive action and programs, (ii) *judge* the adequacy, appropriateness, and effectiveness of such actions and programs, and (iii) *take any*

CONTENTS

NATIONAL DEFENCE

SOURCE GAO, Summaries of Conclusions and Recommendations on Department of Defence Operations (Washington, GAO, 1981).

Figure 1.1 Summaries of GAO work on Department of Defense activities

necessary action (through new legislation if necessary) on the basis of what has been learned' including the reform of 'governmental administration'.[46] By the late 1970s, 80% of GAO's effort was spent on efficiency auditing, but even at this level of activity the Comptroller noted that the GAO could not act in the place of Congress and that better programme accountability would come about if congresssional committees analysed the potential of their own legislation so as to avoid developing unrealistic expectations of the programmes they authorised. He also recommended Congress to specify in new legislation the form of evaluation and reporting that agencies should carry out, and that congressional committees make better use of the information already available to them.[47] However, the work of the GAO is vital to Congress in carrying out its programme accountability role and, when it concerns major defence procurement issues, the ability of the GAO to conduct contract auditing and comprehensive managerial audits is of particular importance since these audits can be conducted on the defence contractor's production sites. In addition to this, the Comptroller General is the chairman of the Costs Accounting Standards Board (CASB) which sets out guideline for the cost accounting systems used by defence contractors.

The GAO plays a vital role in congressional processes designed to hold the executive accountable and especially so in defence. Of the 5074 GAO staff employed in 1979, 1200 were concerned with defence auditing, and of the 983 reports submitted in fiscal year 1979, 230 were on defence issue excluding those classified reports sent directly to the DOD.[48] Some idea of the scale and scope of defence audit and review work can be gained from the table of contents of the fiscal year 1981 report submitted to Congress by the GAO under the heading 'Summaries of Conclusions and Recommendations on Department of Defense Operations'.[49]

The hallmark of these reports is their thoroughness and also that they make clear recommendations to specific congressional committees to take any necessary remedial action. Thus in a report on DOD profit policy, the GAO recommended that 'the Appropriations Committees should direct the DOD to reduce negotiated profit objectives based on costs to compensate for the increase in profits being allowed on contractor's investment in facilities'.[50]

The status of the GAO as an investigative arm of Congress, the scale and nature of its 'audit' operations and its ability to scrutinise and approve the accounting systems of the DOD and defence contractors makes it vitally important for defence accountability in the United States. Above all else however, its two greatest assets are its ability to respond to congressional requests for assistance, and the exercise of its own initiative to inform and guide all congressional committees, including those for defence, in a way that allows them to discharge their oversight responsibilities most effectively. Compared to the role of the A&ED and the GAO, the availability of independent sources of information for MPs and Congressmen is of less importance for programme and financial accountability, but still has relevance at the policy level. Each parliamentary and congressional committee that deals with defence has some information resources of its own, but there are also the facilities of the House of Commons library in the United Kingdom, and those of the Congressional Research Service (CRS) and The Office of Technology Assessment (OTA) in the United States.

HOUSE OF COMMONS INFORMATION RESOURCES

The House of Commons library has been in existance for 160 years, yet its terms of reference are rather vague. In November 1945, the Select Committee on the Library defined its 'essential purpose' as that of supplying 'Members with information rapidly on any of the multifarious matters which come before the House or to which their attentions are drawn by their parliamentary duties',[51] and there has been little attempt to refine it since. The library is divided into a Research and a Parliamentary Division, with a combined staff compliment in 1980 of 100, few of whom had anything other than a library qualification. The staff are liable to be transferred from division to division within the library. One of the five departments of the Research Division is titled 'Science and Technology Section (including defence)', and, like the others is headed by a Deputy Assistant Librarian who is helped by 'two or three library clerks'.[52] Because the library is open long hours there is always a danger that a particular specialist is not available and therefore all staff must 'be ready to turn their hand quickly to subjects other than their own'. The Deputy Librarian of the House of Commons library has recognised that the results of such a system can at best resemble 'serious journalism',[53] and that the quality of Library research work is further limited by the fact that staff cannot undertake research field-work. The library contains only some 150 000 volumes and the Specialist Scientific Section, which also covers defence issues, is very small.[54]

The Research Division does, however, attempt to provide members with Reference Sheets and Background Papers on several issues including defence, and these are prepared in anticipation of member's needs rather than in response to requests. Inevitably, given the staff and resource limitations, the operation is on a small scale and the Reference Sheets do little more than sort out sources and references for members. The Background Papers are an extension of this and are versions of Reference Sheets 'written up' by '. . . a few staff members who have had to get to grips with a subject over a period of time', and who exercise their own discretion about the sources to list and comment upon. Of eight Background Papers produced between 1977 and 1979, only one was concerned with defence, and of twenty-six Reference Sheets issued in the Sessions 1977–78 and 1978–79, again only one was on defence affairs.[55]

It is clear that the Library can do little to inform the private Member of Parliament, and its resources for defence are particularly limited. Even so, it has offered to do more. In evidence to the Select Committee on Assistance to Private Members in 1975, the Library suggested that members of its research staff could be seconded to serve committees such as SCOE. The Select Committee failed to respond to the offer and its dismissive attitude was reinforced by the Report of the Select Committee on Procedure in the 1977–78 session which recognised that the House of Commons Library was the only existing pool of full-time expert staff directly under the control of the House of Commons and that it could provide useful background information to select committees. It recommended, however, that such work should not be provided 'at the expense of the Library's service to individual members'.[56] Even the provision of reading places for the research assistants of MPs has proved difficult and the decision to allow restricted time and a limited number of places for 150 research assistants in 1978 was seen to be a threat to the privacy that members have come to expect in the House of Commons Library.[57] Clearly the Library has been able to do little more than provide interested members with a good reading knowledge of defence issues. It is prevented by the lack of resources and by the unresponsive attitude of Parliament from providing expert knowledge of any consequence to those committees dealing with defence.

CONGRESSIONAL INFORMATION RESOURCES

In addition to the GAO, congressional committees can call upon the assistance of the Congressional Research Service (CRS), the Office of Technology Assessment (OTA), and the Congressional Budget Office (CBO). The latter is dealt with at length in Chapter 3. The CRS is a department within the Library of Congress and draws upon its vast documentary resources. It works exclusively as a reference and research arm for the members, committees and staff of Congress. In fiscal year 1980, it had a budget of over $27 million and a staff of 614 research and information specialists supported by over 250 clerical and administrative staff. The service responds to inquiries from members and committees and is usually able to produce substantive research studies within two to four weeks on all major policy areas.

The Legislative Reorganisation Act of 1970 transformed the Legislative Reference Service of the Library of Congress into the CRS and also widened its responsibilities and duties to Congress. In common with the GAO, the CRS was given broad, but definite responsibility to help congressional committees 'to recognise and solve their informational problems and to identify and meet their informational needs'.[58] The same Act also charges the CRS

> to make available to each committee of the Senate and House of Representatives and each joint committee of the two Houses, at the opening of a new Congress, a list of subjects and policy areas which the committee might profitably analyse in depth.[59]

The Service is divided into several divisions, one of which deals with inquiries concerning United States' foreign policy, foreign assistance programmes, arms control, weapons acquisition, defence budgets and United States defence posture and policy. This is the Foreign Affairs and National Defence Division (FAND), and its strength 'lies in its ability to define policy choices for Congress in a manner that avoids artificial compartimentalization along traditional "foreign policy" and "national defence" lines. By emphasising the cross-cutting, interactive nature of foreign and defense policy decision-making, the division addresses the major trade-offs inherent in most policy choices'.[60] The work of FAND has, throughout the 1970s, assisted congressional committees in defence programme and policy accountability issues, but recent CRS reports have addressed the issue of setting a priority on defence in an unusually explicit way.

A recent FANBD report on 'US Defense Posture in the 1980s: a Survey of Alternative Planning Factors', notes that

> in recent years, Congress has shown increasing initiative and assertiveness in shaping US defense posture. With the advent of the new congressional budget process, Congress has for the first time begun, *as an institution*, to address the task of establishing priorities for defense spending within the overall budget ceiling.[61]

It continues, 'This study is intended to assist Congress in that process. The central premise of the study is that before one can set about constructing a coherent, across-the-board defence posture "package", one must first come to grips with an extensive set of essentially subjective policy issues.'[62] The implications for congressional policy setting are very clear, and the CRS reports of this sort have focused congressional attitudes on defence policy issues more cleary than at any time in the past. In addition to these, other FAND reports provide Congressmen and defence committees with evidence that assists them in programme evaluation.

The defence committees of Congress may also use the resources of the OTA, which was established by the Technology Assistance Act of 1972. Its main work is to provide in-depth studies of the advantages and disadvantage to society, the environment and the economy which may result from the application of a particular technology. The length of time that it takes to produce such studies makes them of limited use for accountability purposes and in the field of defence only two reports have been produced so far, one dealing with the effect of nuclear war, and the other with the basing mode for the new MX missile.

The audit services and information resources available to Congress far outweigh those committed to Parliament, and then in conjunction with the essentially strategic role played by Congress and the more managerial role of Parliament, there is a *prima facie* case for supposing that Parliament's ability to hold the executive accountable in any form of its defence policies and programmes is far less than the corresponding ability of Congress. However, the gap, especially at the programme and financial levels, is far less than these disparities would suggest. It is not that Parliament's limited efforts are more effective than those of Congress, but rather that certain problems inherent in defence policy formulation and in defence programme and financial management make them particularly unresponsive to efficient accounting and accountability practices.

PROBLEMS OF DEFENCE ACCOUNTABILITY

Secrecy and National Security

In his book *The Governance of Britain*, Harold Wilson devotes one chapter to the 'Prime Minister and National Security'; it is 203 words long including its final sentence 'There is no further information that can usefully or properly be added before bringing this chapter to an end.'[63] He refers mainly to the secret services, but the anodyne brevity of his comments is symptomatic of an extensive secrecy about national security issues including defence. During parliamentary question time the Secretary of State for Defence has not only refused to disclose information on 'operational matters', but also on aircraft accident rates, the numbers of foreign soldiers training on British soil, the volume and value of arms sales to foreign countries, and the contract price and eventual cost of military equipment.[64] This last issue has been a persistant problem of defence accountability and one of many examples is revealed in an exchange between a British MP and an MOD witness concerned the increase in cost of Britain's share of developing the Tornado. The MOD indicated that '. . . we would be quite happy to provide a breakdown both of total cost and of the UK share of the development cost', but this undertaking is footnoted in the committee's report as 'not reported',[65] and there is no record of the committee requesting that it should be. The executive's reasons for failing to reveal costings on high technology projects sometimes verge on the facetious, as when it claimed that the publication of its costings 'would have weakened the discipline and incentive imposed upon main contractors of trying to complete the programme within the estimated costs'.[66] Complicity in disguising cost over-runs hardly seems the most appropriate incentive to encourage contractors to meet cost limits. It is also quite common during the proceedings of defence committees and the PAC for defence witnesses to request and to be granted that some of the information that they do give should be side-lined as not for publication.

Such requests for and grants of confidentiality on several types of defence information makes policy, programme and financial accountability difficult. The first two issues were broached squarely – by David Greenwood in evidence given to Parliament in 1975, when he said,

> Indeed in the absence of detailed information, worthwhile programme evaluation of any kind is difficult, if not impossible. It has to be of the speculative nature of this paper; emphasising

inferences, generalities, possibilities. Government's monopoly of information, and occasionally curious ways of handling it, make effective Parliamentary involvement in policy discussions difficult, so that expressions of a desire to learn the views of Parliament do not always ring true. The Sub-Committee has persuaded the MOD to provide much more information about its business in recent years. Because of this there is a better basis for the appraisal of policy exercises like the defence review – both in the House and outside. But we still need more information in Defence White Papers, each year. For looking at defence in relation to national priorities we also need our Public Expenditure White Papers, on time. Finally, on major policy matters, Government could give a clear and comprehensive view of their intentions rather than a series of tantalising glimpses such as December's Hansards gave of the present review.[67]

Elsewhere Greenwood has referred to the difficulty of making anything other than crude calculations about defence programme options because 'detailed information on budgeting priorities is not available in the open literature. Nor are authoritative cost data'.[68] This state of affairs is significant because Greenwood is Britain's leading defence economist, and it is upon expertise such as his that Parliament relies.

It is not unusual for partial and misleading information to be published about defence, and Antony Benn, in a lecture to the Royal Institute of Public Administration in January 1980, illustrated the problem by reference to a Cabinet meeting that reviewed a draft Defence White Paper that showed a large discrepancy in the military strength of East and West. The White Paper had failed to credit the entire armed forces of France to the western side. 'This crude misinformation was designed to win public support for a bigger defence budget by suggesting a more serious imbalance than existed.'[69] This compounds the problem of secrecy and renders any accounting for defence extremely difficult.

In the United States there has been considerable change in the availability of information during the 1970s. The enactment of the Freedom of Information Act in 1974 has enabled Congress to acquire much of the information it needs to discharge effectively its oversight function, although this act allows information to be withheld if it contains national security secrets, trade secrets which would be of value to an industrial competitors, reference to employee personal files and reference to inter- and intra-agency communications. All four of these exceptions can and are regularly claimed by the DOD in its dealing with Congress. The DOD has also refused many times to reveal information by claiming executive privilege.[70] There were indeed amendments offered to the Freedom of Information Act which would have placed a statutory restriction on the use of Executive Privilege, and these reflected congressionl anger when the OMB Director, Roy Ash, refused to testify before Congress in April 1973 solely on the grounds of Executive Privilege. Ash's decision was described by Senator Edmund Muskie as indicating the executive's 'preference for secrecy'.[71] The amendments failed and even under President Carter, executive privilege was used to deny the GAO access to the reports of the Air Force Inspector General until November 1978.[72]

Elmer Staats has testified frequently to Congress about the difficulty of getting information on defence,[73] but by comparison with the British system the problems is of moderate proportions, and indeed one of the GAOs major services to Congress has been to assist congressional defence committees with the problem of an 'information overload'[74] by concentrating their oversight effort where it is most likely to be productive. The extensive hearings held by the House and Senate Armed Services Committees, and Appropriations Committees, at which military witnesses are able to give their independent professional advice, helps to provide much information that has relevance to policy, programme and financial accountability. The potential for programme accountability is enhanced in particular by the Selected Acquisition Reporting System (SARS) which has been in operation since 1969 and which is a recurrent summary report to Congress of the progress and cost of DOD weapons systems.[75] However, the House Armed Services Committee has complained recently that 'There seems to be a conscious effort to minimise public knowledge and discussion of defence issues',[76] and it is undoubtedly the case that the Congress has been prepared to accept defence information that is at best partial and at worst thoroughly misleading. The allegations in the last years of Carter's administration that detente had brought the United States to the verge of strategic inferiority *vis-à-vis* the USSR were widely accepted in Congress although the substance of such charges was tenuous indeed.[77]

ASSESSMENT OF DEFENCE OBJECTIVES

Defence objectives are inevitably concerned with influencing the behaviour of other states and it is never possible to determine with certainty if the broad objectives of policy are successful in peacetime. It is even more difficult to determine if weapons systems will perform in wartime as they are projected to in peacetime exercises, for as one Assistant Director of Defence Research and Engineering asked, 'How can one evalute the worth or capacity of a tactial airforce in peacetime? What are the measures?'[78] A similar problem was raised in a GAO report which drew attention to the fact that,

> The Department of Defence spent billions of dollars each year to maintain the readiness of its weapons systems but cannot accurately project how much readiness a dollar will buy or determine how much readiness is needed.[79]

Even within the DOD internal planning procedures different criteria are used to measure the worth of a new weapons system. The Secretary of Defence reviews the weapons system acquisition process and measures an individual project in terms of engineering performance, but not against its contribution to a defined 'combined-arms battle' which is the criteria that the services employ to include a new weapons system in their programme budget requests.[80] Such confusions and lack of clarity about defence objectives and the difficulty of measuring how well programmes meet them, make accountability difficult, but are seriously compounded by the additional, and often disguised, objectives that governments attach to their defence spending.

Defence equipment spending is of great importance for maintaining high-technology industries and employment, and is often used more to exercise some general responsibility for planning the overall health of the economy than for the procurement of cost effective weapons systems.[81] The logic behind the rescue of Rolls Royce aero-engines in 1972 and the later nationalisation of British Aerospace was to protect a strategic and ailing industry. It has also been noted that the design team for the MRCA was the same as that for the cancelled TSR2, and that it had been kept in being by a series of government decisions to fund design exercises such as the UKVG, which were never intended to produce an operational aircraft.[82]

In the United States the DOD has shown the same concern to spread the work of defence contracts across the defence industrial base to prevent its decay even though some sacrifices are made in terms of price competitiveness and cost efficiency.[83] In addition to this the government uses 'the procurement base to help accomplish its socio-economic objectives. Attempts to attack the following and other diverse problems are all built into the procurement process: employee health and safety, environment, small business, minority business and employment, minimum wages, aiding the economy and protecting domestic business, encouraging North Atlantic Treaty Organisation standardisation, rehabilitating prisoners, and employment for the handicapped'.[84] The multiplicity of purposes that governments attach to their defence spending makes the exercise of programme accountability by Defence departments especially difficult in so much as it leads to procurement decisions that are clearly not cost-effective, but which may protect strategic industries and provide national employment and other benefits. The ability of Parliament and Congress to weigh and trade-off these purposes is frequently limited because the purposes themselves are rarely defined by the respective governments.

PROCUREMENT

The executive's preference for secrecy, the difficulty of setting exclusive and unambiguous defence objectives and the difficulty of assessing them are general problems but have received relatively little attention in Parliament and Congress. Much more attention is devoted to the procurement process and the problems of cost-growth and cost-over run during the acquisition of a major weapons system. The defence market differs from the industrial market place in several important ways and they have been set out by J. Ronald Fox (see Figure 1.2, page 30).[85]

Several of these differences present particular difficulties for accountability. The most important is that a great deal of government defence procurement in the United Kingdom and the United States is by negotiation and this form of procurement has tended to increase. In the 1960s 40% of DOD contracts were given to competitive bids, but by 1978 it had declined to only 28%, and the DOD has been resisting the implementation of OMB circular A-109 which attempts to increase the amount of competitive contracting in government agencies.[86] In the United Kngdom there has been very little competitive contracting for major defence procurements and with nationalisation of British Aerospace and British Shipbuilders in 1977, the opportunity for competitiveness has disappeared. In these circumstances there is a high premium on effective accounting and

Market Characterstics

Industrial Market	*Defence Market*
The seller initiates new product innovations, based on analyses of potential markets. He has no certain knowledge of a product's saleability.	The buyer establishes the requirements for a product. The producer then begins development and production.
The buyer has a wide range of choice between products in the same category that have real of advertised differences.	Relatively few products are produced simultaneously for the same mission. Although the buyer sometimes has the option to choose among prototypes, the time and cost of producing new systems once production has begun discourages replacement.
Price is a dominant factor in a buyer's choice because adequate substitutes for a product are often available.	Price is only one of the factors that govern a customer's choice. It may be far less important than quality, availability, or the technology required to realize a specific program objective.
The market tends to be impersonal. Buyers and sellers act independently.	The market is highly personal. The buyer has constant contact with the seller's organization.
The producer finances the development-production effort.	The buyer bears most of the development cost and may provide equipment and facilities for the use of the producer.
The market usually contains several, or many, customers for each product.	The market is essentially one-customer (monopsonistic).
Prices are primarily determined by competition.	Price is determined by an evaluation of anticipated and actual costs.
Demand is either relatively constant (e.g., for staples), or tends to be a function of disposable income (e.g., for non-essentials).	Demand is a function of the technology available, or of estimates of a potential enemy's technological resources.
The basic design of the product changes slowly and requirements for a given model are relatively stable.	The product may be technologically obsolete before production is completed.

SOURCE J. R. Fox, *Arming America* (Harvard University Press, 1974) p. 39.

FIGURE 1.2 The defence market

management techniques to ensure that projects provide value for money and fulfil the objectives set for them. Despite many experiments in the programme management field, cost-overruns and cost-growth are endemic in defence procurement in the United Kingdom and the United States.

Cost-overrun 'refers to cost increases incurred in connection with a particular weapons contract where current cost exceeds the cost estimate that was made at the beginning of the project or when the contract was entered into',[87] and this arises from poor estimating, bad management or inept contracting. Planning estimates and development estimates on both sides of the Atlantic have been notoriously poor. The excessive profits earned by Bristol Siddley and Ferranti on fixed price contracts are an expression of poor estimating where the main problem was the simple overestimation of costs. Indeed the MOD did not go into Ferranti to *ascertain* costs, but simply attempted to estimate them.[88] But in the majority of cases the early estimates are optimistically low and there is clear evidence in America that low estimates are seen as a way to 'buy into' a government defence contract,[89] and the same phenomenon has been known in the UK in the recent past.[90] Such unrealistically low estimates are reinforced by an entrenched cynicism on the part of the executive. In evidence to the Expenditure Committee a British Treasury official said,

> Over the years we have come to apply a discount factor, . . . to the technical advice we are given. When any scientist tells us that such and such a thing can be done within a year, we probably say 2x; and if the technicians say the cost will be y millions, were probably say 5y millions.[91]

And of the situation in America, the Director of the GAOs Procurement and Systems Analysis Division said in evidence, 'the Congress should take, with a great big grain of salt, the promises and cost estimates presented by the DoD early in a major programme'.[92] Without good cost estimates, Congress and Parliament have been authorising decisions on major weapons programmes in a vacuum. Problems in programme management and in contracting have also been legion, and in management the biggest single problem is the willingness of managers to conceed the pressure of service heads that urgency demands that programmes are put into production as quickly as possible so as to prevent 'the Soviets beating us to the punch'. The DOD, in particular, has often started production of a weapons system before it has been fully developed and proven, and significant production problems usually result and drive up the overall production costs.[93]

Cost-growth 'refers to the general phenomenon of rising weapons costs during the acquisition process regardless of cause or the contractural relationship between the Government and the contractors'.[94] The primary cause of cost-growth has been the sophistication of defence technology, and its effect has been felt irrespective of the quality of programme management. There are several aspects of this problem, the first of which is that service heads tend to request 'state of the art' technology irrespective of the military needs. In the United States, for example, aircraft have been acquired with maximum speeds which cannot be used militarily, but in which 20% of the cost has been expended on securing the last 5% of performance.[95] Such high technology specifications are asked for and secured because the services define their own operational requirements so specifically that they predetermine the selection of a particular system.[96] The high technology elements of modern weapons systems means that weapons costs rise faster than inflation generally as can be demonstrated by the XM1 tank which cost seven times more than the Sherman which it replaced, and by the F-15 which cost three times more than the F-4E that it replaced.[97] Some idea of the scale of the problem of military equipment inflation costs can be gained by the fact that it added $11.3 billion to military procurement in America 1979.[98]

The ten or twelve years lead time between the design of a major weapons system and its entry into service also produces pressures for cost growth. Within this time, political factors make it unlikely that a project will recieve a consistent level of funding, and if funding is reduced projects are 'stretchered' and this increases the cost. In February 1980 such quantity changes accounted for 33% of the total cost growth in the $45.2 billion American defence procurement budget.[99] Also within the lead-time period, the assessment of the threat that a particular weapon may face will be up-dated, and engineering changes may have to be made adding substantially to the final cost of the system. The addition of three new anti-submarine devices to the stern of the FFG-7 class frigates during construction is an example of this form of cost growth, and one that was supported by the GAO.[100]

There has been a major effort in the United Kingdom and the United States to combat both cost overruns and cost-growth. Overruns have been tackled by the introduction of parametric estimating, operational analysis and cost-benefit analysis.[101] There have also been major innovations in contracting with the United Kingdom setting up a Review Board for Government Contracts in 1969. In the United States, David Packard introduced concepts such as 'fly before buy' and 'design to cost' in the late 1960s and early 1970s[102] to improve the performance of defence contractors in meeting contractural obligations including cost. The performance of American defence contractors is 'policed' by the Defense Contract Audit Agency (DCAA) which, although part of the DoD, uses a GAO approved audit method.[103] Efforts to contain cost-growth have included investment incentives for defence contractors so that they install modern production equipment designed to improve productivity and cut overall costs. Other attempts have included value engineering techniques, improvements in manufacturing technology, work measurement systems and 'should cost-reviews'. In summing up the likely effect of these methods on the problem of cost growth, the GAO addressed the problems of American defence procurement, but its conclusions apply equally well to the British defence scene '. . . they appear to be very worthwhile and should be continued. . . . We do not believe, however, that they can have a truly substantial impact on overall costs'.[104] By implication the impact of these methods will be correspondingly small on the ability of the MOD and DoD to account for defence procurement to Parliament and to Congress.

CONCLUSION

It is clear that there is a problem with defence accountability. At first sight it might appear that by strengthening legislature oversight defence accountability can be achieved. This seems particularly true when one recognises the poor quality of assistance on the audit and information sides which the British Parliament recieves. Yet it may be that the defence field is particularly resistant to direct accountability. As we saw Congress has a multitude of Audit, accounting and information services but it still displays an inability to discover the relevant facts. Why should this be so? Obviously Congress suffers from information overload and the 'politics of the pork barrel' as special interests fight to ensure through lobbying that their claims on policy and expenditure are supported. This means that simply providing information does not ensure that the legislature is able to discharge its intended function of making defence accountable.

There are a number of reasons for this, which will become more apparent in the rest of this study. For our purposes here the most salient are the unwillingness of legislators to spend the time to discharge their functions properly, the lack of expertise outside the defence establishment who can make sense of defence related information and the paucity of independent agencies who can provide information on defence that is not filtered through existing defence channels.

But, even if it is possible to overcome these problems (which is doubtful as we shall see), the executive branch normally has two cards it can always play to undermine effective accountability. The first, clearly, is the 'national security' card which can be used to minimise the dissemination of information which is regarded as embarrassing. The second is the fact that legislators tend to be self-selecting in terms of committee work. The legislators who sit on defence related committees tend to be interested in and fairly favourable to the defence establishment. This means that bodies created to scrutinise defence can often be relied upon to endorse the defence establishment's desire to minimise scrutiny.

There is, however, one final problem which is worth remarking upon and which can militate against effective accountablility. Even if it is possible to achieve a fully informed, staffed and highly motivated legislature, if the executive branch is itself failing to fulfil its own responsibilities of financial policy and programme accountability and control, then the ability of the legislature to solve this problem is undermined. The evidence presented here seems to indicate that due to archaic accounting and audit procedures, those reforms which have been achieved in the British and American legislatures have been undermined by a relatively incompetent and self-interested executive and bureaucracy. In these circumstances embarrassing evidence can all too easily be masked by the 'national security' card or the argument (which legislators sometimes accept) that to admit publicly that mistakes have been made is to lend support and succour to the enemy. As we shall see in our detailed analysis of the 1970s and 1980s reforms in defence in Britain and America many of these problems did arise and the desire for greater legislative oversight was undone. First, however, it is necessary for us to explain the historical background to the reform movement and its significance for defence accountability.

NOTES

1. See for example E. Leslie Normanton, 'Public Accountability and Audit: a Reconnaissance', in L. R. Smith and D. C. Hague (eds) *The Dilemma of Accountability in Modern Government* (Macmilllan 1971).
2. See Nevil Johnson, 'Financial Accountability to Parliament', ibid.
3. Ibid. p. 284.

4. Select Committee on Congressional Operations, 'General Accounting Office Services to Congress: an Assessment', (US Government Printing Office, Washington, 1978) p. 16. See also Elmer B. Staats, 'New Problems of Accountability for Federal Programs', in Bruce L. R. Smith (ed.) *The New Political Economy: The Public Use of the Private Sector* (Macmillan, 1975) p. 65.
5. See for example Smith and Hague, op. cit., p. 299.
6. See Staats in Smith op. cit., p.67.
7. See Joseph Pois, 'Trends in General Accounting Office Audits', in Smith op. cit., especially p. 268.
8. See General Accounting Office, 'Operations Auditing by the Defense Contract Audit Agency: GAO, Accomplishments, Problems and Actions to Improve', (Washington; PSAD–76–35, 1975) *passim.*
9. See First Special Report from the Committee of Public Accounts, 1980-81, *The Role of the Comptroller and Auditor General*, vol. 1, *Report*, JC 115–16, *passim.*
10. See ibid., vol. 2, *Miniatures of Evidence*, HC 115-11, *passim.*
11. Cmnd 7845, *The Role of the Comptroller and Auditor General*, para. 12.
12. Ibid., paras 11 and 16.
13. Ibid., par. 10.
14. Ibid., p. 56.
15. First Special Report from the Committee of Public Accounts, op. cit., vol. 3, *Appendices to the Minutes*, HC 115-111, Appendix XXVII.
16. Ibid., note to Appendix XXVII.
17. Vilma Flegmann, *Called to Account: the Public Accounts Committee of the House of Commons 1965–66 to 1977–78* (Gower, 1978) p 91.
18. *Cmnd 7845*, para. 62.
19. The list of major project studies includes: cost of production of Chieftain Tank, HMS Ark Royal refit costs, Mark 31 Torpedo, Special Refit of Tiger Class Cruisers, International Collaborative Projects.
20. Flegmann, op. cit., p. 100.
21. *Cmnd* 7845, para. 8.
22. This quotation comes from *Cmnd* 7845. para. 1, but similar views are expressed in the *Second Report of the Select Committee on Expenditure*, 1976–77 (HC 535) paras 153–8 and 160; the *First Report of the Select Committee on Procedure*, 1977–78 (HC 558), paras 8.7–8.21; and the *Second Report from the Public Accounts Committee*, 1978–79 (HC 330) *passim.*
23. Flegmann, op. cit., p. 84.
24. See *Cmnd* 7845, Annex A, para. 8.
25. The First Report from the PAC 1980–81, op. cit., vol 1, para. 1.6.
26. Flegmann, op. cit., p. 92.
27. The Hoover Commission, *General Management of the American Executive Branch*, introduction (Washington: GPO, 1949).
28. Flegmann, op. cit., p. 25.
29. *Cmnd* 7845, para 21.
30. Ibid., para. 63.
31. See Flegmann, op. cit., p. 28.
32. Ibid., p. 97.
33. Select Committee on Congressional Operations, op. cit., Appendix 4.

34. Ibid., p. 6.
35. See General Accounting Office, *Progress in Improving Program and Budget Information for Congressional Use* (Washington: GAO, PAD–79–79, 1979) p. 15 for an assessment of the effect of this legislation.
36. The General Accounting Office has produced several reports to assist congressional committees to improve their ability to assess the evaluative reports from agencies. For example; *Guidelines for Model Evaluation* (PAD–79–17, Nov. 1978); *Status and Issues in Program Evaluation* (PAD–78–1, Oct, 1978).
37. GAO, op. cit., (PAD–79–79, 1979) p. 20.
38. See section 202(4) of the *Legislative Reorganisation Act* 1970, Public Law 91-510, as amended 1974.
39. General Accounting Office, *Annual Report 1979* (Washington: GAO, Jan. 1980) p. 2.
40. Select Committee on Congressional Operations, op. cit., p. 4.
41. Ibid., pp 14-15.
42. Ibid., p. 6.
43. General Accounting Office, Progress in Improving Programme and Budget Information for Congressional Use, 1980, p. 7.
44. General Accounting Office, *Audit Manual* (Washington: GAO, 1979) p. 14.
45. See evidence of Jerome H. Stolorow, Director PSAD, before the House Committee on Government Operations, 25 June 1979, 'Weapons Systems Costs', p. 4.
46. See 'Assuring Program Accountability', Statement of Elmer B. Staats before the Sub-Committee on Rules of the House, Committee on Rules, House of Representatives, 15 Nov. 1979, p. 3.
47. Ibid., *passim.*
48. GAO, *Annual Report 1979*, p. 55.
49. GAO, *Summaries of Conclusions and Recommendations on Department of Defense* Washington: GAO, OISS–80–01, 21 Jan. 1980).
50. Ibid., p. 139.
51. Dermot Englefield, *Parliament and Information*, (London: The Library Association, 1981) p. 25.
52. Ibid., p. 28.
53. Ibid., p. 28.
54. Ibid., p. 30.
55. Ibid., pp. 43–4.
56. Ibid., pp. 44–5.
57. Ibid., p. 52.
58. See 'Congressional Support Agencies', a compilation of papers, Commission on the Operation of Senate, 94th Congress, 2nd Session (US Government Printing Office, 80–189, 1976) pp. 31–55.
59. See sections 202 (c) and (d) of the Legislative Reorganisation Act, 1970 as amended by Title VIII of the Budget and Impoundment Control Act of 1974.
60. Jane Ann Lindsey, 'The Congressional Research Service', (Washington: CRS, CRS–80–131 D, July 1980) p. 7.

61. Stuart D. Goldman, 'US Defense Posture in the 1980s: a Survey of Alternative Planning Factors' (Washington: CRS, UV 80–202F, Nov. 1980) p. vi.
62. Ibid., p. viii.
63. Harold Wilson, *The Governance of Britain* (London: Weidenfeld & Nicolson, 1976) ch. 9, pp. 167–8.
64. David Leigh, *The Frontiers of Secrecy* (London: Junction Books, 1980) p. 10.
65. Second Report from the Select Committee on Expenditure, 1975–76, *Defence* (HC 155) pp. 133–4, para. 499.
66. Quoted in John Jewkes, *Government and High Technology, Occasional Paper No. 37 (Institute of Economic Affairs, 1972) p. 16.*
67. *Second Report from The Select Committee on Expenditure, 1974–75*, (HC 259) p. 7, para. 20.
68. David Greenwood, 'Defence Programme Options to 1980–81', in Mary Kaldor *et. al.* (eds), *Democratic Socialism and the Cost of Defence* (London: Croom Helm, 1979) p. 142.
69. David Leigh, op. cit., p. 34.
70. Bruce L. R. Smith (ed.) op. cit., p. 302.
71. See Judith H. Paris, 'The Office of Management and Budget (OMB): Background, Responsibilities and Recent Issues', (Washington: CRS, July 1978), for an account of the legislative–executive battle over the use of executive privilege, especially pp 59–60 from which Muskie's quotation is taken.
72. GAO, 'Summaries of Conclusions . . .', op. cit., p. 113.
73. See for example GAO, 'Financial Status of Major Federal Acquisitions, September 30, 1978', p. 2, and Smith op. cit., p. 259.
74. See 'Assuring Program Accountability', op. cit., p. 22.
75. See GAO, 'How to Improve the Selected Acquisition Reporting System', (Washington: GAO, PSAD 75-63, 1975) *passim.*
76. Quoted in J. Ronald Fox, *Arming America: How the US Buys Weapons*, (Harvard University Press, 1974) pp. 138–9.
77. See for example the *Strategic Survey* for 1979, and also for 1980–81, especially pp. 14–15 in the latter for an assessment of the extent to which the US has become vulnerable to the USSR. *Strategic Survey* is a annual publication of the International Institute for Strategic Studies, London.
78. Hearings, House Budget Committee, *Tactical Air Warfare*, 21, 23 and 28 June 1977, p. 7.
79. GAO, 'DODs Material Readiness Report to Congress . . .', (Washington: GAO, LCD 80–5, Oct. 1979) p. i.
80. GAO, 'Models, Data, and War: a Critique of the Foundation for Defense Analyses' (Washington: GAO, PAD–80–21, Mar. 1980) p. 38.
81. Smith, op. cit., p. 20.
82. This argument has been put forward by Dan Smith, *The Defence of the Realm in the 1980s* (London: Croom Helm, 1985) p. 164, among others, but there is little official information to support it.
83. See GAO, 'Impediments to Reducing the Cost of Weapons Systems', (Washington: GAO, PSAD, Nov. 1979) p. 16.

84. Ibid., pp. 18–19.
85. Fox, op. cit., p. 39.
86. Hearings, *Competitive Procurement*, Task Force on Government Efficiency, House Budget Committee, 9 Nov. 1979, p. 2.
87. Bert H. Cooper, 'Cost Growth in Weapons Programs', (Washington: CRS, Dec. 1974) p. 4.
88. See Smith and Hague, op. cit., p. 153.
89. Cooper, op. cit., p. 19, and 'Weapons Systems Costs', op. cit., p. 6.
90. Dan Smith, op. cit., p. 157.
91. Quoted in Jewkes, op. cit., p. 14.
92. 'Weapons System Costs', op. cit. p. 6.
93. 'Impediments to Reducing the Cost of Weapons Systems', op. cit., p. 9.
94. Cooper, op. cit., p. 5.
95. Ibid., pp. 16–17.
96. 'Impediments . . .', op. cit., p. 10.
97. Cooper, op. cit., p. 4.
98. GAO, 'Financial Status of Major Federal Acquisitions, Sept. 30 1979' (Washington: GAO, PSAD–80–25, Feb. 1980) p. 1.
99. Ibid., pp. 1 and 4.
100. GAO, 'Summaries of Conclusions . . .', op. cit., p. 133.
101. See Gavin Kennedy, 'The Use and Limitations of Economic Analysis for Defence Policy Planning', and J. W. Gibson, 'Systems Analysis in British Defence policy Making: Some Achievements and Limitations', in Laurence Martin, (ed.) *The Management of Defence* (London: Macmillan, 1976), for an assessment of these techniques in the UK.
102. See Smith, op. cit., p. 57 for a comment on these methods in the US.
103. GAO, 'DODs Material Readiness Report . . .', op. cit., p. 3.
104. GAO, 'Impediments . . .', op. cit., p. 42.

2 The Background to Congressional and Parliamentary Reform of Legislative Oversight

In the 1970s both Britain and the United States experienced dissatisfaction with existing arrangements and innovated to reform and enhance legislative oversight of their executive branches. This desire for reform was experienced first in Britain in the early 1960s and culminated in the sweeping away of the old Estimates Committee of the House of Commons and its replacement with a new Expenditure Committee in 1971. This committee was in turn replaced in 1979. In the brief period in which it was in operation (and despite the fact that there was always confusion about what its role was intended to be in detail)[1] it had the general goal of extending Parliamentary scrutiny of government policies and expenditure of public funds. In the United States the demand for reform and its culmination in new institutional procedural relationships came somewhat later.

The 1974 reforms in Congressional procedures also saw the creation of a new committee structure – with the institution of new Budget Committees in both the House of Representatives and the Senate – as well as a new budgetary timetable and the creation of a new advisory/research agency – the Congressional Budget Office. The American reform, however, was intended to achieve more than those in Britain. It was envisaged that this new system would, first of all, end the fragmentation of budgetary relationships within Congress and, by centralising, ensure that Congress rather than the executive branch set national policy and expenditure priorities.

This pinpoints something which will become only too apparent within this study. Although there were similar problems facing the legislative and executive branches in Britain and America prior to the

1970s, the fact that the American Congress has always had far more extensive policy-making and priority setting powers *vis-à-vis* the executive, as compared with the relatively ineffectual and limited role of Parliament in Britain, means that the analyst is not always comparing like with like. Thus, while there was an attempt to enhance the legislative role in both countries, the exact goals of reform and the institutional and procedural innovations adopted were somewhat dissimilar and this makes it difficult to compare the two systems and reforms easily.

One further caveat is worth making. This study, while concerned with the fate of legislative reform in both countries, is not a general and inclusive study of either the Expenditure Committee or the Congressional Budget System, (such studies exist elsewhere).[2] The focus of this study is rather the problem which defence poses for legislative innovations in oversight and control. As we outlined in Chapter 1, defence creates peculiar difficulties for legislative oversight which may be insuperable; not least due to the problems of excessive executive secrecy over information and national security. Obviously, however, before we can judge the degree of difficulty which defence creates we must, first of all, understand the general reforming movement in both countries in the 1970s.

THE ANGLO-AMERICAN BUDGETARY SYSTEMS PRIOR TO REFORM

Before assessing the basic reasons why reforming movements developed in Britain and America, it is first of all necessary to outline the formal relationship between the executive and the legislature in these two countries is so far as policy-making for expenditure and revenue raising was concerned before the 1970s. As we shall see the American Congress had far more extensive priority setting powers in theory than constitutional arrangements allowed for in Britain.

Peter Else has argued that theoretically we can conceive of executive/legislative relationships in three broad aspects:[3]

(1) The legislature can have a *legal* or audit role ensuring that money is only spent by the executive for the purpose for which it was intended.
(2) The legislature can have a *managerial* role ensuring the scrutiny of the efficient/value for money use of funds allocated to the executive without waste.

(3) The legislature can have a *strategic* role involved in the actual allocation of expenditure and revenue resources in policy terms and the assessment of output efficiency.

The British Parliament has historically been confined to *legal* and *managerial* roles; while the Congress in the United States has historically had a share with the executive branch in all three of these roles.

To put the matter simply: since the nineteenth century Parliament has been limited to checking the value for money of central government policies and auditing the actual expenditure involved. The Congress has normally been involved in setting expenditure and revenue priorities, as well as auditing and checking the value for money of executive expenditure. In recent years however both Parliament and Congress have found that these historic roles have been gradually circumscribed and undermined. In order to understand how the executive branches in both countries have tended to usurp the role of their respective legislatures it is necessary to outline first of all the normal/historic relationships which have operated over expenditure and revenue policy-making in each country.

The British Expenditure and Revenue Cycle

While it has been true historically that Parliament has had the 'power of the purse' this power has existed in only the most formal of senses – particularly since the growth of well organised two party alignments in the House of Commons after 1868.[4] While Parliament has theoretically had the power to control the executive, in practice this power has always been seriously circumscribed by the fact that Parliament was unable to raise taxes or expenditure on its own initiative. Only the crown (government) was in a position to fulfil this *strategic* role. Parliament's traditional role has been limited to making amendments to government Finance Bills; requesting increased taxation; or to recommending reductions in government assessments of expenditure requirements.[5] This meant that since the middle of the nineteenth century the British Parliament's role has been limited to the scrutiny of government policy, revenue and expenditure decisions; the legitimation of state actions through the provision of statues; and, the provision of information for informed public debate. In other words Parliament has – in Else's terms – had *legal* and *managerial* roles. This can be indicated clearly by describing in detail the role of Parliament in expenditure and revenue policy formulation.

The process of granting expenditure requests to fulfil policy is, in Britain, an annual process and money allocated in one year cannot be held over until another. Parliament passes the relevant expenditure (Consolidated Fund Act) and revenue (Finance Act) legislation in each year after the government of the day has formulated its priorities for spending and taxation. The process is outlined in Figure 2.1 and can be summarised as follows.

The Strategic Role

In Britain the allocation of priorities and revenue obligations is wholly located within the executive branch of government because, even though the British government is characterised as Parliamentary Government, the government is drawn from Parliament rather than Parliament controlling and dictating to the government of the day. In normal times a working Parliamentary majority ensures that the government of the day can win most of the important debates brought in the House of Commons.[6] As a result the formulation of expenditure and revenue policy (the budget) is located within Whitehall with the major spending decisions being taken by the Cabinet up to eighteen months before their submission to Parliament. The crucial decision points in this process are normally in the summer, prior to the relevant financial year, and just before the formulation of the public expenditure White Paper in the winter, prior to the relevant financial year. In this process the Prime Minister, the Chancellor, the Bank of England and Treasury play crucial roles.[7]

The Managerial Role

The scrutiny and efficiency role is normally confined to Parliament throughout the financial year. The process commences somewhat before the official financial year begins on 1 April each year. In January and February each year the government sends Winter Supplementary Estimates of its required spending plans for Parliamentary perusal. These estimates relate to additional spending

Budgetary Roles	*Timespan in Fiscal Year*	*Location*
Strategic Role	Up to 18 months prior to the relevant fiscal year	*Executive Branch:* The Cabinet, guided by the Treasury, the Chancellor of the Exchequer and the Bank of England decides on resource allocation between various departments in the light of Treasury economic forecasts. A Public Expenditure White Paper and individual Department Estimates of future spending needs are formulated. Treasury and Chancellor, with Prime Minister and Bank of England also, formulate Budget proposals for the April of the fiscal year.
Managerial Role	From the January prior to the April commencement of the relevant fiscal year on 31 March	*Legislative Branch:* Parliament scrutinises the Departmental Estimates introduced in January/February for the coming fiscal year (and any subsequent supplementary Estimates in Spring, Summer and Winter as the government may introduce). Parliament review is by debates in the Full House of Commons and by the passing of two wholly separate Bills: the Finance Act for revenue after the April Budget (passed and debated in May and June): for expenditure (debated and passed by 5 August – bar for supplementary expenditure Bills). These debates are assisted by a Select Committee on Estimates which reviews the Estimates in detail and provides Reports for Parliamentary debates.
Legal Role	Continuous and up to two years after the fiscal year	*Legislative Branch:* The Estimates Committee reports assist in the audit process but the major role is by the Comptroller and Auditor General and the Exchequer and Audit Department which reports on Departmental Estimates to the Public Accounts Committee of Parliament, which in return undertakes subject/issue reviews which are for Commons debate.

FIGURE 2.1 The formal budgetary system in Britain prior to 1971 (fiscal year: 1 April–31 March)

requests for the current financial year. In the same period however the main estimates for the forthcoming financial year (civil and defence) are introduced. Each Department of State draws up estimates of its likely expenditure requirements for the coming financial year and these are presented together in the form of votes. In other words, the departmental estimates are consolidated into omnibus votes to be debated on and passed by Parliament in the 29 supply day debates set aside to discuss the etimates in the Parliamentary financial year.[8] The debates on the estimates provide the opposition and backbench MPs with the opportunity to scrutinise and criticise government policies, without normally allowing for Parliament to usurp the central government's allocation role, due to the executive's ability to out-vote the opposition on these crucial issues. This process begins on the 1 April each year after the closure of the previous financial year on 31 March. To assist the government a vote on account is formally passed by Parliament to support the expenditure of the government until the estimates are formally passed. At the same time the final Spring Supplementary Estimates are introduced from the previous year and the Budget (or main revenue raising government statement), is normally introduced at the beginning of April. In May and June the House of Commons debates the budget provisions as contained in the Finance Bill and once again the government can normally ensure a sufficient majority to see this bill enacted. Following this, in July, the Summer Supplementary Estimates for the current year are introduced and debated prior to the passing of the Consolidated Fund Bill which serves for the appropriation of new spending. This process normally has to be completed by the 5 August each year (apart from the subsequent Winter and Spring Supplementary Estimates).

Finally, to assist in the scrutiny of what the government is doing, since 1912 the House of Commons was normally assisted by a Select Committee on Estimates which through its sub-committees provided reports to guide, influence and inform the Full House of Commons debates on the estimates. Unfortunately, as we shall see, the limitations on this *managerial* role were legion because the Supply Day Debates were rarely used by the Opposition to scrutinise what the government was doing in detail. In practice the time was used for set piece adversarial conflicts between the relevant front-bench teams. The Estimates Committee Reports were rarely used or read as a result. One final point is worth making here (which further underlines the problem of oversight). The revenue and expenditure processes in the British Parliament are wholly separate and never co-ordinated even though they involve the same institution of the whole House of Commons.

The Legal Role

This role of checking the legality of expenditure entered into, after Parliamentary approval for spending has been granted, is a 'post-hoc' audit role performed by the Comptroller and Auditor General (C and AG) assisted by the Exchequer and Audit Department. The C and AG provides an Annual Report for Parliament which traditionally is scrutinised and analysed by the Public Accounts Committee (PAC) of the House of Commons which was created in 1861.[9] The major role here for the PAC to assess waste and extravagance and provide its own reports for Parliament which while being rarely read or debated (only one day is set aside each session for this report), have sometimes had an impact on government behaviour.[10] In general this legal role is adequately performed by the PAC but its reports are sometimes two years behind the actual date of expenditure and are fairly technical in character.

The American Revenue and Expenditure Cycle

If Britain's legislature has been formally constrained to fulfil only a *legal* and limited *managerial* role the American Congress has had no such formal limits on its powers. Indeed in theory the Congress and President (executive) in America are supposed to share all three roles, with the Congress having ultimate power to set expenditure and revenue priorities in the light of Presidential requests and priority assessments.

The process is outlined in summary form in Figure 2.2 and can be outlined in the following way:

The Strategic Role

The executive, working through the President's Office of Management and Budget (OMB), receive Agency requests by the 1 October in the year prior to the commencement of the fiscal year on the 1 July. The President receives advice from the OMB, the Heads of the Federal Agencies, the Treasury Department and the Council of Economic Advisers. A Federal or Presidential Budget request is formulated by the Winter months for submission to Congress in the third week of the January in which the fiscal year in July begins. This

Budgetary roles	*Timespan in fiscal year*	*Location*
Stragetic role	1 October–December in the fiscal year preceding. (Although may be up to eighteen months prior to this date in executive gestation.)	*Executive Branch:* President, OMB, Council of Economic Advisers, Treasury Department and all Federal Agencies prepare Budget Request for Congress.
	January–July prior to the relevant fiscal year.	*Legislative Branch:* Congress in House Ways and Means and Senate Finance Bills. House and Senate Authorisation Committees provide authority for spending on specific programmes. House and Senate Appropriations Committees agree on appropriations. Each Chamber resolves conflicts between equivalent committees by Conference Committees. Decisions taken can either raise or lower expenditure and revenue and add-on or rescind specific programmes.
Managerial role:	Continuous process	*Executive Branch:* The President has the power of limited veto and impoundment of Congressional programmes and expenditure plans.
	Continuous process	*Legislative Branch:* All committees hold Hearings and Inquiries and have powers to question and call witnesses and see papers and are assisted by GAO studies and reviews.
Legal role:	Up to two years afterthe fiscal year	*Legislative Branch:* The GAO assists the Comptroller-General who audits the accounts of Federal Agencies and Reports to Congress.

FIGURE 2.2 The formal budgetary system in America prior to 1974 (fiscal year: 1 July–30 June)

budget has, since 1939, contained a centralised and co-ordinated request for both revenue and expenditure.[11] The *strategic* role is not confined to the executive branch in the United States however because the Congress has the formal powers (which it does use) to raise and lower expenditure and revenue requests, and also to shift the allocation of these requests between different priorities. The means by which this is achieved occurs in the normal legislative process in Congress.

Before any money can be appropriated for a particular purpose in America it must be authorised by one of the legislative committees of the Senate and House of Representatives. These authorising or legislative committees (Senate and House Armed Services Committee for example) have the power to authorise programmes and entitlements which the President does not support or to refuse to authorise those that he may desire.[12] Further *strategic* influence is however granted to Congress in the Appropriation Committees of each House. Both the Senate and House Appropriations Committees and their sub-committees have the power to refuse to grant appropriations requested by the President and to add-on expenditure and programmes to those requested. Clearly, then, there is within Congress a myriad of checks and balances which force compromise between different committees in Congress and between and amongst Federal Agencies and the President. Thus there may be different expenditure totals emanating from House and Senate Authorisation and Appropriation Committees and between all of these committees and the Presidential budgetary request. The normal process of reconciliation of these conflicts of interest is for conferences to be held between the two Houses and the various committees to arrive at agreed totals.[13] In general it is argued that in Congress the Appropriation Committees have a slight edge in influence and, because the House Appropriations Committee starts the process, that it may hold a slight edge over the equivalent Senate Committee.[14]

A similar mutual inter-relationship between various contres of power is also experienced in terms of revenue allocations. From the President's Budget request tax bills are formulated and sent to the House Ways and Means Commitee which can also raise or lower taxes in its final Bill. This Bill is then reviewed by the Senate Finance Committee and conflicts are resolved between the two committees and then *vis-à-vis* the appropriated and authorised programmes by relevant conference committees.[15] This process is completed by 1 July each year and agreed bills are then sent to the President for his signature and their approval as *obligated* outlays (i.e. this means there is an authority for Federal agencies to spend up to a certain amount of expenditure but these outlays – unlike in Britain – need not fall in the fiscal year under review). The strategic process in the United States therefore involves a mutual and continuous interrelationshp between Congress and Executive.

The Managerial Role

This role is also shared between the Executive and the Congress although it does not occur in any convenient or codified timespan. The scrutiny of what the executive agencies are doing with money and whether it is cost-effective is a continuous process in Congress. The scrutiny function is to be found within the committee hearing and inquiries which are held at both the authorisation and appropriation stages. Similarly, since the Congress can also make policy and allocation decisions the President has been granted the power under the 1905 and 1906 Anti-Deficiency Acts to create contingency reserves when authorised and appropriated expenditure is not necessary on cost-effective grounds or due to changed socio-economic circumstances.[16] Furthermore, the President has a limited power to veto and impound funds and temporarily limit expenditure on certain programmes when he feels this is in the national interest. Finally a form of *post-hoc* cost-effectiveness and scrutiny role has been provided by the General Accounting Office in modern times.[17]

The Legal Role

The role of auditing Federal Agency accounts and of ensuring that money voted for particular programmes is spent where it was intended has been performed since 1921 by the Comptroller-General working with the General Accounting Office and reporting to Congress.

In theory then there are marked differences between the roles of the British Parliament and the American Congress. The British Parliament has been formally limited to a *legal* and *managerial* role. The American Congress has traditionally shared the *strategic* and *managerial* roles with the President and the Federal Agencies and maintained for itself a *legal* role overseeing executive spending. But, by the 1960s and early 1970s it became apparent that these traditional roles, while somewhat different, were being questioned by executive encrochments and by an ever growing complexity of state and society. For this reason and in response to a similar reforming renaissance on both sides of the Atlantic, by the mid-1970s both Parliament and Congress had created for themelves new institutional and procedural relationships aimed at reforging their traditional roles.

THE NEED FOR REFORM:

The British Experience

While in the past the Parliament has normally effectively scrutinised and audited executive policy and expenditure decisions, by the end of the 1960s it was increasingly clear that Parliament's role was in danger of becoming moribund. A number of developments in the post-war environment were responsible for the undermining of Parliament's *managerial* and *legal* roles.

Public expenditure rose massively from 14.5% GNP in 1900, until, by 1978, it had reached approximately 50% GNP.[18] This growth, while fairly consistently upward, was not exponential because it rose and fell at certain times (see Figures 2.3, 2.4 and Table 2.1). The key periods of growth in expenditure (ratchets)[19] came during the First and Second World Wars. After 1945 however the trends of expenditure continued on an upward curve, with a large increase for Korean re-armament in the early 1950s. After 1955 there seemed to be an exponential growth of expenditure as social welfare and other state spending increased under the Keynesian consensus agreed by all major political parties at this time. This trend did not end until around 1975 when expenditure finally peaked as the weakness of the British economy and electoral antipathy became constraining invariables on public spending and increased taxation.[20]

Despite this decline in expenditure in the 1970s it was still the case that the state's role has massively increased. This undermined the rather limited and antiquated public expenditure procedures and committees in the House of Commons. By the 1950s it was becoming increasingly clear that not only had the size of expenditure and revenue increased, which was in itself a major problem for adequate and consistent Parliamentary scrutiny, but that the scope and complexity of the executive had increased. The growth in the number of civil servants and the rise in the responsibilities of local government meant that, by 1975, local authorities were accounting for approximately one-third of public spending and Parliament had no direct scrutiny over this expenditure as compared with central government Estimates.[21] Furthermore, as the state's Keynesian role developed in the management of macro-economic problems after 1945, it became inevitable that, as soon as the state saw a failure in micro-economic relationships, this would presage a move to even more directive state intervention. The form of this intervention –

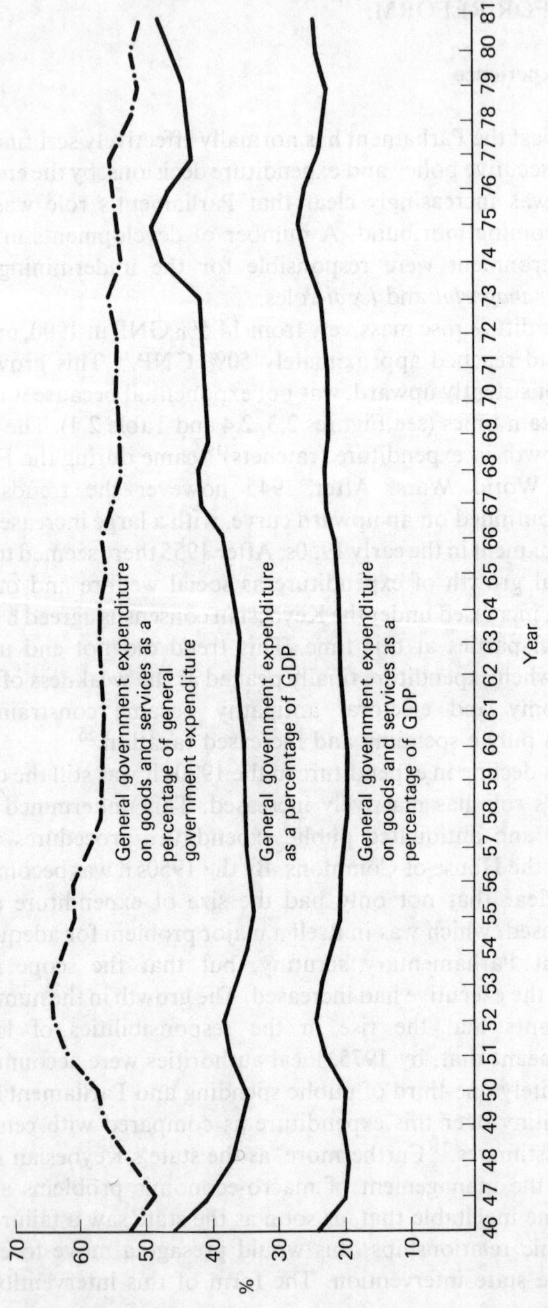

SOURCE David Heald, *Public Expenditure* (London: Martin Robertson, 1983) p. 25.

FIGURE 2.3 British general government expenditure/GDP ratios (1946–81)

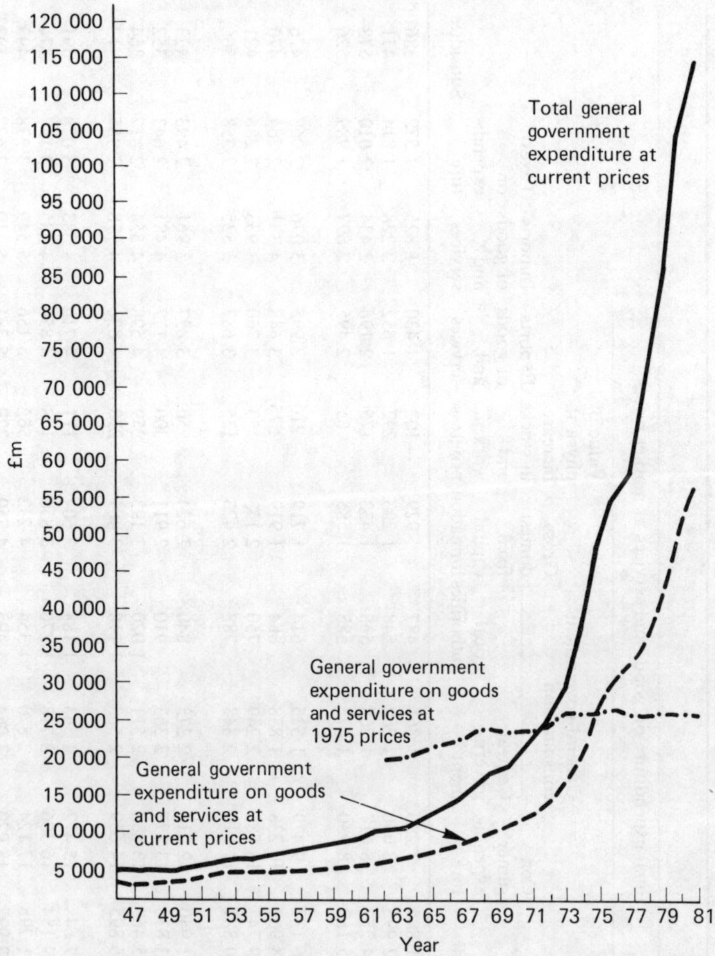

SOURCE David Heald, *Public Expenditure* (London: Martin Robertson, 1983) p. 24.
Notes: The series for general government expenditure on goods and services at 1975 prices can only be taken back to 1962 through a lack of constant price figures for earlier years covering general government domestic fixed capital formation. The Central Statistical Office do not publish any estimates of total general government expenditure (i.e. including, *inter alia*, transfers) at 1975 prices.

FIGURE 2.4 The growth of general government expenditure in Britain (1964–81)

aimed at solving supply-side problems – was in the shape of semi-autonomous, arms-length public agencies known as quangos, which were not accountable to Parliament in the same way that central

TABLE 2.1 *Expenditure on the Gross Domestic Product in Britain* (1946–83)

£ million, current prices

	Gross domestic product		Final expenditure on goods and services at market prices									
	At market prices[1]	At factor costs[2]	Total	Consumer's expenditure	General government consumption: Central government	General government consumption: Local authorities	Gross domestic fixed capital formation	Value of physical increase in stocks and work in progress	Exports of goods and services	Imports of goods and services	Taxes on expenditure	Subsidies
1946	10 060	8 874	11 885	7 280	1 861	487	929	—102	1 430	1 825	1 572	386
1947	10 765	9 422	12 993	8 036	1 262	548	1 203	292	1 652	2 228	1 814	471
1948	11 386	10 823	14 257	8 617	1 268	568	1 433	175	2 196	2 434	2 010	573
1949	12 492	11 029	15 189	8 980	1 473	588	1 588	65	2 495	2 697	1 989	526
1950	13 056	11 472	16 132	9 479	1 535	614	1 719	—210	2 995	3 076	2 060	476
1951	14 571	12 777	18 902	10 238	1 838	684	1 919	575	3 648	4 331	2 264	470
1952	15 814	13 949	19 747	10 785	2 249	750	2 153	50	3 760	3 933	2 286	421
1953	17 046	15 054	20 881	11 510	2 348	788	2 423	125	3 687	3 835	2 358	366
1954	17 979	15 909	21 940	12 210	2 373	840	2 624	56	3 837	3 961	2 493	423
1955	19 357	17 066	23 838	13 177	2 363	910	2 911	300	4 177	4 481	2 643	352
1956	20 915	18 462	25 469	13 888	2 511	1 020	3 193	259	4 598	4 554	2 817	364
1957	22 117	19 574	26 895	14 659	2 563	1 118	3 481	238	4 836	4 778	2 955	412
1958	23 065	20 428	27 648	15 472	2 563	1 188	3 604	111	4 710	4 583	3 028	391
1959	24 299	21 486	29 184	16 306	2 718	1 270	3 856	178	4 856	4 885	3 187	374
1960	25 749	22 864	31 298	17 124	2 870	1 354	4 232	562	5 156	5 549	3 378	493
1961	27 487	24 453	32 997	18 020	3 064	1 493	4 750	279	5 391	5 510	3 627	593

1962	28 806	25 535	34 414	19 110	3 234	1 638	4 904	—8	5 526	5 608	3 879	608
1963	30 613	27 155	36 640	20 319	3 341	1 978	5 144	161	5 877	6 027	4 027	569
1964	33 389	29 468	40 208	21 693	3 539	1 927	6 123	700	6 226	6 819	4 437	516
1965	35 887	31 499	42 858	23 110	3 851	2 143	6 618	461	6 675	6 971	4 959	571
1966	38 245	33 383	45 505	24 462	4 120	2 401	7 051	288	7 183	7 260	5 421	559
1967	40 473	35 277	48 328	25 704	4 518	2 695	7 701	286	7 424	7 855	5 997	801
1968	43 950	38 037	53 330	27 679	4 759	2 903	8 512	452	9 025	9 380	6 808	895
1969	46 957	40 019	56 887	29 379	4 873	3 123	8 832	537	10 143	9 930	7 780	842
1970	51 503	43 974	62 650	31 935	5 447	3 557	9 735	382	11 594	11 147	8 413	884
1971	57 838	50 037	70 031	35 748	6 194	4 078	10 889	114	13 008	12 193	8 740	939
1972	64 047	55 939	77 819	40 411	6 967	4 744	11 947	25	13 725	13 772	9 255	1 147
1973	73 997	65 310	93 030	46 004	7 872	5 557	14 835	1 529	17 233	19 033	10 124	1 437
1974	84 095	75 641	111 493	53 072	10 106	6 595	17 308	1 290	23 122	27 398	11 452	2 998
1975	106 264	95 812	135 269	65 216	13 493	9 592	21 312	—1 531	27 187	29 005	14 131	3 679
1976	126 798	113 799	163 693	75 712	16 140	10 865	24 718	789	35 469	36 895	16 458	3 459
1977	145 854	129 129	188 431	86 537	17 787	11 633	27 021	1 804	43 649	42 577	20 026	3 301
1978	167 963	148 668	213 474	99 486	20 069	13 285	31 137	1 690	47 827	45 511	22 958	3 663
1979	196 398	170 965	250 940	117 912	23 351	15 424	36 882	2 123	55 248	54 542	29 884	4 451
1980	230 197	199 317	287 626	136 789	29 851	18 959	41 628	—2 899	63 298	57 429	36 197	5 317
1981	254 203	218 020	314 135	152 125	33 826	21 496	41 794	—3 148	68 042	59 932	42 087	5 904
1982	277 334	235 759	344 353	166 477	36 950	23 252	45 993	—1 428	73 109	67 019	46 991	5 416
1983	301 298	257 489	377 880	182 427	40 623	25 236	49 559	267	79 768	76 582	49 865	6 056

[1] Equals total final expenditure on goods and services at market prices less imports of goods and services.
[2] Equals gross domestic product at market prices less taxes on expenditure plus subsidies.
SOURCE CSO; *Economic Trends, Annual Supplement (1985)* p. 8.

departments and the traditional nationalised industries had been.[22] As a result, there was a feeling that not only was public expenditure out of control but that public institutions were increasingly unaccountable.[23] Similar problems were also manifested as the post-war consensus ensured the permanent acceptance of welfare and social service programmes (pensions, unemployment benefits and social benefits) which were largely uncontrolled by Parliament. As the number of eligible people increased so did expenditure and taxation requirements with no effective central government or Parliamentary control. At the same time, Parliament faced an ever increasing technological and scientific complexity in the policy decisions that governments were forced to make. Not only did technological sophistication contribute to inflation and rising expenditure but it also ensured that a relatively amateur and 'club-like' Parliament, with procedures more fitting to an age of economy of spending rather than budgetary/fiscal economic 'fine-tuning', would be unable to maintain its *managerial* and *legal* roles effectively.

These trends were further compounded by factors which seemed to lead to an ever increasing executive centralisation of key policy and expenditure decisions. The first of these factors was the growth of functional representation and the trend towards a centrally dominated Corporate State.[24] In the 1960s academics were beginning to argue that this trend towards key policy and expenditure decisions being made increasingly by organised functional interest groups in Whitehall was a threat to territorial and Parliamentary democracy.[25] Some writers saw this as inevitable due to industrial concentration and mergers causing the executive increasingly to dominate the legislature.[26]

The limited measures available for control and influence over executive policy-making were increasingly seen as inadequate: question time was no longer an ordeal for well briefed Ministers; supply days were increasingly used not to debate the estimates in detail but for the opposition to indulge in ritual adversorial conflict over broad policy issues; adjournment debates were used increasingly for local/constituency issues rather than for national priority considerations; and, MPs lacked adequate staff and research back-up to keep abreast of the growing sophistication and complexity of modern policy-making.[27]

More worrying, perhaps, for those who were concerned with the inability of Parliament to discharge its function of controlling public expenditure was the fact that expenditure and policy planning as an administrative exercise was becoming increasingly esoteric and mysterious. It was gradually dawning on Parliament that decision-making in an age of massive forward expenditure commitments meant that policy was being formulated with five to ten year implications. This development could tie the hands of future Parliaments and limit the discussion of policy to incremental adjustments at the margins of on-going expenditure plans.[28] Furthermore, by the early 1960s, Whitehall was experimenting with a new five year forward planning system – the Public Expenditure Survey Committee (PESC) – which allowed departments to plan their expenditure on the basis of five year forward looks. This system had been encouraged by Parliament in the 1950s and by the Whitehall sponsored Plowden Report on *The Control of Public Expenditure*, which appeared in 1961.[29] While this development of esoteric management tools was obviously much needed to ensure that the long term expenditure consequences of individual policy decisions were fully appreciated in the light of likely economic growth, inflation and unemployment trends, it meant that Parliament and its Public Accounts, Estimates and Nationalised Industry Committees were unable to fully scrutinise expenditure and policy. They simply did not have the tools or information on which to assess the governments programmes satisfactorily. In particular the PESC figures were not presented to Parliament, nor were the Treasury forecasts. Furthermore these estimates which were available were only presented on an annual 'cash' basis, while the government now had both 'cash' and output budgeting figures.[30]

This meant that, while the executive branch in Britain was taking steps to maintain some control and future planning of its expenditure and revenue policy decisions, a large Parliamentary role in influencing government policies or controlling the 'power of the purse' was increasingly being seen as a sham. More worrying, perhaps, was the fact that state intervention and rising public expenditure was now making it ever more difficult for Parliament to fulfil even its limited *managerial* and *legal* roles adequately.

The inadequacies of Parliament were clearly apparent by the middle of the 1960s. Parliament lacked any means of setting priorities or of adequately scrutinising information or Departments because there was no means of tying expenditure and revenue policy together in the same institutional discussions. In fact while the Budget statement was clearly an important debating point, expenditure plans (with their 'guns versus butter' implications) were not given any consistent forum in Parliament.[31] Furthermore, under normal circumstances the government of the day could defeat any critical motion or reports by the use of party discipline and the Whips.[32] Ironicaly enough even when specialist subject committees existed to scrutinise government accounts (like the Science and Technology, Nationalised Industries, Estimates and Public Accounts Committees) they consistently lacked the detailed specialist staff, research facilities, or members who were sufficiently expert to question government priorities.

On top of this then came the problem that most public expenditure scrutiny in Britain was *post-hoc*. The Estimates and Public Accounts Committees only scrutinised expenditure plans after decisions had been taken. Further, the time available for the scrutiny of the estimates by these two committees was itself inadequate. The eventual reports from the Estimates and Public Accounts Committees were only provided with two and one days for debate respectively in any one session.[33] Ultimately this meant that while it had always been true that the executive has been able to dominate policy-making in modern times (through its control over a majority in the House of Commons; the Parliamentary timetable; the gestation of legislation; and, the provision of information)[34] Parliament's ability to fulfil its *legal* and *managerial* roles was now questioned as well. Procedures and institutions created by Gladstone over a hundred years before in the 1860s were clearly inadequate to the needs of the 1960s and 1970s.

The American Experience

The United States Congress, while always maintaining a share of the priority setting *strategic* role, as well as the *legal* and *managerial* roles, also experienced a diminuition of its ability to discharge these three roles in the post-war period. In particular the Congress failed to fulfil its prime role of setting national priorities for expenditure and revenue policy. As in Britain the United States has witnessed a fairly steady, if not exponential, increase in public revenue and expenditure (See Figure 2.5 and 2.6). In less than fifty years public expenditure rose from $3 billion in the 1920s to $300 billion in the 1970s. Between 1933 and 1973 the tax burden for revenue purposes rose from $2 billion to $250 billion. The national debt rose from $11 billion to approximately $500 billion in 1973, with deficits being recorded in 37 of the 54 years between 1925 and 1979.[35] This has meant of course

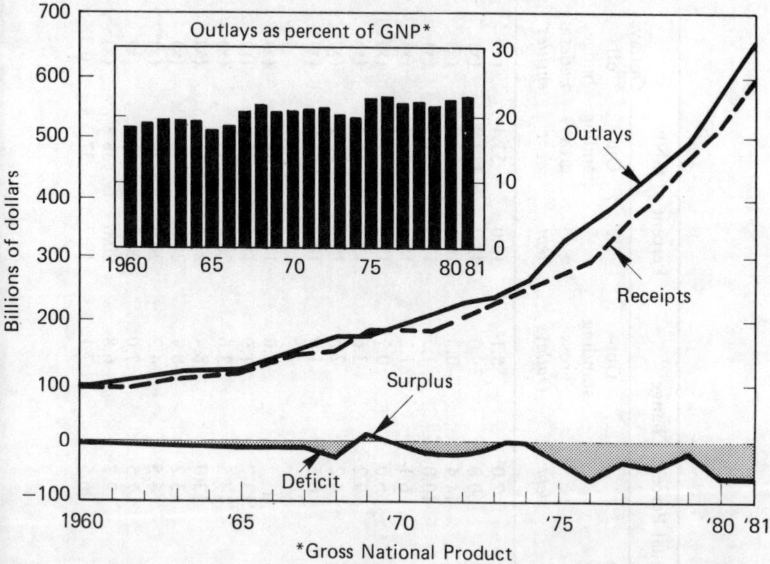

SOURCE *Statistical Abstract of the United States* (Bureau of Census) p. 244.

FIGURE 2.5 Federal budget receipts and outlay (1960–81)

that the number and range of decisions which Congress has been called upon to make in conjunction with the executive has risen massively. More worrying perhaps has been the fact that this increase in public expenditure has presaged an increase in the number and range of public agencies (quangos) to be scrutinised – many of which are at 'arms length' and not subject to detailed Congressional scrutiny.[36] But perhaps the most worrying element for Congress in this rapidly rising expenditure total has been the incidence of 'uncontrollable' expenditure. It is argued that over 55% of the annual budget is 'uncontrollable' due to entitlement (welfare, unemployment) programmes and the tendency for contracts and loans for public and private agencies to be authorised outside the normal appropriations process in Congress.[37] While this creates problems for Congressional control it is not problematic until economic growth declines and inflation rises making it difficult for all of these measures to be funded. After 1960 however deficit budgets were the order of the day as inflation rose and growth declined. This forced Congress to reconsider its role in the budget process as the demand for more and

Year	Receipts	( )	Surplus or deficit debt[1]	Out-standing gross *Receipts*	Annual Percent Change[2] *Outlays*	*debt*	Out-standing gross *Outlays*	Percent of GNP[3] *debt*	Out-standing gross *debt*	Outlays off-budget Federal *entities*[4]
1940	6.4	9.5	—3.1	50.7	37.8[5]	7.0[5]	5.1[5]	10.0	53.4	(x)
1945	45.2	92.7	—47.5	260.1	48.0	60.0	39.0	42.7	119.9	(x)
1950	39.5	42.6	—3.1	256.9	—2.7	—14.4	—0.3	16.1	96.9	(x)
1955	65.5	5	—3.0	274.4	10.6	10.0	1.3	17.9	71.9	(x)
1960	92.5	92.2	0.3	290.9	7.2	6.1	1.2	18.5	58.3	(x)
1961	94.4	97.8	—3.4	292.9	2.1	6.0	0.7	19.2	57.4	(x)
1962	99.7	106.8	—7.1	303.3	5.6	9.2	3.6	19.5	55.7	(x)
1963	106.6	111.3	—4.8	310.8	6.9	4.2	2.5	19.2	53.7	(x)
1964	112.7	118.6	—5.9	316.8	5.7	6.5	1.9	19.2	51.2	(x)
1965	116.8	118.4	—1.6	323.2	3.7	1	2.0	17.9	48.9	(x)
1966	130.9	134.7	—3.8	329.5	12.0	13.7	1.9	18.6	45.4	(x)
1967	149. 6	158.3	—8.7	341.3	13.4	17.5	3.6	20.4	44.0	(x)
1968	153.7	178.8	—25.2	369.8	2.8	13.0	8.4	21.4	44.3	(x)
1969	187.8	184.5	3.2	367.1	22.0	3.2	—0.7	20.3	40.3	(x)
1970	193.7	196.6	—2.8	382.6	3.2	6.5	4.2	20.3	39.5	(x)
1971	188.4	211.4	223.0	409.5	—2.8	7.5	7.0	20.5	39.7	(x)
1972	208.6	232.0	—23.4	437.3	10.8	9.7	6.8	20.6	38.8	(x)
1973	232.2	247.1	—14.8	468.4	11.3	6.5	7.1	19.7	37.3	0.1

1974	264.9	269.6	—4.7	486.2	14.1	9.1	3.8	19.5	35.2	1.4
1975	281.0	326.2	—45.2	544.1	6.1	21.0	11.9	22.0	36.8	8.1
1976	300.0	366.4	—66.4	631.9	6.8	12.4	16.1	22.3	38.5	7.3
1976, TQ[6]	81.7	94.7	—13.0	646.4	(x)	(x)	(x)	(x)	(x)	1.8
1977	357.8	402.7	—44.9	709.1	19.3	9.9	12.2	21.6	38.0	8.7
1978	402.0	450.8	—48.8	780.4	12.4	11.9	10.1	21.6	37.4	10.4
1979	465.9	493.6	—27.7	833.8	15.9	9.5	6.8	20.9	35.4	12.5
1980	520.1	579.6	—59.6	914.3	11.6	17.4	9.7	22.6	35.6	14.2
1981[7]	600.3	655.2	—54.9	992.6	15.4	13.0	8.6	23.0	34.9	23.6

X Not applicable. [1] End of fiscal year; see text. [2] For explanation of average annual percent change, see Guide to Tabular Presentation. [3] Gross national product as of fiscal year; for calendar year GNP, see table 699. [4] Federal Government allocations other than those reflected in budget outlays; see text for explanation. [5] Change from 1939, from previous year shown for all other years. [6] Transition quarter, July–Sept. [7] In March 1981 the 1982 budget request (submitted January 1981) was revised for most budget items. Where possible, information for 1981 is based on March revisions; otherwise January estimates are shown.

SOURCE *Statistical Abstract of the United States* (Bureau of Census) p. 245.

FIGURE 2.6 *Federal budget receipts, outlays, and debt (1940–1981)*
(In billions of dollars, except per cent. Through 1976, for years ending 30 June, except as noted; beginning 1977, ending 30 September. Minus sign (—) denotes deficit. See also *Historical Statistics, Colonial Times to 1970*, series Y 339-332)

more expenditure was increasingly matched by an electoral unwillingness to pay higher and higher taxation.

This process of re-appraisal of the Congressional role in budget policy was also necessitated as it became apparent that the acceptance of Keynesian policies in the post-war period had led to ever growing executive centralisation and control of budget and expenditure policies. Nor was this surprising because, as we saw earlier, while Congress formally had the 'power of the purse' and the final ability to set policy priorities, this process was immensely fragmented in the legislature in practice. The Senate Finance and the House Ways and Means Committee deal with revenue issues, while the Senate and House Authorisation and Appropriations Committees are responsible for expenditure decisions. Thus, while taxation and revenue proposals were sent to Congress in one budget, in practice they were dealt with separately and only finally reconciled once all spending decisions had been taken; they were never debated or discussed together as spending priorities were assessed. In other words the budget came out of the Congress with expenditure and revenue proposals, but this was not an integrated or co-ordinated process, rather it was the sum of diverse, unconnected, uniformed and 'client-related' decisions located in numerous centres of power within the Congress.[38]

This 'politics of the pork barrel', by which individual committees and Congressmen ensure that the special interests and districts they represent benefit from Congressional actions has always been a problem for Congress. It has become more difficult in the modern era, however, because it has implied an ever upward ratchet to public expenditure, at a time when the public has become less willing to pay the increased taxation which these spending decisions require. To overcome this inability to choose between buying off clients and friends or refusing to spend money to keep down taxation Congress traditionally turned to the executive in the hope that the President would be able to set these priorities and take the blame if clients were not adequately rewarded. This was one reason for the 1905 and 1906 Anti-Deficiency Acts, which gave the President the power to veto Congressional expenditure to create a 'contingency reserve' in the national interest. Similarly, in 1921 the Budget and Accounting Act extended the central economic and budget management role of the President. This Act allowed the President, assisted by a new Bureau of the Budget, to create his own budget request for Congress and to set policy priorities after studying Federal Agency requests. Franklin

Roosevelt extended this executive pre-eminence in budget/fiscal policy in the 1930s as he adopted Keynesian policies. In 1939 Roosevelt centralised further by bringing the Bureau of the Budget into the President's office out of the Treasury Department.[39]

It was with this growth of a Keynesian role – as underlined by the 1946 Employment Act which committed the President to maintain growth, low inflation and low unemployment – that Congress increasingly found itself at a disadvantage *vis-à-vis* the President and executive branch Congress failed to create for itself a similar institutional system as the Bureau of the Budget to co-ordinate expenditure and revenue proposals and set priorities. Post-war Presidents were increasingly 'fine-tuning' the economy and setting and re-setting their priorities which clearly indicated that Congress, for all its formal powers, was no longer the major actor in budget policy-making. Increasingly, the President and his Office of Management and Budget (the BOB was renamed in 1970), with the Council of Economic Advisers, the Treasury Department and the heads of the Federal Agencies were the major actors in the budget process.[40]

Congressional fear of central control was compounded in the 1960s by the trend to new budgetary techniques and management systems within the executive branch. We saw that the British had experimented with PESC as a new management system and this was *pari passu* with a similar trend towards reform and forward analysis of management systems in American Federal Agencies at the end of the 1950s and beginning of the 1960s. This new belief in 'output budgeting' (of looking at the expenditure consequences of future commitments and the costs and benefits of alternative approaches to fulfil the same goals, as well as the functional costs of agency goals rather than their administrative costs) was known in American as a Planning, Programming and Budgeting System (PPBS) and resulted in budgeting moving from a qualitative, administrative exercise to become increasingly esoteric, quantitative and computer based.[41]

This process of providing the budgetary system with an army of economic, computer and statistical advisers began in earnest in the Department of Defence in 1961 as a number of PPBS experts from the Rand Corporation were brought in with Kennedy's Defence Secretary, Robert MacNamara. The goal for these analysts was to compare and contrast alternative programmes for efficiency and provide costed options for the Secretary of Defence.[42] Eventually, by 1965 President Johnson was so impressed by this approach that he ordered all Federal Agencies to adopt PPBS by the 1 July 1967 under BOB supervision. By May 1969, 26 such Agencies had adopted forms of this system despite the lack of experts available in these techniques and opposition from a number of Congressional Committees which feared the consequences of the further development of PPBS.[43] This trend could not be overturned however; not even by Richard Nixon who turned against this approach himself in 1971.[44]

Like the British Parliament in the 1960s therefore the American Congress began to fear for its traditional role of *strategic, managerial* and *legal* scrutiny of the executive. Congress itself began to recognise by the early 1970s, a number of key reasons for this diminuition of its role. While Congress still retained the formal power to set priorities, and while it clearly could add-on to and subtract from Presidential budgetary requests, in practice the executive branch was normally in a position to dominate budgetary decisions because the president was the only actor in the process who could take an overview of budgetary (revenue and expenditure) requirements in the light of broader economic conditions. Clearly, this was a crucial weapon for the President when discussions and disagreements occurred over budget requests or omissions with the Congress (Eisenhower in particular used this power to restrain defence spending in the 1950s).[45] As a result Congress spent its time operating within specialist and blinkered committees which assiduously defended their 'turf' but were incapable of taking an overview. Furthermore the time available for their deliberations was totally inadequate because the decisions on the budget had normally to be taken between the end of January and the 1 of July. This timetable was rarely kept to and continually brought the Congress into disrepute.[46]

Further problems became manifest in this period as the problems of economic management became matters of increased public concern as economic growth slowed and inflation rose. It was apparent that Congress lacked any alternative source of economic advise and relied on Presidential/executive information. Despite the fact that Congress did have large committee staffs these normally consisted of subject or procedure specialists rather than macro- and micro-economic experts. This limited the ability of Congressmen to comprehend policy and budgetary choices. During this period the legislative Committees often authorised spending up to $10 billion above the level that the Appropriation Committees were prepared to fund.[47] But perhaps of more concern was the fact that Congress felt itself not only unable to understand budget choices but increasingly unable to control the level of expenditure. In part, as we saw this was due to the fragmentation of power in Congress and the 'politics of the pork barrel', but it also arose from the growth of 'uncontrollable' spending outside Congressional annual appropriation processes. In Fiscal year 1974 it was estimated that through entitlement programmes, contract authority and loan authority, at least 55% of the budget was not controllable.[48] Further problems were manifest also: Congress was totally unable to 'fine-tune' the economy because it had no control over the actual outlay of funds in any one year. This arose because in America (unlike Britain where expenditure is voted on a cash/annual basis only) Congress each year gives authority to agencies to spend a certain amount of money on specific programmes and that spending can occur in any year. This means that Congress has no immediate control over expenditure in any one year and can quite easily find expenditure rising in a year in which it wishes to retrench and vice versa. Finally, the process of appropriating funds by voting for specific items in detail was increasingly overtaken by the pressure of time, which meant that the former ability of Congress to scrutinise expenditure in detail was undone as it was forced to allow appropriations to be passed in blocks to speed up the process. This clearly left the executive with fairly wide discretionary powers to move funds around within any particular function – thereby undermining detailed Congressional control of expenditure.[49] For all of these reasons the American Congress in the early 1970s felt a need to re-assert its former role in budgetary politics – this was not however a completely new desire in either the United States or Britain.

THE DEMAND FOR REFORM

The British Experience

The British Parliament experienced a glorious two decades of *strategic* influence over government policy-making between 1848 and 1868 but this role was not to last after this period as the two party system, with fairly tight voting behaviour, was entrenched after 1868.[50] Indeed even during this period Parliament was losing powers to the executive and finding itself limited to a *legal* and *managerial* role. During the Crimean War, for example, Parliament found its power to call for any papers it wished; to demand debates; and, to create specialist committees to revicw any subject it thought important replaced by question time, when Ministers could be questioned about their actions.[51] Ultimately in the 1860s Gladstone created the Parliamentary scrutiny system of executive expenditure and policy enshired in the 1861 creation of the Public Accounts Committee and the 1866 institution of the Comptroller and Auditor-General and the exchequer and Audit Department. With the adoption of the Estimates Committee in 1912 after the Budget crisis of 1910 and 1911, to allow Parliament to devote more time to scrutinising the Department Estimates (but *not* the policy behind the Estimates), the 'circle' of scrutiny powers for Parliament was created.[52] While Parliament then had new institutions and procedures to scrutinise expenditure, in effect this was a diminuition of the ability of Parliament to question and control policy-making which had been experienced in earlier times. Now uncertainty of roles was replaced by a fairly clear demarcation of the relationship between legislature and Parliament: the executive decided; the legislature scrutinised and audited.

Since 1912 there have been demands for reform of this system in Britain and in general terms these have followed two lines of argument. First of all, there have been those who have railed against the limitations imposed on Parliament's influence over policy-making: the Lloyd-George Liberal reform proposals of the 1930s and the more recent Liberal, Walkland and Economist reform proposals for electoral reform and proportional representation aimed at giving back to Parliament a *strategic* role fall within this school of thought.[53] Secondly, and the most influential school of thought in the context of actual reforms adopted in Britain, have been those who recognised the need for a strong executive but who wish to see internal structural and procedural reforms to strengthen the *managerial* and *legal* roles of Parliament, which are perceived to be in abeyance due to executive encroachments. Within this broad church of internal reformers there have however been important differences of emphasis; ranging from those who merely wanted procedural reforms (Jennings) through to those who desired more aggressively scrutinising committees on either a subject or department orientated oversight basis (Crick, the Study of Parliament Group, Hill and Winchelow, Johnson, Crossman and Wheare),[54] to those (like John Mackintosh) who were concerned not only to extend internal committee reforms to encompass a more successful *managerial* role but also to copy the *strategic* role adopted in the American Congressional committee system.[55]

In terms of actual historic influence and pressure it is the internal reformers who have been the most active in pressing their case and in influencing Parliamentary arrangements in Britain. As early as 1917 the internal Whitehall Haldane Report on government machinery was calling for Parliament to be given more extensive powers to call for papers and executive information to enable it to fulfil its scrutiny role effectively.[56] In 1918 and again in 1943/44 wartime Select Committees on National Expenditure questioned the existing legislative control and scrutiny of expenditure and the estimates. Indeed it is interesting to note that both Committees (and as early as the First World War) questioned the utility of Parliament being given Estimates based on general administrative 'cash' requirements without costings for expenditure either being assigned to intended executive functions or to the future expenditure consequences of policies decided upon. In general the executive took little notice of these recommendations to restructure the estimates in a radical way to allow Parliament to maintain an effective *managerial* role. While the Army estimates were presented in a functional, 'output' format for a while they were eventually withdrawn on economy grounds in 1926/27, and an internal committee of inquiry (the Crick Committee on the machinery of government) in 1950 rejected the arguments of the 1943/44 Select Committee on similar economy grounds.[57]

Despite this bureaucratic opposition to internal structural reforms a number of developments in Parliament were successfully adopted in an attempt to allow Parliament to have a more effective *managerial* role. In 1944, a Select Committee on Statutory Instruments was created as it became clear that with the growth of the state's role in society and the burgeoning of public expenditure there was little chance of Parliament adequately covering the growth of delegated legislation in any detail. Eventually, in line with this general trend to update Parliament structures to take account of modern trends Conservative backbenchers forced their own government to create a scrutiny Select Committee on Nationalised Industries in 1956.[58]

Notwithstanding these successes for the internal reformers it was soon apparent that these were of only limited value. Changes taking place within the bureaucracy and its management of public expenditure in the late 1950s and early 1960s required additional reforms if Parliament was not to lose any credibility as manager and auditor of government actions. As the 1964/65 Select Committee on Procedure argued (taking much of its evidence and arguments from the servants of Parliament and concerned academics and MPs) most of the existing Select Committees lacked adequate expert advice and information; were ignored by the government; and, their reports were also ignored by the generality of MPs in the House of Commons. As a result there was not consistent scrutiny of government expenditure or policy decisions as the work of the committees were *ad-hoc* with no standardisation of approach. The Committee called for *one* Select Committee based on the format of the old Estimates Committee to look at expenditure and the estimates in more detail with specialist advisers and more research back-up.[59] This was of course seen as particularly important in the light of the new 'forward-look' (PESC) system which was beginning to be adopted in the light of the Plowden Report recommendations in 1961.[60] It is worth pointing out, however, that even at this stage, when the executive's own internal management reforms were seriously questioning Parliament's role, there was no unity of purpose or approach in Parliament: four minority members of the 1964/65 Procedure Committee argued not for one committee but for a full range of specialist committees on either a subject or departmental basis.[61]

In spite of mounting pressure and expectation of reform within Parliament – which was itself fuelled by the electoral commitment to reform by the Labour government which was returned to office in October 1964 – the reforming Labour administration soon procrastinated once in office as it seized the reins of executive power for the first time in thirteen years. There was therefore no early acceptance of the 1964/65 Procedure Committee recommendations, although the Estimates Committee was allowed to extend its sub-committees on a subject basis.[62] The government was not however fully committed to these reforms as the continuing miserliness of the executive over funding overseas travel and the failure to respond to sub-committee reports indicated.[63] The fear that reform might create Congressional style investigatory and strategic committees, which would limit a reforming Labour administration, explains much in the antipathy of the Wilson government to further reforms. After the decisive election victory in 1966 and the appointment of a reformer – Richard Crossman – as Leader of the House of Commons, the Labour government felt more confident in extending Parliament's ability to fulfil its *managerial* and *legal*, if not, *strategic* roles. In December 1966 an experiment in Select Committees was introduced. A new Science and Technology Committee to oversee a specific subject area and a new Agriculture Committee to oversee the work of a Department of State, were created.[64]

This did not mean however that the Labour government intended that it should give up any of its executive prerogatives as the experience of the Agriculture Committee revealed. This committee came into open conflict with the Ministry of Agriculture and the Foreign and Commonwealth Office. First with its desire to see papers relating to FCO submissions to Cabinet discussions on the agricultural consequences of EEC membership and, also, for its desire to visit Brussels to look into the problems of the Common Agriculture Policy against the Ministry of Agriculture's wishes. The committee was subsequently abolished in February 1969.[65] The experience of this committee did not lead to a total rejection of reform by Labour but it pinpointed that there were limited beyond which the executive was not prepared to be pushed. The Science and Technology Committee was maintained throughout the period because it confined its activities to fairly anondine, technical studies. As a result, the government allowed further committees to be created on an *ad-hoc* basis in 1968 and 1969. Some of these committees were departmental based (Education and Science and Overseas Development) while others were subject or function orientated (Scottish Affairs, Race Relations and Immigration and the Parliamentary Commissioner for Administration's Activities).[66] Overall however these committees, taken together, did not meet the requirements of the 1964/65 Procedure Committee because they maintained the unsatisfactory *ad-hoc* approach to executive scrutiny; they still lacked adequate research and expert back-up; and, the government and Parliament tended to ignore their reports and recommendations as it had in the past. Furthermore the innovation in special committees had resulted in the unfortunate side effect of diminishing the role and capability of the Estimates Committee. The number of MPs serving on the Estimate Committee was continually reduced from 43 to 36 in 1967/68 and 33 in 1968/69. At the same time the Estimates Sub-Committees were abolished after 1967 on the grounds that they either overlapped with or took members away from the experimental Select Committees.[67]

In a sense then the British Parliament, despite winning internal reforms from the executive in the 1960s, found itself in no better (indeed in perhaps a worse) position than it had hithertofore. The government gave with one hand and took away with the other in such a manner that, despite the pressure for consistent and uniform scrutiny powers, the legislature found itself with even more fragmented powers and committees than had ever been the case – a classic case of divide and rule? As a result a new Select Committee on

Procedure was instituted in the House of Commons and in 1968/69 it came forward with further recommendations for reform.[68] Influencing this new Committee's delibertions was a growing awareness of Parliament's inability, not only to scrutinise policy decisions, but to keeep abreast of the changes taking place in Whitehall and the management of public expenditure. In December 1963 a White Paper on Public Expenditure had been produced by the Chancellor which revealed the government's move to forward expenditure planning (expenditure was presented in twelve blocks with for the first time up to three years of forward projections included). This was followed in September 1965 by National Plan under the new Labour government, which presented chapters on public expenditure projections up to five years in advance and in far more detail. In February 1966 a further Public Expenditure White Paper was introduced in which the full five year PESC summary was reproduced with rolling programmes. Finally a Green Paper for Consultation was introduced in 1969 setting out the case for an annual Public Expenditure White Paper with far more information than had been the case in the past.[69] At the same time the government was also conducting its own inquiry into the workings of the civil service under the Fulton Committee. This Committee reporting in 1968 was to conclude that the bureaucracy was excessively secretive and that this had been exacerbated by the development of PESC. Furthermore it was argued that Parliament required a new information system for public expenditure decision-making if it was to fulfil its *managerial* and *legal* roles effectively.[70]

As a result of these new developments the Procedure Committee came forward with number of novel recommendations. The overall aim was for Parliament to be given a more effective scrutiny role and this was to be achieved by allowing the legislature to get more fully at policy decisions and their expenditure consequences than had been possible under the old Estimates Committee.

Thus on top of the demand for an annual Public Expenditure White Paper to be presented in November of each year came a request for an annual two day debate on the White Paper, which would in turn be assisted each year by reports drawn from a new Select Committee on Expenditure which would replace the old Estimates Committee. This new Committee (SCOE) would have a Steering Committee and nine sub-committees each containing nine members. The sub-committees would scrutinise the estimates of departments and also (and this was new) have the power to examine the means adopted to implement policy; any relevant public expenditure documents; and, make retrospective scrutiny of the results achieved. If this involved the questioning of Ministers over policy (this had never been allowed the Estimates Committee) and the calling for relevant papers, this was also taken to be necessary. Any final reports were to be prepared in time for them to inform the annual debate on the Public Expenditure White Paper.[71] Clearly, as the Committee recommendations indicated, there was a desire implicit in these proposals that there would be an end to the *ad-hoc* scrutiny of public expenditure and policy. True, it was always envisaged that the old PAC, Nationalised Industries and Statutory Instruments Committees would remain in operation – along with other Select Committees – but the new SCOE was to replace the old Estimates Committee in an attempt to allow Parliament to assess the overall level of public expenditure and its allocation amongst different uses. While this did not mean that Parliament should set priorities or take on the *strategic* role, which some of the reformers in Parliament (like Mackintosh) had always desired, it certainly meant that if they were instituted these reforms would take Parliament much further towards that role. Furthermore, these reforms, at the very least would ensure that for the first time Parliament would be in a position to discharge its *managerial* and *legal* roles effectively.[72]

The Labour government, due to the fear that it might weaken its own position, procrastinated once again. Reform was, however, made inevitable in June 1970 with the electoral success of a reform minded Conservative government led by Edward Heath which was commited to Fulton style management reforms. In October 1970 a Green Paper was produced spelling out what the new government was prepared to accept and, after a debate in November 1970, the new proposals were accepted and a Select Committee on Expenditure – with the goal of extending Parliament's scrutiny and information role – was created in early 1971.[73]

The American Experience

As we saw earlier there had been a number of reforms in the budgetary system in the United States before the Second World War. In general most of these reforms were aimed at extending the co-ordinating role of the President in order to overcome the fragmentary nature of existing Congressional–Executive relationships. Thus the

1905 and 1906 Anti-Deficiency Acts and the 1921 Budget and Accounting Act were attempts to end the upward spiral of spending and an attempt to introduce a degree of co-ordination into budget making. Despite these trends there were always demands in Congress for internal, structural reforms to ensure that Congress itself would set its own house in order rather than allowing the President to do it for the legislature. In part this obviously arose from a fear that the executive would come to dominate the *strategic* allocation of resources and usurp the constitutional role of Congress. Part of this pressure had been witnessed throughout the eighteenth and nineteenth centuries with pressure within Congress to reduce deficits.[74]

While there were similar trends to reduce deficits in the twentieth century to a large extent these goals were superseded by the move to Keynesian deficit financing by Roosevelt in the 1930s. Thus the pressure to restore a more co-ordinated and fiscally conservative Congressional role, as well as to restore legislative prerogatives lost to the President at the beginning of the century, became enshrined in post-1945 attempts to restructure the Congressional budgetary role. The first attempt to achieve a more co-ordinated Congressional role in budgeting came in the 1946 Legislative Reorganisation Act. This act tried to give back to Congress its overall *strategic* role of allocating priorities within overall expenditure and revenue total by ending the unsatisfactory fragmentation of powers in the legislature. In future, under this Act, a Joint Committee of both Houses on the Budget would be created which would set expenditure and revenue ceilings by the 15 February each year. This would clearly become the most important committee in Congress, because its ceilings would effectively delimit the scope for action by all the other Congressional budget committees. As a result it was hardly surprising that this proposal faced severe opposition from existing committees in the process and failed in operation. For the 1948 fiscal year the Joint Committee called for a $6 billion reduction in President Truman's budget but the conference committee set up to agree on the cuts could not do so and no legislative budget was adopted by Congress that year. For fiscal year 1949 an agreed $2.5 billion cut was agreed upon but it was soon discovered that the Joint Committee had no powers with which to enforce its decisions and the experiment failed to work as the authorising and appropriation committees ignored the ceiling. The Act fell into abeyance as a consequence.[75] This experiment was followed quickly by a second approach in 1950. In this year the House

Appropriations Committee tried to ensure an overview of spending by putting all the sub-committee appropriation proposals into one compendium bill rather than into several bills. The Senate procrastinated and refused to adopt a similar approach by the deadline of May which had been set and this second approach to overview and co-ordination fell into disrepute.[76]

Despite the desire to reforge the strategic pre-eminence of Congress after the Second World War there were a number of reasons why these innovations were likely to fail. First of all the Joint Committee system was unwieldly because it involved over 20% of Congressmen and its ceilings on expenditure came at a very early stage in the financial year. This had two weaknesses. It superseded the role of the Appropriation Committees which were powerful and, by setting early and rigid ceilings, it brought Congress into disrepute in a period when budgets were increasingly used for 'fine-tuning' economic problems at various times of the year. More problematic perhaps was the fact that no successful coalition of the diverse interests in Congress could ever be shaped in this period because the Party of the President in Congress always saw any Congressional reform as an attempt by the opposition to defeat their own executive's policy priorities. It would take peculiar circumstances for any workable cross-party consensus to be created sufficient to bring about the necessary reform of Congress.[77] Furthermore it was always difficult for Congress to act independently of the President and executive due to their lack of independent information sources. Finally Congressmen have never really been national policy orientated and have tended to concentrate on local constituency interests which makes a national budget role extremely difficult for the legislature to achieve.[78]

Why then was it possible in the early 1970s for Congress to institute a fundamental structural reform in the shape of the 1974 Congressional Budget and Impoundment Control Act, which did aim to restore the *strategic* role to Congress against executive pre-eminence? Obviously, the factors specified earlier – the growth in budget deficits and rising taxation, the problems of inflation and the realisation of presidential control over priority setting – were all of importance. Alone however these pressures would not of themselves have been likely to generate a cross-party desire for institutional reform because they had been fairly consistent features of the post-war period. On their own it is doubtful that they would have been likely to overcome the desire by Congressmen themselves to spend on their own special interests and constituencies. Indeed while there was growing pressure to limit federal spending in the early 1970s (which culminated in legislation to limit federal spending, demands for a Constitutional Convention on the need to balance the budget and California's tax-cutting Proposition 13 in the mid-1970s), alone these pressures would not have been sufficient.[79]

Two further factors – one a necessary condition, the other the sufficient condition – were responsible ultimately for the desire to reform Congressional strategic policy-making powers for the budget. The first necessary condition was a growing realisation of the need to ensure that Congress was in a position to scrutinise and check the institution of PPBS within the executive branch. The realisation that Congress would have to put its own house in order if it was to keep abreast of executive reforms in budgetary management was seen plainly in Senator William Proxmire's, Joint Economic Committee (sub-committee on economy and government) Report of 1969. In this Report Proxmire called for the dissemination of more information from the executive on PPBS and five year forward expenditure costings as opposed to the annual budget information in normal use. This new information was to be analysed by more Congressional staff assistance and a new committee structure to allow Congress to fulfil its constitutional role of controlling the budget.[80] This alone would not have been sufficient to cause all-party agreement on the need for reform; the sufficient cause was the impact of the imperial Presidency of Richard Nixon (1968/74) and the 'battle of the budget' between 1972/73, resulting in a controversy over the impoundment of Congressional expenditure by the president.

Nixon eventually united both Democrats and Republican, fiscal-conservatives, good-budgeters and liberal, anti-defence pro-welfare spenders into one united front in 1973 and 1974. Initially, there had been little chance of fiscal-conservatives in the Republican Party supporting Liberal-Democrats who wanted to reduce defence expenditure or 'good-budgeters' of all parties who wanted to restore the centrality of Congressional control over the budget, because they saw these measures as simply another guise for anti-Vietnam, anti-Nixon interests. Nixon, however, eventually eroded his own support in Congress amongst Republicans. This came about due to his Watergate involvement and exposure and, more importantly in the context of the budget, due to his decision to impound Congressional expenditure on programmes which he decided required curtailment.[81] Impoundment of itself was not the true cause of this waning support for Nixon because there had been a long history of Presidents impounding and vetoing expenditure on the grounds of sound financial management or higher national priorities.

Since the 1930s there had always been legitimate uses of impoundment powers: Roosevelt during the Second World War had stopped expenditure on public works to use the money for the war effort; in the 1950s and 1960s Presidents had vetoed spending on weapons systems and programmes approved by 'pork-barrel' Congressional action; and, Johnson had deferred billions of dollars worth of expenditure in order to reduce the level of demand in the economy which was seen to be contributing to inflation at the end of the 1960s. All of these actions were legitimate however because they were either temporary in duration or were taken for higher national priorities and/or in close consultation with Congressional leaders.[82]

Nixon went too far because in July 1972 he called for a ceiling of $250 billion, which entailed a cut in Congressional budget appropriations of $10 billion. Not only did Nixon do this but he also specified which programmes he wanted to end, reduce or curtail in an estimated $18 billion of impoundments. But, while Nixon argued he was doing this to reduce inflation the balance of the cuts fell heavily on domestic welfare rather than upon defence programmes.[83] This indicated that the President was flouting Congressional priorities in an attempt to impose his own ideological preferences on Congress and thereby undermine the formal relationships in the Constitution. Numerous bills were subsequently introduced into Congress to stop and reverse impoundment and court cases were introduced in the Supreme Court to test the legality of this action. Finally, in July 1972, a Joint Study Committee on Budget Control was instituted which reported in April 1973.[84] This Committee, while recognising the need to reassert the *strategic* role of Congress, was both aware of the earlier failure of reform and seized of the need to ensure that any reform would work. This meant of course that the reform could only be implemented successfully if any newly proposed Committees to oversee the budget were added on to, rather than supplanting, the traditionally powerful money committees.[85]

It was, however, generally agreed that the President had taken his powers too far and that he had been encouraged to do so by the fragmented nature of the Congressional budget process. These problems were to be overcome in the future then by the imposition on the existing budgetary process of a new fiscal timetable (giving Congress more time to look at priorities and to study the spending and revenue consequences of different programmes); assisted by new Budget Committees in each House of Congress (which would formulate resolutions setting limits on the authority to spend, the actual outlays of expenditure, the level of revenues and the size of the national deficit each year to guide the work of the existing committees so that they did not take decisions without awareness of the broader consequences of their actions). There was later a proposal to tie with this new restrictions on the President's power to impound funds.[86] This was eventually approved in July 1974.

THE NEW BUDGETARY PROCESS IN BRITAIN AND AMERICA

The Role and Structure of the Select Committee on Expenditure in Britain

The Conservative government after June 1970 followed the broad outlines of the 1968/69 Procedure Committee Report although a number of modifications limiting the scope of SCOE were noticeable in the final structure that was created. Instead of over 80 MPs being allowed to work on SCOE only 49 would serve. This arose because of the 9 sub-committees with nine members proposed only 6 sub-committees were created with eight members and one overall chairman.[87] This meant that the sub-committee would have to broadly subject orientated rather than departmental scrutinisers as had been the intention of the Procedure Committee. In this sense the more moderate reformers had seen their goals prevail over the more radical internal reformers who envisaged effective scrutiny of departments and an overall alternative priority setting role to that of the executive. Whatever the limitations of SCOE – and as we shall see they were to be legion – the 1971 reform did mean that Parliament had been given an institutional innovation which aimed at strengthening its ability to fulfil its *managerial* and *legal*, if not any *strategic*, roles.

The structure created was one which saw the demise of the old Estimates Committee and its replacement by a Select Committee on Expenditure. SCOE consisted of an overall (15 man) liaison/steering committee plus one general sub-committee for public expenditure as a whole. There were also sub-committees for Defence and External Affairs, Trade and Industry, Education and Arts, Employment and Social Services, and Environment and Home Office. Each committee was to be allowed to study any relevant estimates and public expenditure papers and to be allowed to discuss the policy behind the expenditure and to question and call Ministers and civil servants as witnesses. This meant that while the new system did not mirror the new PESC system, which was departmentally based, it did allow for a more extensive scrutiny role than the Estimates Committee. In particular there were more members and the sub-comittees were able to travel fairly freely. In addition each sub-committee was assisted, not only by the normal clerk to the House of Commons, but also by a specialist adviser and was to have access to the House of Commons library. While these research and advisory services were plainly inadequate when compared with Congressional support services they were nonetheless a distinct improvement on earlier times and did ensure that more informed reports would be provided for Parliament as a result. Set against this however was the failure to provide any time in the sessions of Parliament to debate the reports or to ensure any satisfactory framework of executive replies to SCOE recommendations.[88]

Nevertheless, for the first time Parliament had, alongside the traditional PAC and other *ad-hoc* Select Committees, a new structure in SCOE which had the capability of more effectively scrutinising the Estimates as well as the PESC system. Furthermore, if the institution was used as some intended it was possible to take government expenditure in the round and to set out alternative spending priorities to those of the government. This was not, as we shall see, to be achieved in practice and SCOE became merely an updated Estimates Committee. Nevertheless, the potential for a more effective *managerial* and *legal* role was built into this innovation and the provision of a more informed Parliamentary debate about 'guns and butter' priority issues was possible. In the end the high hopes which were entertained for this reform were to be defeated by a combination of executive recalcitrance, obduracy and MP myopia.

The Role and Structure of the Congressional Budget System

The purpose of the 1974 Congressional Budget and Impoundment Act was to (a) establish a legislative budget process to determine national policies and priorities and (b) provide a process to allow Congress to review Presidential impoundment of funds. Simply put, it was an attempt to reforge the *strategic* budgetary role of Congress under modern conditions. The way in which this was to be achieved was via four major provisions. The first of these provisions established two new committees, The House and Senate Budget Commitees (HBC and SBC), and the Congressional Budget Office (CBO). The second established a strict timetable and a new procedure for various phases of the congressional budget process, and the third created a new fiscal year, specified the scope of information to be included in the President's budget request and improved programme review and evaluation procedures. The final section established a procedure for the review and control by Congress of presidential impoundments of funds.[89]

The budget committee have the duty to report at least two 'concurrent resolutions' on the budget each year which must take into account the effect of existing and proposed legislation on budget outlays. The first to be adopted by 15 May, takes into account the President's budget request and the views of the authorising committees, and is intended to guide the subsequent appropriations of Congress.

The second, to be adopted by 15 September after all the regular appropriations have been completed, sets a ceiling on congressional budget action. The budget committees are assisted by the CBO which has a staff of 208 and which acts as the principal source of information for Congress on the budget and on taxation and expenditure legislation. By 1 April each year the CBO reports to the budget committees on fiscal policy and national priorities for the coming financial year, including alternative overall budget levels and also for each functional category (see Figure 2.7).

The first step in the new congressional budget year is the preparation by each authorising committee of its views and estimates on the budget matters within its jurisdiction and these will take into account the 'current services' budget, or the President's estimates of the cost of continuing existing services at their present levels, and his January budget which also covers requests for new budget authority.

With this information to hand and with the CBO 1 April report, the budget committees report the first concurrent resolution by 15 April, allowing for a full month for action on the floor of both Houses and for the conference meeting between the two committees before the resolution is adopted in May. The resolution sets targets for total new budget authority and budget outlays and also sets appropriate levels of federal revenue, public debt, and the size of the budget surplus or deficit. In addition, the new budget authority and outlays are allocated among the major budget functions. These resolutions do

The new budget calendar established by the Acts sets out the fiscal year in the following way:

On or before	*Actions to be completed*
10 November	President submits current services budget.
Fifteenth day after Congress meets	President submits his budget
15 March	Committees submit reports to budget committees.
1 April	COD submits reports to budget committees.
15 April	Budget committees report first concurrent resolution to their respective Houses.
15 May	Committees report Bills authorizing new budget authority.
15 May	Congress adopts first concurrent resolution on the budget.
7th day after Labor Day	Congress completes action on Bills providing budget authority and spending authority.
15 September	Congress completes action on second concurrent resolution.
25 September	Congress completes action on reconciliation process implementing second concurrent resolution.
1 October	Fiscal year begins.

FIGURE 2.7 *The Congressional budget timetable after 1974*

not have the force of law nor do they directly limit federal expenditure, but they do provide a coherent framework which orders congressional action on revenue, spending, and debt legislation.

The second budget resolution to be adopted by 15 September may retain or revise the levels set earlier in the year and can include directions to the appropriations committees, and to other committees, to recommend changes in budget authority, federal revenues, and public debt. Such changes are reported in a reconciliation Bill to be enacted by 25 September after which the budget process is complete.

The enactment of a reconciliation Bill also prevents Congress considering any spending or revenue legislation that would exceed the levels specified by the second resolution. Congress may, however, adopt a new budget resolution at any time during the fiscal year. The Act also restricts the various forms of 'backdoor' spending such as new contract or loan authority, encourages Congress to authorise programmes at least one year in advance of the fiscal year to which they will apply, and regulates the impoundment of funds by the Executive by requiring that they be reported to Congress and approved by it.

The Act therefore has the macro-economic objective of bringing order to, and restoring control over, the congressional budget process as a whole and of allowing Congress to set in a realistic way priorities for national spending. It also has implications for the defence budget.

First, the Act is intended to enable Congress to weigh the merits of spending programmes one against the other and to allow the national defence budget to be assessed not just against the Administration's request, but against the claims and merits of other public spending programmes in much the same fashion as was intended to SCOE in Britain. It was also intended to enable authorisation committees and the appropriations sub-committees for defence to estimate more fully the implications of their spending programmes on the budget as a whole, thereby making their actions more responsible and responsive to the priorities set by Congress. Finally the Act's provisions dealing with the standardisation of budget data, greater information from the Executive, and the control of Executive impoundments, were intended to enable the committee to assess, establish, and defend more effectively than before the priorities within each budget function.

In other words, therefore, the Act seeks to extend further the legislature's role is setting national priorities, as opposed to simply adding to or subtracting from the Presidential budget. In this sense, the 1974 Act in the US was less revolutionary than the 1971 reform in Britain because, in Britain, reform required that Parliament be given a national priority-setting capacity, as well as creating new scrutiny committees. In the US the priority-setting scrutiny committees were already in existence, what was required was some means of ordering the chaotic independence of these committees. As we shall see the implementation of reform in Congress has fallen short of the original intention owing to the two similar restraints that operate in Britain – the attitude and procedures of legislators and, more importantly, the independence of the Executive. Two crucial constraints when reinforced as well by the peculiar problems of reforming legislative oversight in the defence field.

The nature of these difficulties was outlined in general in Chapter 1, in the following chapters the acute difficulties facing attempted reforms of legislative oversight to render defence expenditure, procurement and policy-making more accountable to public scrutiny are documented in detail.

NOTES

1. Ann Robinson, *Parliament and Public Spending* (London: Heinemann, 1978) pp. 42–53.

2. Robinson, ibid. Paul Byrne, 'The Expenditure Committee: a Preliminary Assessment', *Parliamentary Affairs*, vol. 27 (Summer 1974) pp. 273–86; Nevil Johnson, 'Select Committee as Tools of Parliamentary Reform: Some Further Reflections', in S. A. Walkland and M. Ryle (eds), *The Commons in the 70's* (London: Fontana, 1977); and, S. A. Walkland, 'Whither the Commons', ibid., deal with the British experiment. Lance Le Loup, *The Fiscal Congress: Legislative Control of the Budget* (London: Greenwood Press, 1980), Aaron Wildavsky, *The Politics of the Budgetary Process*, 3rd edn (Boston: Little Brown, 1979); and, Joel Havemann, deal with the American experiment.
3. Peter Else, *Public Expenditure, Parliament and PPB*, vol. 36 (London: PEP, Nov. 1970) p. 2.
4. Philip Norton, *The Commons in Perspective* (London: Martin Robertson, 1981) ch. 2.
5. Kenneth Bradshaw and David Pring, *Parliament and Congress* (London: Constable, 1972) pp. 309–10.
6. Ibid., pp. 342–7.
7. Norton, op. cit., ch. 2.
8. Bradshaw and Pring, op. cit., pp. 317–23 and 342–7.
9. Else, op. cit., pp. 4–10
10. In particular the Public Accounts Committee discovered irregularities by Ferranti Limited in defence contracting and money overpaid was returned to the Exchequer in 1964 and changes were made as a result in government contracting. Bradshaw and Pring, op. cit., pp. 333–4.
11. Wildavsky, op. cit., pp. xii–xvi; and, Else, op. cit., pp. 68–9.
12. Bradshaw and Pring, op. cit., pp. 324–7.
13. Ibid., pp. 324–7.
14. Ibid., pp. 324–7.
15. Ibid., pp. 347–50.
16. George Cross, *The Congressional Budget and Impoundment Control Act of 1974: a General Explanation* (Washington: United States House of Representatives Committee on the Budget, Feb. 1975) p. 2.
17. Wildavsky, op. cit.
18. Mark Hodgkinson *et al.*, 'Public Expenditure in the United Kingdom: Myth and Reality', *Barclays Review*, vol. 55 (May 1980) pp. 33–4.
19. The best summary of the early growth of British public expenditure and the development of the concept of 'ratchet effects' is presented in Alan Peacock and Jack Wiseman, *The Growth of Public Expenditure* (London: Allen & Unwin, 1961).
20. P. K. Else and G. P. Marshall, *The Management of Public Expenditure* (London: Policy Studies Institute Report no. 580, Mar. 1979) pp. 5–7.
21. Robinson, op. cit., pp. 15–16.
22. Christopher Hood, 'The Rise and Rise of British Quango', *New Society* (16 Aug. 1973) pp. 386–8.
23. B. L. Smith and D. C. Hague (eds), *The Dilemma of Accountability in Modern Governments* (London: Macmillan, 1971).
24. Andrew Cox, 'Corporatism as Reductionism: the Analytic Limits of the Corporatist Thesis', *Government and Opposition*, vol. 16, no. 1 (Winter 1981) pp. 83–95.

25. John P. Mackintosh, 'Failure of a Reform: MP's Specialist Committees', *New Society*, p. 79.
26. On industrial concentration see: Leslie Hannah, *The Rise of the Corporate Economy* (London: Methuen, 1976); and on the state's growing intervention see: Stephen Young with Anne Lowe, *Intervention in the Mixed Economy* (London: Croom Helm, 19??).
27. Tam Dalyell, 'Making Parliament Work', *New Statesman*, vol. 76 (23 Aug. 1968) p. 218.
28. Hugh Heclo and Aaron Wildavsky, *The Private Government of Public Spending* (London: Macmillan, 1974) *passim*.
29. The Plowden Report: *The Control of Public Expenditure*, Cmnd 1432 (1961).
30. Peter Jay, 'Public Expenditure and Administration', *Political Quarterly*, vol. 41 (Apr./June 1970) pp. 200–2.
31. Robinson, op. cit., pp. 15–16.
32. Mackintosh, op. cit., p. 791.
33. Arthur Silkin, 'The Expenditure Committee: a New Development', *Public Administration*, vol. 53 (1975) pp. 46–7.
34. 'Parliament Redivivus', *The Economist*, vol. 274 (9 Feb. 1980) pp. 28–9.
35. Cross, op. cit., p. 1; and, *The Congressional Budget and Impoundment Control Act of 1974: Legislative History* (Washington: Committee on the Budget, HR 7130-S 1546, Jan. 1979).
36. B. L. Smith (ed.), *The New Political Economy* (London: Macmillan, 1974).
37. Le Loup, op. cit., p. 9.
38. Ibid., pp. 5–7. For a more detailed discussion of the American appropriations process see: Richard F. Fenno, The Power of the Purse (Boston: Little Brown, 1966).
39. Le Loup, ibid., pp. 5–7.
40. Wildavsky, op. cit., pp. x–xiii.
41. Ibid., *passim*: and, Else, op. cit., *passim*.
42. Else, ibid., pp. 69–72.
43. Ibid., pp. 73–4.
44. Else and Marshall, op. cit., p. 108.
45. Wildavsky, op. cit., pp. x–xiii.
46. Le Loup, op. cit., p. 6 and 19.
47. Wildavsky, op cit., p. x and p. 124.
48. *The Congressional Budget . . . Legislative History*, op. cit., pp. 21–4.
49. Ibid., p. 20 and 24.
50. Ronald Butt, *The Power of Parliament* (London: Constable, 1969) ch. 2.
51. 'Blowing up a Tyranny', *The Economist*, vol. 265 (5 Nov. 1977) pp. 11–12.
52. Else, op. cit., pp. 1–2 and 7.
53. Details of the various schools of thought are provided in Norton, op. cit., pp. 200–35.
54. Ibid., 200–9.
55. J. P. Mackintosh, 'What's wrong with British Parliamentary Democracy?', *Westminster Bank Review* (May 1968) pp. 20–35.
56. 'Making Parliament Work', *The Economist*, vol. 268 (5 August 1978) p. 16.

57. Else, op. cit., pp. 20–3.
58. Ibid., p. 7 and 21–3.
59. Report of the Select Committee on Procedure, *Specialist Committees* (H.C. 303, 1964/65).
60. Plowden Report, op. cit.
61. Mackintosh, 'The Failure of Reform', op. cit., p. 79.
62. The subject committees were for Social Affairs, Economic Affairs, Technology and Scientific Affairs, Defence and Overseas Affairs and Building and Natural Resources. See Martin Partington, 'Parliamentary Committees: Recent Developments', *Parliamentary Affairs*, vol. 23, no. 4. (Autumn 1970) pp. 366–9.
63. Ibid., pp. 370–5.
64. Donald R. Shell, 'Specialist Select Committees', *Parliamentary Affairs, vol. 23, no. 4 (Autumn 1980) p. 381: and, Gavin Drewry, 'The Outsider and House of Commons Reform', Parliamentary Affairs*, vol. 31 (Autumn 1978) pp. 424–8.
65. Mackintosh, op. cit.
66. Norton, op. cit., p. 131.
67. Partington, op. cit., p. 371; and, Walkland, op. cit., p. 247.
68. Shell, op. cit., pp. 396–404.
69. Jay, op. cit., pp. 201–203.
70. J. M. Lee, 'Select Committees and the Constitution'. *Political Quarterly*, vol. 41 (April/June 1970) pp. 188–91.
71. Report of the Select Committee on Procedure: *The Scrutiny of Public Expenditure and Administration* (H.C. 410, 1968/69).
72. Lee, op. cit., pp. 189–92. It is important to stress at this point that there was some overall confusion in what was intended. Maximialist reformers clearly wanted to push towards a more Congressional system, while moderate reformers wanted simply to extend the scrutiny of the executive or provide more information for debates. Robinson, op. cit., pp. 44–6 is useful on this.
73. Robinson, op. cit., p. 26.
74. John D. Fisk, *Legislation to Limit Federal Expenditure: Past and Present* (Washington: Congressional Research Services, Report No. 79-19E, 18th January 1979), pp. 1–8.
75. Le Loup, op. cit., pp. 6–7.
76. Ibid.
77. pp. 8–9
78. pp. 10–11.
79. Fisk, op. cit., and Le Loup, pp. 8–10.
80. Else, op. cit., p. 77.
81. Le Loup, op. cit., pp. 9 and 20.
82. Allen Schick, *The Impoundment Control Act of 1974: Legislative History and Implementation* (Washington: Congressional Research Services, Report No. HJ8 USA-76-45S, 27 Feb. 1976) pp. 1–8.
83. Ibid., pp. 3–8. The actual cuts attempted by Nixon were as follows: half of the $18 billion authorized for water treatment facilities; and moratorium on subsidies to housing; a cutback to disaster assistance; suspension of community and rural development activities; approximately $2 billion from the budgets of Labour and HEW Departments;

and, the curtailment of programmes assisting rural environmental protection and electrification, water and sewerage works, farm developments and water bank construction.
84. *The Congressional Budget . . . Legislative History*, op. cit., pp. 17–18.
85. Ibid., pp. 17–35.
86. Le Loup, op. cit., pp. 21–22.
87. Byrne, op. cit., p. 276.
88. Silkin, op. cit., pp. 45–7.
89. See *The Congressional Budget and Impoundment Control Act* (1974): Public Law 93–344.

Part II
Legislative Oversight and Defence Expenditure

3 The Impact of Reform on Congressional Oversight of Defence Expenditure

The major incentive for budget reform in the 1970s was the desire of Congress to regain control of the budget process, to exercise efficient control over functional budgets, and to set budget priorities in an effective and responsible manner. In particular the Congress was determined to have a much greater influence upon setting the priorities on defence and social welfare spending, and greater control of the defence budget itself than had been the case during the two administrations of President Nixon. This chapter will examine briefly the criteria against which the defence budget priority should be set, and also the manner in which the defence priority was set and defence budget controlled before and after the 1974 reforms. (For details of trends see Table 3.1 and Figures 3.1 and 3.2.)

SETTING A PRIORITY ON DEFENCE

The criteria for deciding what the defence priority *should* be rest upon the answers one gives to certain questions. The most important is defence of what? The security of the state is the fundamental and obvious answer, but itself begs the question about the nature of security and how it may be achieved. In this sense the defence priority can only be assessed in terms of the committments and the justifications of committments expressed in the state's foreign policy. In the recent past this has varied for the United States from 'Fortress America' to the idea of security in the 'greater than physical sense'.[1] That is to say the difference between defending the physical integrity of mainland America from external attack, and securing America's

TABLE 3.1 *Defence budget trends, fiscal years (1950–88) (in billions of fiscal year 1983 dollars)*

	Budget authority					
	Total		Investment accounts[a]		Operating accounts[b]	
Year	Amount	Per cent change	Amount	Per cent change	Amount	Percent change
1950	79.4		20.8		58.6	
1951	224.5	182.9	107.7	418.3	116.8	99.4
1952	288.8	28.6	150.1	39.3	138.7	18.8
1953	235.0	—18.6	106.7	—28.9	128.3	—6.5
1954	175.9	—251.	51.3	—51.9	124.6	—2.9
1955	149.5	—15.0	40.2	—21.7	109.3	—12.2
1956	153.6	2.7	49.1	22.1	104.5	—4.4
1957	163.2	6.3	57.6	17.4	105.6	1.1
1958	159.6	—2.2	59.4	3.2	100.1	—5.2
1959	170.9	7.1	73.0	22.8	97.9	—2.3
1960	166.0	—2.8	69.0	—5.5	97.1	—0.8
1961	165.5	—0.3	69.1	0.2	96.4	—0.7
1962	188.5	13.9	83.7	21.1	104.8	8.7
1963	191.8	1.7	89.8	7.3	102.0	—2.7
1964	184.6	—3.7	82.4	—8.2	102.2	0.1
1965	177.0	—4.1	72.5	—12.1	104.5	2.3
1966	213.1	20.4	93.2	28.7	119.9	14.7

1967	232.3	9.0	94.0	0.8	138.4	15.4
1968	235.4	1.3	92.2	—1.9	143.2	3.5
1969	226.5	—3.8	79.5	—13.8	147.0	2.7
1970	204.4	—9.7	69.2	—12.9	135.3	—8.0
1971	183.8	—10.1	60.3	—12.8	123.5	—8.7
1972	178.9	—2.7	63.3	4.9	115.6	—6.4
1973	170.8	—4.5	59.6	—5.8	111.2	—3.8
1974	165.2	—3.3	56.4	—5.3	108.8	—2.2
1975	161.5	—2.3	53.2	—5.7	108.3	—0.5
1976	168.2	4.2	60.0	12.8	108.2	—0.1
1977	177.2	5.3	67.7	12.8	109.5	1.2
1978	174.2	—1.7	65.0	—4.0	109.2	—0.3
1979	174.4	0.1	64.3	—1.1	110.1	0.8
1980	178.3	2.3	64.5	0.3	113.8	3.4
1981	200.3	12.3	78.8	22.2	121.5	6.8
1982	223.8	11.7	96.8	22.8	127.1	4.6
1983c	239.4	7.0	111.1	14.8	128.3	1.0
1984d	263.6	10.1	125.4	12.8	138.2	7.8
1985d	292.6	11.0	148.4	18.4	144.2	4.3
1986d	308.4	5.4	157.6	6.2	150.9	4.6
1987d	320.7	4.0	163.2	3.6	157.6	4.4
1988d	333.5	4.0	172.0	5.4	161.5	2.5

Continued

	Outlays					
	Total		*Investment accounts*[a]		*Operating accounts*[b]	
Year	*Amount*	*Per cent change*	*Amount*	*Per cent change*	*Amount*	*Percent change*
1950	69.1		13.2		55.9	
1951	107.3	55.3	21.6	64.3	85.6	53.2
1952	193.9	80.7	58.7	171.4	135.1	57.8
1953	207.3	6.9	81.1	38.0	126.3	—6.6
1954	194.9	—6.0	77.2	—4.8	117.7	—6.8
1955	168.4	—13.6	64.9	—15.9	103.5	—12.1
1956	162.5	—3.5	60.7	—6.5	101.8	—1.6
1957	166.5	2.5	62.4	2.8	104.1	2.3
1958	162.7	—22.3	63.1	1.2	99.6	—4.4
1959	165.4	1.7	66.4	5.1	99.1	—0.5
1960	164.3	—0.7	68.1	2.6	96.2	—2.9
1961	166.9	1.6	70.7	3.8	96.2	0.0
1962	179.6	7.7	75.5	6.7	104.2	8.3
1963	182.6	1.6	82.5	9.3	100.1	—3.9
1964	181.6	—0.6	78.8	—4.4	102.7	2.6
1965	165.6	—8.8	63.6	—19.3	102.0	—0.7
1966	183.2	10.7	69.4	9.1	113.8	11.6
1967	216.1	18.0	82.0	18.2	134.1	17.9
1968	236.0	9.2	90.8	10.8	145.2	8.3

1969	229.6	—2.7	89.5	—1.4	140.1	—3.5
1970	211.6	—7.8	78.1	—12.8	133.5	—4.7
1971	191.9	—9.3	67.7	—13.2	124.2	—7.0
1972	179.4	—6.5	62.0	—8.4	117.4	—5.5
1973	164.0	—8.6	56.9	—8.2	107.1	—8.8
1974	160.5	—2.1	53.9	—5.3	106.5	—0.5
1975	160.6	0.1	52.0	—3.6	108.6	1.9
1976	155.1	—3.4	49.7	—4.4	105.4	—3.0
1977	157.9	1.8	51.8	4.2	106.1	0.7
1978	158.7	0.5	52.4	1.1	106.3	0.2
1979	165.0	3.9	57.5	9.8	107.4	1.0
1980	170.0	3.0	59.8	4.0	110.2	2.5
1981	177.8	4.6	63.8	6.6	114.0	3.5
1982	191.1	7.5	69.5	9.0	121.6	6.7
1983[c]	208.9	9.3	83.2	19.7	125.7	3.4
1984[d]	230.2	10.2	96.2	15.6	134.0	6.6
1985[d]	252.1	9.5	111.3	15.7	140.8	5.1
1986[d]	271.8	7.8	124.7	12.1	147.1	4.5
1987[d]	284.8	4.8	131.3	5.4	153.4	4.3
1988[d]	295.8	3.9	138.0	5.1	157.8	2.9

[a] Includes the following accounts: procurement; research, development, testing, and evaluation military construction; family housing.
[b] All accounts not included in footnote a, primarily the following: military personnel, retired pay, operations and maintenance.
[c] Estimated. Includes Administration's proposed supplemental appropriations.
[d] Projected.
SOURCES: Department of Defense; and CBO projections based on DoD estimates.

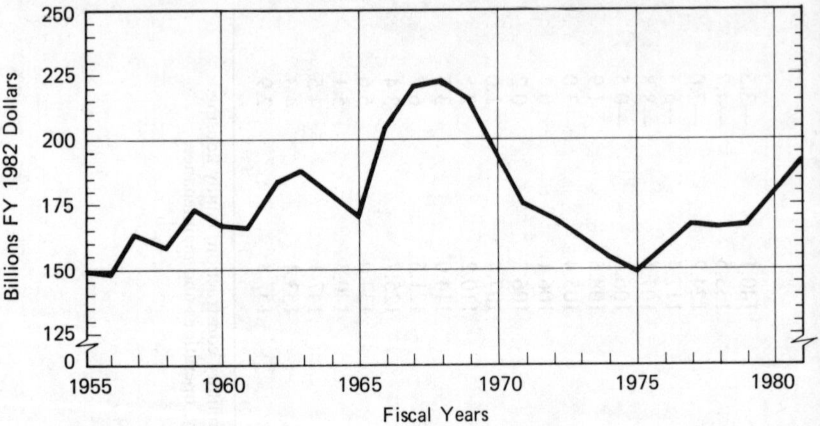

FIGURE 3.1 *Budget authority of national defence (Function 050) (1966–81)*

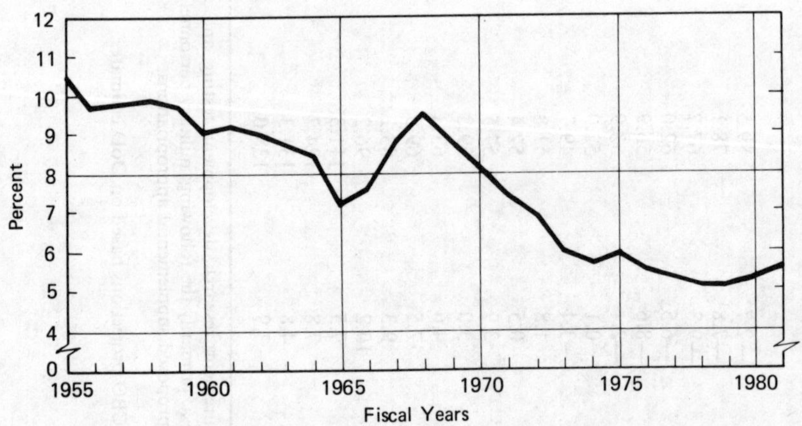

Source *CBO, Resources for Defence: a Review of Key Issues for Fiscal Years: 1982–1986* (GPO: January 1981).

FIGURE 3.2 *Outlays for national defence (function 050) as a percentage of GNP (1955–81)*

present 'way of life' as a wealthy liberal democracy in a liberal-democratic free-enterprise international system. The first requires the defence of the continental United States, the second defence of the 'free world' and the resources upon which it depends. A level of defence spending and capability that expresses a high priority for the security of 'Fortress America' would indicate a very low priority when applied to the 'free world' conception of security.

One must also answer the question defence against what?, and here the assessment of existing and potential threats to the state and its wider security interests are vital. The assessment may have both an abstract and a concrete dimension, as with the present 'one-and-a-half war' capability required of America's general purpose forces, and the specific assessment of the threat that a portion of those forces face in the NATO theatre. The assessment of a threat is always accompanied by a statement of the way that it should be countered, and at the level of strategic weapons, for example, the United States has fluctuated between policies of 'sufficiency' and 'superiority'. But concepts such as these can only be translated into military capacity by understanding what one's forces have to be sufficient for or superior to. This is not simply a question of calculating military capability, but raises the delicate and sensitive questions of assessing the intentions and interpreting the strategies of adversary states. The fact that capabilities and intensions are constantly changing means that the adequacy of a particular level of defence capability will also change and with it the priority that it communicates. It may be perfectly possible for the priority attached to defence to increase as defence spending and capability go down, if the threats against which they are deployed are declining even faster.

The third and perhaps the most perplexing set of questions concerns the standard against which the defence priority should be compared and the way in which priorities should be measured; that is to say, defence as a priority compared to what and by how much? In the context of the budget debate measurement is usually done in terms of resources expressed as dollars or as a percentage of GNP. The standard against which the defence priority is measured is less easy to identify. In the budget debates of the 1970s the defence priority has been considered most often in the classical 'guns versus butter' context in which current financial resources devoted to defence are compared to the current financial resources devoted to other public spending programmes. But in the attempt to define the defence priority there have also been comparisons of the relative growth of defence and non-defence resources, especially in the period after the Vietnam war when social welfare programmes grew very rapidly. The current level of defence resources has sometimes been compared to the level of defence resources allocated in the past or to those promised for the future. Supporters of higher defence spending have frequently assessed the defence priority by comparing what the President asks for and what the Congress grants.

The defence and budget debates of the 1970s less often, indeed hardly ever, assessed the defence priority in terms either of the capacity, the 'disposable power', that dollar resources bought, or the degree to which that capacity allowed the Department of Defense to fulfil its policies and commitments and meet the threats to American security. And although Congress has frequently expressed concern about defence cost-growth and cost overruns, that is its control of the defence budget, it has most often been to control the dollar volume of the budget rather than to preserve the military capability that it buys, or to acquire a specified capability more economically. Even the assessments of American and Soviet defence capabilities is most often conducted in terms of crude dollar-roubel comparisons, and the debate about respective military capabilities and intentions has been conducted at a very superficial level. The same is true of the comparison of various spending programmes where Congress endlessly debated dollar allocations but hardly ever compared the degree to which defence and other programmes were able to meet their objectives. These debates also lacked any deep consideration of the objectives themselves or an assessment of their adequacy and realism, but rather concentrated on marginal cuts or additions to functional budgets and programmes that otherwise made thier way through Congress largely by the force of inertia.[2] An examination of executive priority setting and defence budget formulation together with an examination of the pre– and post–reform methods employed by Congress to set the defence priority and control the defence budget will help explain these deficiencies.

Decisions about budget priorities and the control of functional budgets, including defence, have been shared in America since 1921 by the executive and legislature. Within the executive, decisions about the defence budget involve the Department of Defense, the President and the Executive Office. Within Congress, the defence budget is handled by the House and Senate Armed Services Committees, the defense sub-committees of the House and Senate Appropriations Committees and, since 1974, by the new Budget Committees of the House and Senate. These committees can draw upon the various support agencies of Congress, as well as on their own considerable staffs. The Executive budget expresses priorities for national spending and offers detailed budgets for each government agency, but Congress is able to rework departmental budgets in its legislative committees, and the thirteen annual appropriations Acts produced by the Appropriations Committees can express very different spending priorities to those of the President. In practice the congressional budget usually resembles that of the President, but the ability of Congress to make changes is considerable.

THE EXECUTIVE DEFENCE BUDGET

The DoD budget cycle has been based on a Planning, Programming and Budgeting system (PPBS) since 1961 and has been modified to some extent by each Secretary of Defense.[3] Harold Brown introduced some changes in September 1977 but retained the broad outlines of the system which is set out below. It is worth noting, however, that in 1977 President Carter introduced zero-base budgeting to all departments but its application in the Pentagon was a difficult and costly one. The end result was that very few of its methods were grafted onto the PPB system and then only at the margin. At its best the system allowed the cental budgeting staff of the Pentagon to establish three zero-based budget levels ranging from 10% above to 10% below the current year budget and only within this range were 'ranked' decision packages from programmes produced in order to allow the Secretary of Defense to increase or decrease spending and, at the same time, retain both the balance among and the priority of. Below this range, that is 90% of the defence budget, programmes were considered to be both essential and cost-effective.

PLANNING STAGE

November
The Joint Chiefs of Staff submit the *Joint Strategic Planning Document* (JSPD) which examines the existing Five Year Defense Program and assesses the military threat to the USA and proposes a strategy to counter it.

December-to-January
The Office of the Secretary of Defence reviews the Joint Chief's advice and drafts the *Consolidated Guidance* (CG) on defence policy and strategic guidance which serves as the central document in the planning stage.

March
The Secretary of Defense meets Service Heads and the Joint Chiefs to discuss disagreements on policy and military objectives expressed in the draft Consolidated Guidance. The Consolidated Guidance is sent to the Whitehouse for the *Spring Review* which is conducted by the President with the advice of the OMB, the Secretary of the Treasury and the Council of Economic Advisors. The OMB independently estimates the likely spending of the 13 largest domestic departments, but takes advice from the Secretary of Defense before calculating the total for defence. After the differences with the Services have been reconciled, or overruled, and the Spring Review completed, the Secretary of Defense issues the final version of the Consolidated Guidance including fiscal guidance.

PROGRAMME STAGE

March to May
The Joint Chiefs submit the *Joint Forces Memorandum* (JFM) which assesses the level of forces which can be provided for each of the ten programme categories within the limits of the Consolidated Guidance. The memorandum also assesses the risks associated with deploying forces at these levels, and it is at this stage that the Joint Chiefs traditionally make a strong case for additional funds.

May
Military Departments and Defense Agencies submit *Program Objective Memorandum* (POM) which are based on the strategic advice contained in the Consolidated Guidance and set out programme requirements for the next five years.

May to June
The Joint Chiefs submit the *Joint Program Assessment Memorandum* (JPAM) which assesses the balance of forces provided by the POMs and the ability of those forces to execute approved military strategies. The Office of the Secretary of Defense drafts *Issue Papers* which analyse the memorandum in the light of the Consolidated Guidance, and identify any trade-offs between modernisation, efficiency and readiness that will require the intervention of the Secretary of Defense.

July to August
The Secretary of Defense issues draft *Program Decision Memorandum* (PDM) which are sent to the Service and Defense Agency heads for comment. The Reclama book is opened to register Service appeals against the PDMs, and after consultations with Service heads the final version of the Memorandum is issued in late August to guide the preparation of budget estimates.

BUDGET STAGE

15 September
Services and Defense Agencies submit detailed budget estimates.

October to December
The Office of the Secretary of Defense and the OMB conduct the *Fall Review* of estimates to ensure that they are correctly priced and that production targets are realistic. As each estimate is approved it is entered in a Budget Decision Documents.

December
The Secretary of Defense submits his budget to the President for review within the context of the Federal budget. The OMB makes its 'hard choices' on defence at this stage and is constantly lobbied whilst it does so. The Pentagon/OMB dialogue responds to changes in domestic spending and the performance of the economy which allows marginal, and usually upward, revisions of the defence budget until virtually the eve of its presentation to Congress. After the DoD's budget request has been made final, the Defense and Service controllers translate the ten 'output' programme budgets into the six 'input' appropriation accounts and the 'line items' that are dealt with by Congress. The Five Year Defense Program is updated and becomes the base for the next PPBS cycle.

The PPB system is theoretically one of output budgeting, and should allow fiscally unconstrained planning, the objective assessment of military threats, needs and missions, and the provision of alternative costed options for each of the missions.[4] This is, however, far from accurate and overlooks the fact that budget cycles overlap and that budgeting is a continuous and political process. This is graphically illustrated by thc Five Year Defense Program which is the central document in the Pentagon's budget process because it is revised at the end of each cycle according to the most recent fiscal guidance for defence, and thereafter becomes the base for the next round of budgeting. This was tacitly accepted by the Assistant Secretary of Defense in evidence in Congress in 1977 when he said,

> The Department has long recognised that the appropriation structure specified by the Congress is input oriented. The FYDP structure attempts to convert these input oriented displays.[5]

The attempts to convert and display are very different kinds of exercise from output budgeting. The Joint Chiefs are also obliged to operate on the basis of the five year programme in the planning phase and must exercise 'fiscal responsibility' when drafting the Joint Strategic Planning Document.[6]

The importance of inputs in the budget system is reinforced by the final version of the Consolidated Guidance which contains fiscal, or input, guidance and remains in force as a planning and programming guide until revised by the Secretary of Defense. Even though the planning stage precedes the formal announcement of any year's *specific* fiscal guidance, the document remains a powerful benchmark in military and DoD planning. This shows that the budget phase rather than the planning phase is the beginning of the PPB cycle and that it informs the stages of planning and programming; indeed this is a view supported by a recent Director of Program and Financial Control.[7]

The restriction of zero-based methods to the upper margin of the defence budget means that the base is continually approved and that the operational plan which it reflects is not subject to scrutiny. The Pentagon has argued that this is reasonable, for to attempt a 'ranking or prioritization' over more than this limited band of the budget leads to a conflict between 'real world and reasonableness versus textbook'[8]. This comment makes the important and realistic point that an effort of unacceptable proportions would be needed to rank all programmes each year but nevertheless, the acceptance of the 'base' *budget*, that is prior inputs, necessarily forecloses many *planning* options.

In the 'Spring Review' the defence total is established by political negotiation between the Secretary of Defense and the President's staff, and past levels of defence spending play a particulalry crucial part. Similar calculations are made when re-allocating resources among agencies during the 'Fall Review' in December and a clearer example of political budgeting by input and by increment is difficult to find. Further confirmation is provided by the translation of the Pentagon programme budget – supposedly developed by output budgeting methods – into the input appropriation accounts and line items that are dealt with by Congress. This is partly to provide Congress with a budget that it can recognise and deal with, but also because the DoD understands that incrementalism, or making additions to a base that is 'given', is the most successful way to protect or increase the defence budget. The annual demand for more is not diluted by the need to justify what already exists.

The defence budget is not only incremental and highly political, it is also very flexible. This reflects the interplay of Pentagon, Service and congressional politics, changed political and economic circumstances, and changing public attitudes about defence needs, but it also reflects the important part that military play in defence budget planning. When political conditions are favourable for the expansion or redirection of the defence role, the Joint Chiefs can exert considerable influence and demonstrate remarkable agility in adapting military planning assumptions. Within a period of less than five years it was programmed that the USAF should contribute to the Strategic Offensive mission with a new manned bomber under Ford, without one under Carter, and with two under Reagan. The influence and flexibility of the military was demonstrated by the testimony of the Chairman of the Joint Chiefs of Staff on SALT II in the summer of 1979 and by his posture statement of 1980, only weeks after Afghanistan. These were crucial in radically redefining and redirecting the executive's defence policies,[9] and the speed of these reorientations belie any claim that the Pentagon's civilian and military heads used PPBS methods to make a comprehensive and exhaustive comparison of alternative policies and programmes.

The reclama system, which allows Service heads to appeal against programme and budget requests that have been denied by the Secretary of Defense, introduces an additional element of flexibility into the system since it provides the Services with an opportunity to reverse programme and budget decisions that go against them. This opportunity is sufficiently effective for the OMB to refuse to take any 'hard' budget decisions during the Spring Review simply to avoid being inundated by Service pressure.[10] The OMB exercises its influence during the November/December budget phase when such decisions become unavoidable and are essentially input based. Even when the executive budget is complete, the Services still have ample opportunity to fight their 'lost' causes in Congress and, during Carter's presidency, were very successful in restoring programmes deleted in the programme and budgeting phase.[11]

The budget process is also very lengthy and, with congressional action, occupies nearly two years. Within this time political and economic circumstances inevitably after the planning assumptions upon which programme and budget decisions are supposed to rest. For example, the 1974 mid-term elections brought to Congress many new members pledged to restrain defence expenditure, but within a year Cambodia and South Vietnam had fallen and the USA had been embarrassed by the Mayaguz affair and the public and congressional mood began to change; so much so that in 1976 President Ford increased the defence budget dramatically to appease rising congressional demands. President Carter also found the public and congressional ground-swell for a strong defence irresistable despite his election pledge to cut defence spending by 5% each year.[12] Such politically induced decisions divorce budgeting from planning and programming and have enabled the Services to acquire resources that will effect the defence posture over the long-term and in ways that did not appear in the Five Year Defense Program or in defence policy documents.

It is clear therefore that the Pentagon's budget is incremental, political and flexible, and that by far the largest part of it can not be closely examined by Congress to assess defence missions nor, therefore, the degree to which defence resources are matched to missions. The flexibility and sensitivity of defence policy to changes in congressional and public mood further undermined the ability of committees and Congress to make a seasoned assessment of the defence priority. Consequently, it is very difficult for Congress to make any effective judgement about the priority that the overall level of defence expenditure represents; it *should*, however, be able to exercise control over the incremental additions or reductions that are made each year to the defence budget. In practice, deficiencies in Congresses' own budget process make not only the defence base budget but also the annual defence increment uncontrollable, and neither element of the budget reflects any systematic attempt by Congress to set priorities.

THE PRE-1974 CONGRESSIONAL BUDGET PROCESS

The major problem in the congressional budget process as we saw in Chapter 2 was that there was no integrated or controlled process for coordinating the work of the many committees involved. Both spending and revenue committees operated separately over many months and produced a bewildering number of legislative measures, each reported to the House and Senate at different times and debated and enacted in isolation. Not even the 13 annual Appropriations Bills were considered together either by the Appropriations Committees or by Congress. The result was that,

> Budget action never explicitly decided the size of the budget, whether it should be in surplus or in deficit, and precisely by what amount. The budget process was, in fact, merely the sum of dozens of isolated and usually unrelated actions . . .[13]

The fragmented nature of the process allowed each committee autonomy over a segment of the budget, and allowed committee members to exert influence mainly to satisfy constituency and lobby interests.[14] Many interests, such as public assistance and farm support prices, were protected in the form of legal entitlement rather than through the annual appropriations process. This type of expenditure is 'uncontrollable' in the context of the budget process since changes in entitlements require separate legislation, nevertheless, most entitlements continued 'from year to year without being seriously reviewed or curtailed'.[15] The Office of Management and Budget estimated that the 'uncontrollable' portion of the budget had grown from $93 billions in 1967 to $332 billions in 1978, when it represented 75% of all budget outlays.[16] Fragmentation and loss of control made it almost impossible for Congress to identify priorities in the budget let alone readjust them.

Yet at the same time the ability of the executive to control the budget increased and the President's budget, and each of its functional budgets, became the major cue to congressional action. This was, and remains, the case even though the amount of detailed information contained in the executive's defence request has declined as its overall size has grown. The $100 billion plus Defence Department budget of 1976 had only some fifty block accounts which lacked the detail of, for example, the more than 40 'lines' of a

$200 000 appropriation for a Military Academy contained in the 1976 defence budget.[17] The authorising committees were, and are, supposed to review and establish policy for each department in a comprehensive and systematic manner, and the appropriations committees should use these reviews to make specific allocations of money and define the use of expenditures. However, both types of committee operate on an annual basis, begin their work long after the President has submitted his budget and focus on current rather than future spending and policy.

The Armed Services committees control the largest annual authorisations in Congress and indeed the House Armed Services Committee began the move towards greater annual authorisations when it won the right in 1959 to authorise the procurement of aircraft, missiles and naval vessels. This move was clearly intended to strengthen control over the Pentagon and to expand legislative influence over the defence budget, and both the House and Senate committees have traditionally used this influence to support the growth of defence spending. However, the time that the Armed Services committees took to make their recommendations, and the recommendations themselves limited and inhibited the work of the Appropriations committees which are the main protectors of the congressional purse.

The work and jurisdiction of the Armed Services Committees reduced the competence and the time available for the Appropriations Committees to consider the defence budget. It is the authorisation committees that are charged with the responsibility of exercising 'oversight' of executive departments to the exclusion of both appropriations and, later, the new budget committees.[18] This means that the review of defence programmes and management has been the responsibility of committees that have traditionally seen their role as concerned more with expanding the defence budget than with its effective scrutiny. This and the fact that the lengthy annual defence authorisation hearings have reduced the time available to the Appropriations committees has meant that the authorisations legislation has set the broad outlines of the defence policy and budget. In a 1977 report the House Budget Committee observed that,

> the basic shape of the defence procurement policy is determined at the authorisations stage and, in most years, the reporting and floor consideration of the defence appropriations bill occurs only weeks after the necessary authorisations have been enacted. Generally,

the floor debate on the defence authorisations bill is much more extensive than that for the equivalent appropriations measures.[19]

For these reasons the authorisations of the Armed Services committees create an expectation of high defence spending that it is difficult for the Appropriations Committees to ignore.[20]

Even so, appropriations respond even more strongly to the President's budget request and to the amount that was appropriated the previous year. This made congressional consideration of the budget in general and of defence in particular excessively incremental to the extent that 'the zone of discretion within which the Committees function ranges between last year's spending level and this year's budget request'.[21] Even when Congress attempted to change presidential priorities by cutting the defence request and protecting welfare programmes, committee action was predictable enough to allow counter-balancing action, and throughout the 1970s Presidents submitted 'unrealistically high Defense requests in expectation of later reduction by Congress'.[22]

Congressional control of the defence budget was also very tenuous not only because there was little that could be done to prevent cost-growth and cost-over-runs of military equipment and the escalation of military salary accounts as shown in chapter one, but also because the actual outlay of defence expenditure was entirely in the hands of the executive. The United States operates an obligation based budget rather than the expenditure based budget employed by most other states. Therefore, Congress may appropriate funds and pass legislation which authorises agencies to enter into obligations, but it does not control actual spending. This is decided by the rate at which individual agencies obligate the funds to specific programmes, and the speed with which those programmes are completed. For most major defence construction projects appropriations are made to cover the full costs and the appropriation may remain available for three years before it is obligated and specific contracts entered into. Outlays occur only when the DoD's contractors submit their bills, and the first of these may not be until some five years after the original appropriation was made.[23]

The discretion that this gives to the executive to vary outlays in any one year is particularly great in defence where the lead-time of modern weapons systems means that the DoD always has very large 'unobligated balances' on hand, balances which stood at $74 billion in fiscal year 1978.[24] The fact that Congress budgets one year at a time compounds this problem because executive outlays in any single year are made up of fractions of budget authority from several past years. Congress has found that 'the choices made in prior years restrain the cope of action in the [current] budget year', and that the goal of developing a budget that expresses congressional spending priorities cannot 'be achieved if budgeting is pursued one year at a time'.[25] The size and unusual nature of the degence budget made it particularly difficult to alter national priorities. The House Budget Committee noted as late a December 1979 that little had changed.

> The Congress still has difficulty debating important national budgetary choices, because the tremendous inertia of the Federal Budget makes it almost impossible to make major changes in the size or composition of the budget in any one year'.[26]

The Executive has also been able to use the provisions of the Anti-Deficiency Acts of 1905 and 1950 to reserve or impounded funds that were not needed to accomplish legislative objectives. The definition of what is needed to fulfil those objectives is a sensitive issue, and has been made most often by Presidents on their own initiative. In the field of defence the exercise of this initiative has met with a mixed reception from Congress. In the 1950s and 1960s there were several sharp controversies over the refusal of Presidents Eisenhower and Kennedy to spend money on particular weapons systems authorised by Congress, but Johnson's use of multi-billion dollar impoundments during the Vietnam War, designed to deflate an overheated economy, were taken in consultation with an supported by the Congress. However, Nixon's swinging programme of impoundments that affected defence hardly at all but made deep cuts in dozens of domestic programmes, was the single most important issue that galvanised Congress to reform the budget process.[27]

THE 1974 BUDGET REFORM

These problems produced the political coalition in Congress that formulated and passed the Congressional Budget and Impoundment Control Act of 1974 and the substance of the reform is now well documented.[28] The Act created the House and Senate Budget Committees to be assisted by a new Congressional Budget Office

(CBO), which was to be the principle source of information to Congress on the budget and also on spending and tax legislation. The Act also established a new budget timetable and fiscal year in order to co-ordinate the work of Congress, and a set of provisions to review and control presidential impoundments.[29]

The Act identifies five fundamental purposes which are the effective control of the congressional budget process, determination of appropriate levels of federal revenues and expenditures, impoundment control, setting national priorities and acquiring information from the executive.[30] The broad intention of the Act was to provide a coherent framework within which the long-estalished authorisation and appropriations committees could work and to allow Congress to see and control the global effects of their work. The essence of such control was seen to be a procedure to establish budget totals that reflected budget priorities established by Congress. The main effort to achieve this is centered on the adoption of two Concurrent Resolutions on the Budget by the House and Senate Budget Committeess which recommend levels of revenue and public debt, a surplus or deficit for the next financial year and, above all, levels of budget authority and outlay in aggregate and by function. It is the specification of functional budget levels within the overall federal budget that allows priorities to be expressed. At the beginning of the new system a 'target' resolution was to be adopted in the spring, and a 'ceiling' resolution in the autumn.

The work of the Congressional Budget Office is also important since it is charged with submitting a report to the two budget committees on fiscal policy and national priorities for the next fiscal year.[31] It also undertakes a 'score-keeping' function which involves the tracking of the numerous congressional spending decisions and relates them to the budget authority and outlay targets established in the most recent concurrent resolution. This serves the vital role of keeping the Budget Committees and Congress informed of the cumulative effect of its many budget decisions, and give early warning of legislation that may 'break' the budget ceilings or alter priorities. The CBO is also intended to assist the various legislative committees of Congress with budget information and to alert them to major budget issues that will arise in their area of jurisdiction in the next budget year.[32]

However, it was clear even in 1974 that the role of the new committees would be limited and a House study published in February 1975 emphasised,

> . . . the Budget Committees *are not intended to diminish in any way the responsibilities or prerogatives of other committees.* They are intended to perform new fiscal policy and priority-setting functions which, properly executed, will enable other committees to perform their tasks with greater focus and effect.[33]

In January 1981 the fundamental purpose of the budget system was described as the provision of 'order, guidance and information' to enable Members of Congress to make informed and responsible choices and to set priorities which are in tune with political and economic realities. It was hoped that this would give Congress 'a capacity to propose a coherent congressional alternative to the President's budget based on an examination of the whole budget rather than unrelated and often isolated parts'.[34]

The essence of the reform, therefore, was an attempt to instill self-discipline and responsibility into Members of Congress and the committees in which they worked, by establishing a process which provided independent budget information and which allowed the global consequences of separate committee actions to become visible. It was hoped that better information and a capacity for 'over-view' would enable Congress to set *aggregate* targets and ceilings for expenditure and receipts, and a *hierarchy* of functional targets for expenditure. The new process should have meant that Congress no longer had to legislate in ignorance, but could acknowledge the consequences of its actions.[35] However, Senator Henry Bellmon, the ranking Republican member of the Senate Budget Committee for most of the 1970s, observed that '. . . the level of general dissatisfaction which provided strong support for the passage of the act, did not reflect a consensus with respect to the manner in which the process once established should ultimately function'.[36] This observation was nowhere more true than in the consideration of defence issues.

THE BUDGET PROCESS AND DEFENCE

Limited Powers

A major restriction on the effectiveness of the new process is the limited constitutional powers of the Budget Committees and the effect that this has on their relationships with other committees and the party leaders in both Houses. Indeed, the composition of the Budget Committees, especially that in the House, is unusual and reflects the attempts of the established spending and revenue committees to limit their influence.

The House Committee has 30 members of which ten are nominated by the Appropriations and Ways and Means Committees, eighteen are nominated by other standing committees, including Armed Services, and the majority and minority leadership each nominate one representative. The parties have tended to use their caucases rather than the normal Committee on Committees to select their representatives. These unusual procedures have been described as necessary to recognise '. . . the special need to coordinate revenue and expenditure actions [and] to assure that all interests and views are represented by the making of fiscal decisions'.[37] In fact the procedures are to ensure that the interests of the fiscal and other standing committees are represented in the House Budget Committee and that it does not restrict or rival their work.

A further limitation on the House Committee, also introduced by fiscal committee representatives during the drafting of the Budget Act, is that no member may serve more than six years in five successive Congresses. This was intended to prevent members developing either a long-term interest in the work of the committee or expertise in budgetary matters.[38] So effective was this limitation that the House Committee was informed in 1980 that it had not developed into a 'supercommittee', as some established chairmen in the House had feared, but that temporary status had weakened attachment of some members to it and that there was concern about the ability of the committtee's representatives to defend effectively the views of the House in conference.[39]

The Senate Budget Committee has 22 members selected from the Senate at large in the same manner as other standing committees, but in the first years of the process the Democratic appointments were made by the Senate Democratic Steering Committee, whilst the Republican Conference made a special provision to allow its members of the Finance and Appropriations Committees each to nominate one Republication member of the Budget Committee. In both cases the intention was to ensure that the traditional committees had representation and influence on the new Budget Committee.[40] The effects of these limitations can be seen in the relationships between the two Budget Committees and other committees and especially in the formulation of the First Concurrent Resolution on the Budget.

Committee Relationships

The legislative committees of the House have been very cautious in their dealings with the Budget Committee and have not been willing to surrender any power to it. The House Budget Committee has been equally careful not to exceed its limited jurisdiction. This was graphically demonstrated in FY 1980 when pressure to balance the budget led the Senate to attempt to enforce 'reconciliation'.[41] This would have required legislative committees to limit their spending to the levels specified in the most recent Budget Resolution, but the House Committee would not accept the procedure. The official explanation was that it 'would not be appropriate or productive for the House',[42] but this simply disguised the fact that the Budget Committee feared the more powerful legislative committees, and that 'many Democrats, led by their respective committee chairmen, would vote against the entire resolution if their committees were directed to take reconciliation action'.[43] This can be explained in part by the fact that House Budget Committee chairmen tend to be the nominees of or show deference to more senior chairmen. For example, the first chairman, Al Ullman, was proposed by Wilbur Mills of the House Ways and Means Committee and acted in his shadow.[44]

However, when reconciliation was forced on the House in FY 1981 by the power of public opinion in favour of a balanced budget, Robert Giaimo the Budget Committee Chairman expressed the belief that budget cuts would best be made by the authorising committees, but added that,

> It is no secret that these committees will be under intense pressure from well-intentioned special interests to resist *any* reform or modification of existing programs

He reluctantly accepted the need for reconciliation but added the hope that it would 'be perceived' not as the efforts of one committee to accrue power at the expense of others'.[45] Yet this is precisely how it was viewed, and the Chairman of Armed Services was one signatory of a letter which described reconciliation as an act that 'undermines the committee system' and 'infringes on the legitimate roles of authority and appropriations processes'.[46]

The record of the Senate Budget Committee demonstrates an equal sensitivity to the interest of other committees and politial leaders, despite the fact that it was chaired for many years by Edmund

Muskie, a senior and respected Senator. From the very beginning Muskie resolutely refused to consider the 'line-item' budget details of the authorisation and appropriation legislation to prevent an intrusion into the jurisdiction of other committees. In 1978 he said,

> I suspect that the first substantial move we would make in that direction would be resented and resented by the authorising committees.
>
> So, I am not inclined to do it at this point because we have troubles enough with authorising committees in trying to maintain present roles.[47]

Even so, the committee had occasional need to look at the broad categories of functional budgets to estimate if the totals were realistic. After one such cursory examination of the estimates for defence spending, the Armed Services Committee noted in its report on the Fiscal Year 1980 authorisations,

> the committee desires to emphasize the need for the Budget Committee to avoid line-item review of budgets. Such review is not only inappropriate, in the light of the work of the authorizing and appropriating committees, but also slows the major congressional effort of reviewing overall budget levels.[48]

The Armed Services Committee seemed to be unaware that the work of the Budget Committee was intended to be a central part of that effort.

The First Concurrent Resolution

The work of the Budget Committees on the First Budget Resolution has also suffered from lack of co-operation from the legislative committees. This resolution is intended to guide the appropriations of Congress and set global spending, revenue and debt targets. It is accompanied by a joint statement of party managers, which distributes the total budget authority and outlays contained in the Resolution to the various committees of the House; it is this document that expresses congressional spending priorities. Not only is the Resolution formulated after the President has published his budget but it is also based upon the reports of spending intentions of the authorising committees themselves. Yet these reports are prepared early in the budget process, by 15 March, and usually before the authorising committees have completed their hearings. The reports are therefore speculative, often brief, and usually err considerably on the side of generosity.

Some committees, Armed Services most prominant among them, progressively decreased the amount of detail in their reports of the Budget Committees. In Fiscal Year 1981, the House Armed Services Committee reported a $175.3 billion defence estimate, $13.5 billion over the President's request, in a three page letter with one brief table of statistics attached.[49] Despite the brevity of and frequent over-estimation in the reports, they were invariably accepted as the basis of the first budget resolution. In 1978 the House Budget chairman expressed the belief that Budget Resolutions might have become 'Christmas trees' which gave legislative committees all they asked for, and a year later the ranking Republican on the committee said that 'through the estimates process, we find ways to accommodate all the committees'. It is clear that, lacking authority and containing representatives from other more powerful committees, the House Budget Committee very quickly adopted the habit of attempting to accommodate all the spending requests submitted to it.[50]

William Proxmire refered to a similar tendency in the Senate and noted that he had lived to regret the submission of low estimate for his own committee,

> ever since then I have been a little gunshy and I have attempted to come in high rather than low, and I think that is a common tendency. That means that the estimates can be unusually high.[51]

The Senate Armed Services Committee also made very brief reports to its Budget Committee, and a comment that 'some committees report in the greatest detail and others do little but give you a one-sentence statement that the committee's position is to support the administration's request', was a thinly veiled reference to this. Yet the Senate Budget Committee's self-imposed inability to examine line-items made it difficut to evaluate the spending requests of the authorising committees, which, in the first year, exceeded President Ford's budget request by $60 billion. Without the ability to examine the detail of spending proposals the Senate Committee has to rely upon the authorising committees it is supposed to oversee to formulate more realistic functional budgets. The order of spending priorities expressed in the Senate's First Budget Resolutions were the result of this *ad hoc* and uncoordinate procedure. One analyst has concluded that the Senate Committee's methods 'choked off any opportunity that the budget resolution might provide for the full Senate to debate spending priorities'.[52]

Furthermore, much of the information available to Congress is, or at least is regarded to be, tainted and of poor quality. Most Republicans and many conservative Democrats regard the CBO as 'Keynesian' – largely because its Director, Alice Rivlin, was a Brookings academic – and dismiss its economic and defence budgeting advice. Defence analysts on the House Armed Services Committee staff regarded the CBO defence experts as too young and inexperienced to be reliable and worked without their help or advice.[53] Each committee involved with the defence budget has its own staff and this is a further complication since information is used to protect a committee's 'turf', and there is not always as free an exchange of information between committees as the effective examination of the defence budget requires.

Budget Floor Action

The House Committee had to accommodate the spending requests of as many other committees as possible because it works and its reports were intensely partisan and votes in the committee and on the floor of the House had to be bought with an accommodating First Resolution.[54] In addition, the House Budget Committee cannot match the technical expertise of the Armed Services Committee on line-item defence equipment issues, and its members dare not challenge specific military requests on the floor even if they think that particular weapons programmes are poorly managed and do not meet defence policy goals. This was clearly expressed by one staff member who said, 'We're aware that we'll get killed if we take on the other Committees head-to-head. All we have to work with is the good will of the other Committees.'[55]

Yet, the work of the Budget Committee has intensified party divisions and dispute, and aggravated the competition of authorising committees for scarce resources. A member of the Congressional Research Service observed that, 'The budget process has fuelled an increase in budgetary conflict on Capital Hill',[56] and it has been a conflict fought out on traditional special-interest committee lines rather than on the basis of different views of budget priorities. Dr Alice Rivlin refered to this when she said in 1979 that,

> the floor debates on the resolution have been inordinately concerned about changing minor line items and adding to and subtracting from the functional totals. Sometimes the basic decision about fiscal policy kind of gets lost there.[57]

The chairman of the House Appropriations Committee described the traditional inter-committee conflict in the resolution debates rather more graphically when he said 'We had a bloodletting on some of those votes.'[58]

Senator Muskie on the other hand did, at first, attempt to enforce the targets of the first budget resolution against the decisions of other committees on the floor of the Senate. In August 1975, the first year of the new system, Muskie took-on the chairman of the Senate Armed Services Committee when the annual military procurement Bill was reported on the floor authorising funds that exceeded the first resolution. Budget Committee Republicans and Democrats supported Muskie on the Floor and, by a vote of 48 to 42, the military procurement Bill was amended to conform to the resolution target. However, Muskie's attempts in 1976 to control the more powerful chairman of the Senate Finance Committee, Russell Long, were to prove less successful and very costly to the prestige and effectiveness of Muskie and his committee. The episode reduced the standing of the Budget Committee and it became very reluctant to challenge other committees on the floor.

The Budget Committees of both houses found it difficult throughout the 1970s to assert any real control over the established authorising and appropriations committees, which continued to construct the budget piecemeal and in terms of parochial and political interests rather than centrally and in terms of national and strategic criteria. The ability of the Budget Committees to *review* the budget centrally did not lessen the fragmented and traditional way that it is *formulated*. This weakness was compounded by several technical problems that arose in the operation of the new budget system.

Technical Problems

One of the major innovations of the new Budget Act was to introduce a strict timetable for the completion of the various stages of the congressional budget. The President's Budget is introduced in January and is considered by Congress until 1 December when the Budget year begins. Two of the most important dates in the calendar are 15 March, by which time spending committees must report their spending intentions to the Budget Committees, and 15 May by which time the spending committees must report Bills recommending new Budget authority, and Congress must adopt the First Concurrent Resolution on the Budget. Most authorising committees authorise funds annually after a lengthy series of hearings, and most still find it extremely difficult to complete their annual review of spending by 15 March. As we have seen this encourages the submission of very generous estimates of spending to the Budget Committees which in turn inflates the First Resolution.

The 15 May deadline also presents problems, and has been a subject of constant criticism by authorising and appropriations committee chairmen. In the first year of the new system the Senate Armed Services Committee reported,

> For the first time, this year the committee had to work within the full procedures established by the Congressional Budget Act of 1974. The committee met the deadline of May 15th for reporting the military authorisation bill, although it was difficult and required a great deal of intense effort. In particular, the committee had to mark-up prior to the final passage of the Congressional Budget resolution and therefore without full knowledge of the final Defense budget targets. The schedule set forth in the Congressional Budget Act is difficult to maintain and ought to be reviewed.[59]

In its Fiscal Year 1980 report on the military authorisation bill, the same committee added, with a note of resignation, that the first budget resolution 'was again not passed by both houses in time to be of use as a guide to action', and reported that a budget waiver had been obtained which allowed the defence authorisation to be set without reference to the budget resolution that was supposed to set a priority on it, and once again allowing authorising legislation to dominate defence priority setting.[60]

The Chairman of the House Appropriations Committee has also made the important point that the failure of the authorising committees to complete their work on time places the appropriations committees under very severe pressure in the new timetable, and that this is an important reason why Congress has often failed to have its appropriations bills enacted by the 1 October deadline. He observed that 'The authorization problem is chronic and shows absolutely no sign of improving on its own. The provisions of the Budget Act have been tested and they are not adequate.' He noted that the FY 190 Department of Defense appropriation bill did not reach the floor of the House until September, and that if his committee had waited for the authorisations to be completed 'half the year would have elapsed before the appropriation could be signed into law. This would be a poor and expensive way to handle legislation with such obvious national security ramifications'. He added that unless a solution to this problem is found, 'Congress will have forefited a rare opportunity to implement effectively its will in setting national priorities and achieving legislative budget control.'[61] To date no solution has been found.

The Senate Appropriations Committee has also experienced pressure under the strict timetable of the new system. In Fiscal Year 1977 the committee struggled to meet the schedule set by the Budget Act and pushed the Military Construction Appropriation Bill through Senate in one hour on a day when attendence was below normal. It has been less inclined to meet the deadline in subsequent years. Despite these problems and criticisms, the timetable has remained unchanged and there has been an increasing tendency for authorising committees to miss the deadline thus putting pressure on the Appropriations Committees which should wait for them to complete action before beginning their own. The same problems made it increasingly difficult in the 1970s to approve the second budget resolution on time and contributed to it becoming nothing much more than an exercise in the addition of Appropriation Bills as they were voted into law. Congress kept to the Budget timetable for FY 1977, but by FY 1980 the final Budget action was taken two months after the deadline set by the Budget Act, and many departments had to exist on 'continuing resolutions' which allow them to spend at the rate of their previous budget year allocation, but which restricts the ability of Congress to consider spending priorities.

THE BUDGET SYSTEM IN OPERATION

Two marked budget tensions emerged in the operation of the new system and they became acute at the end of the 1970s. The first was between the demands of defence, championed largely by the Senate, and those of social welfare spending which were defended strongly by House Committees. The second was the tension between the demands for a balanced budget, which was supported by most Republicans and many fiscal-conservative Democrats, and the inclination of congressional committees, including Armed Services, to increase spending even at the cost of a growing federal deficit. Both tensions reached breaking point in the Fiscal Year 1981 budget cycle which began in January 1980, a little over a month after the thirtieth State legislature had passed a resolution in support of a constitutional amendment to require a balanced federal budget, and only days after the Soviet invasion of Afghanistan which stimulated demands for greatly increased defence spending.

In response to this situation the Budget Committees of the House and Senate held more extensive hearings than usual in preparation for the First Concurrent Resolution on the Budget for Fiscal Year 1981. That resolution would have to establish a balance among the traditional demands for welfare spending and the newer demands for increased defence spending and a reduction of the federal deficit. The House Committee set 'the challenge' of a balanced budget in recognition of the fact that the demand for it was 'broadly based and deeply felt'. The Senate Committee responded more to the public and congressional demand for a stronger defence posture and held a series of six special defence hearings from February to March 1980. Both sets of hearings, but especially those in the Senate, represent the most sustained and responsible attempt by the Budget Committees and Congress to set a priority on defence and for this reason are worthy of close examination. Although unusual in many ways, these hearings and the subsequent congressional action demonstrate clearly the potentialities of and the limitations of the ability of Congress to set a priority on defence.

Nevertheless, the highly charged atmosphere in which the post Afghanistan defence debate took presented a severe challenge to Congress, especially given its susceptibility to public opinion. This was clearly recognised by Senator Henry Bellmon who expressed the hope that the special series of hearings would enable the Budget Committee, Senate and the Congress as a whole 'to escape the trap of evaluating defense needs solely on the basis of the percentage of total growth'. He argued that the level of defence spending should be determined after an evaluation of foreign policy goals and the military capabilities needed to defend them. However he recognised that,

> This defense debate for fiscal year 1981 has already been so couched in terms of real growth that it will be very difficult to bring the consideration back to one of national security goals and capabilities. The administration has become a willing or an unwilling participant in this trend of divorcing the defence budget from the issues which concern it.'[62]

The Senate Budget Committee set itself four questions around which the hearing were organised: a determination of foreign policy objectives and of the military capabilities necessary to support them; an assessment of the threats to American national and global interests and their relationship to foreign policy objectives and military capabilities; an assessment of the ability of US miltary forces to meet foreign policy goals and military threats; and an assessment of the economic and budget effects of increased defence spending. Clearly the major objective was to identify a linkage between foreign policy goals and a level of military capability necessary to support them. There were no grounds for optimism since a CBO report of 1976 noted,

> A comparison of reports written during the 1970s – the presentations of Secretaries Laird, Richardson, Schlesinger, and Rumsfeld – demonstrates that factors such as detente, peace, and alliance systems have been variously interpreted as requiring reduced or expanded defence spending with little explanation of the changed international conditions or the changed assessments which lie behind such reversals. . . . The annual report still provides only the bare outlines of the reasoning by which the recommended defence posture is held appropriate to prevailing international conditions: Congress is still asked to approve these policy judgements on the basis of their conclusions alone.[63]

After six days of hearings on the FY 1981 defense budget request and after careful consideration of Secretary Brown's evidence, the committee concluded that the testimony it received 'did not identify a clear linkage', and noted that 'although our forces are designed primarily to fight wars, there was no testimony on our wartime foreign policy goals and, therefore, no way to link our forces to those goals'.[64]

The major problem confronting the committee was the very broad and vague, indeed almost enigmatic, definition of US defence goals and objectives offered by Harold Brown, the Secretary of Defense, and his military advisors. The Secretary is obliged under the provisions of the Defense Authorisation Act of 1976 to consult each year with the Secretary of State and report to Congress on the foreign policy goals and the military force structure of the United States. Brown's report specifically addressed the problem of the role that was expected of military power in maintaining US security, but he cast the administration's answer in the most all-inclusive of terms because,

> In order to begin answering that question we must ascertain the conditions necessary to US security. That is, we have to define how Americans can maximize their basic values of life, liberty, and the persuit of happiness without undue fear of conquest, loss of territory, or other threats to these activities, and without infringement on the rights of others to similar opportunities.[65]

He identified our international trends which he claimed were pertinent to decisions about US defence capabilities and these were that dependence on foreign raw materials made US security dependent on maintaining the territorial integrity 'of large parts of the world', that the same dependence made it necessary to keep open sea lanes 'with the principal geographic regions of the world', that the US must respond to the 'sustained expansion' of Soviet forces to 'avoid an inferior US military position', and finally the need to combat the ability of the USSR to exploit 'international turbulence' by providing 'the political/military leadership needed for the Free World'. The Senate Budget Committee commented that,

> These general policy statements are said to provide the basis for the FY 1981 Defense Program. These policy statements are so general that it is very difficult to link them specifically with the defence program.[66]

The problem was conceded by the Secretary of Defense in his report when he said that the level of forces necessary to support this conception of security was 'not an easy issue to resolve'. But the resolution of the problem was made no easier by the 'instruments of national security policy' that the administration was using. The first was 'sustained real increases in defence spending', and the *second* priority was 'carefully planned programs that make the best use of the added defense resources and the special national advantages we have'. This clearly reverses any responsible method of priority setting and there is little wonder that the Budget Committee felt that the administration focused principally on the rate of growth of the defence budget rather than on 'an understanding of new military threats or of any improvements that should be made to military forces'.[67]

Precious little accuracy was added to the committee's proceedings by the outside expert witnesses who appeared before it, and this was particularly evident in the three hearings that were devoted to the 'Soviet Threat'. The committee took evidence from Professors George F. Kennan and Richard Pipes, and Doctors Edward Luttwak and Robert Legvold. Kennan and Legvold offered moderate and measured assessments of the threat but with little evident sympathy for their views from the majority of the committee. Pipes and Luttwak on the other hand draw a lurid picture of Soviet intentions that included Professor Pipes' speculation that the Soviet Union was likely to seek to 'control . . . the two ends of the Mediterranean' in order to get Europe 'pretty much in a vice', although he did add that 'That is my guess. I have no evidence.' He also suggested that the Soviet Union was likely to 'fish in the very muddy waters' of Yugoslavia and engineer a situation where it could be invited to intervene in a Croation–Serbian conflict, and added the by then *de rigueur* observation that the invasion of Afghanistan was a major threat to the security of the Persian Gulf and also felt that in some circumstances a Soviet nuclear first strike against the United States was not only possible but likely.

Dr Luttwak was even less precise in his assessment of the Soviet threat and talked in terms of 'a great military power on the move'. For him, the Soviet Union 'was following [its] own logic; we will have to stop them by force. One hopes that it will not be in places where this might lead to nuclear complications'. Some members of the committee were extremely taken with this rhetoric and Senator Exon prefaced one of his questions to Dr Luttwak with the observation 'since there is a distinct possibility of a World War III . . .'[68]. In its review of these hearings, the committee observed that 'The only consensus among the four Soviet experts on this issue was that the Soviet Union seeks to enhance its position in the world as a long term goal', which was a rather tactful way of saying that much of the evidence had been either self-evident and platitudinous, or contradictory and highly speculative. It was certainly of little use in trying to determine either the precise nature of the principal threat to American interests or the appropriate level of US forces that could best counter it. However vague the experts consensus on the nature of the Soviet threat, three of them were agreed that at least $30 billion should be added to the fiscal year 1981 defence budget to meet the threat – whatever it was.[69]

In accordance with this mood and its own first 'instrument of national security policy' the administration was seeking a 5.6% real increase in defence expenditure and the central assumption on which this was based was described in the following way.

> There is no serious disagreement about the need for the United States to maintain the full spectrum of military capabilities, non-nuclear as well as nuclear. The panoply of forces now deployed by the Soviets alone makes this range of capabilities essential. We must simultaneously be in the business of deterring strategic nuclear, theatre nuclear, and non-nuclear war. This kind of diversity means, inevitably, that our total defence needs will be larger than in the past.[70]

This statement did little to identify goals or the way that military forces would relate to them, but it did at least identify three broad areas in which the administration might attempt to improve military capabilities. In the event the extra defence funds allocated to specific defence programmes achieved little more than cosmetic improvements.

In terms of specific programmes, the administration gave much prominence to the Rapid Deployment Force which it had first announced in the autumn of 1979. The force was intended to provide the United States with the ability to deploy up to 100 000 troops outside the areas covered by its alliance agreements. It was clear that adequate sea and air lift capabilities were lacking for such a force but by the time the administration had submitted its defence budget it had done little to indicate how it would remedy these deficiencies. Zbigniew Brzezinski had talked of the need to procure a new long-distance transport aircraft and 14 roll-on/roll-off ships,[71] but there was no discussion of the kinds of situation in which the force would be deployed, what considerations had determined its size or the size of the airlift and sealift programmes.

The debate on conventional forces in the Senate was even less concerned with specific requirements of this kind, and dealt only with the need to provide additional funds in order to raise military salaries aimed at improving the retention rate of service personnel, to increase operation and maintenance accounts and to purchase more military equipment. In other words the military and civilian witnesses simply supported the need for more conventional forces, but there was no attempt to offer a reasoned assessment about why they were needed. During the Committee's review of defence programmes, Senator Bellmon commented on the evidence of Dr John Lehman, a civilian witness, who claimed that the present level of American conventional forces had failed to deter events such as Afghanistan, Cuba, Iran and Ethiopia. Bellmon said,

> I do not think that anything we would have done militarily would have helped in any place like Iran or Afghanistan. Cuba happened in 1962, and we had nuclear superiority all over the place. In Ethiopia, we were there for 40 years or longer, and our armed forces did not help us there. I cannot follow your reasoning.

He followed this with the question 'Do you think Khomeini would have been deterred if we had all this hardware we are talking about?' The essence of Lehman's reply was that the conventional forces he was calling for could do little physically but that they might help change what he believed to be a 'general perception that the United States no longer is in the business of defending its vital interests'.[72]

The assessment of the administration's request for strategic weapons demonstrated a similar propensity to increase spending with relatively little attention given to the mission that these forces are designed to achieve or of their standing against the threat that faced them. The administration case rested on the assumption that deterrence required the US to demonstrate an ability to respond to all conceivable levels of 'Soviet attack', therefore the United States must 'have plans for attacks which pose a more credible threat than all-out attack on Soviet industry and cities.' To fulfil this the US would need 'options to attack the targets that comprise the Soviet military force structure and political power structure, and to hold back a significant reserve'. This request was made at a time when the United States already had what the CBO described as 'an ambitious modernisation program for its strategic forces', and its projection of January 1980 showed that 'spending on strategic force modernisation programs will increase almost 75 percent in real terms by fiscal year 1985'.[73]

Nevertheless the debate about strategic weapons centred almost exclusively on the alleged gap in Soviet and American investment in strategic weapons and Harold Brown asserted that overall Soviet military investment had been some 75% greater than that of the United States, and investment in strategic systems 100% greater. According to Fred C. Ikle, a former Director of the US Arms Control and Disarmament Agency the figures were 80% and 270% respectively. The ways in which these very different conclusions had been reached were not revealed to the committee nor were they asked for. There was no indication of the time scale that the comparisons related to, although it became clear that they were based, however imprecisely, on the 1970s which was a period when the USSR invested heavily in strategic systems to balance the large US investment of the 1960s. It was arcane and essentially misleading comparisons such as these that dominated the debate even though the committee's summary noted that,

> The bulk of Soviet procurement was in this decade . . . while the bulk of US procurement was in the decade of the 1960s. This difference is expected to decline in the '80s as the expenditures for MX missiles, for Trident missiles and submarines, and for cruise missiles increase.[74]

Even the most pessimistic assumptions about the nuclear balance accepted than any Soviet lead would occur in the early 1980s, and the CBO pointed out that this would be remedied by the programmes already funded by Congress and that any resources in excess of this would do little to 'increase US capabilities over the next few years because of the long lead-times necessary to deploy strategic weapons'. No member of the Budget Committee nor any of its witnesses considered the long-term implications of the new strategic resources they were calling for, and which Congress was to provide in abundance.

It is interesting at this stage to note briefly how Congress dealt with the fiscal year 1982 defence request. President Carter's budget, submitted in January 1980, included a defence request of $158.7 billion in budget authority and an outlay target of $142.7 billion and this represented a 5.6% real increase over FY 1980. The request was revised in February to $161.8 and $146.2 respectively to take inflation into account. The House Budget Committee in its First Concurrent Resolution on the Budget set defence budget authority at $160.8 billion and the outlay target at $147.9 billion, compared to the Senates figures of $173.4 billion and $155.7 billion respectively. In the House/Senate conference substitute figures of $171.3 billion and $153.7 billion were accepted reflecting the Senate's determination to have a defence figure considerably above that asked for by the President; a determination that arose from the many long months that it had wrestled with the question of the ratification of the SALT II Treaty.[75] Ratification had been suspended after the invasion of Afghanistan and defence became an increasingly important issue in the presidential electoral campaign with much public support for Ronald Reagan's tough defence line. This was clearly mirrored by Congress which did not pass the second budget resolution until late November 1980 when the defnce provision was increased further and represented an 8% real increase in spending over the fiscal year 1980 level.[76]

Some explanation of the willingness of the Budget Committee, and indeed Congress as a whole, to deal with the defence priority simply in terms of numbers rather than in terms of policy goals and programme capabilities can be found in the pronounced responsiveness of Congress to policies which seem to have the support of public opinion, and also to two unusual qualities of the defence budget itself. The first of these is that the problem of ten to twelve year lead-times for major items of defence equipment makes it difficult to express a higher defence priority in the short-term in anything but dollars and the second is what can best be described as the 'perceptual' quality of much defence spending.

The willingness to elevate the defence priority in response to perceived public demand was no where more evident than in the administration itself. Senator Bellmon made the caustic but nevertheless aposite comment in his opening remarks to the first of the special defence hearings,

> President Carter who ran for office on a platform of cutting defence spending has become, in other people's words a 'born again hawk' and embraced the concept of higher spending without noticeably educating the country or the Congress as to the purposes or goals of the foreign policy framework which he has

operated up until now. How much of the administration's new defense fervour is attributed to the world situation as opposed to the political timeliness of such a stance I cannot say.

The Defence Secretary was pushed on this issue in questions during the hearings and admitted that he felt that 'something like 60 percent of the American people now believe that defense spending should be increased'.[77] Indeed, there was evidence that public opinion had moved in favour of increased defence spending by December 1978, and the activities of pro-defence pressure groups had stimulated public and congressional support for increased spending.[78] It was this sort of pressure that led Brown to make such grandiloquent statements in his defence report as 'This nation must remain the strongest in the world. That, I believe, is the consensus of the country, and of the Congress.' The dilemma for the administration and the Congress was how to demonstrate to the public in some dramatic way that they were acting to fulfil the demands of that consensus; the dilemma was superficially resolved by resort to the 'machismo of numbers', or more simply by throwing dollars not so much at perceived defence problems, but simply into defence.

Nevertheless, there was another important reason why so much emphasis was given to the dollar volume of the budget rather than to the military capacity that it bought. There is no doubt that many members of the administration and Congress, and many of the civilian experts believe that the size of the budget has an important influence on the Soviet Union's 'perception', and that of other states, of America's determination to fulfil her defence commitments. Lawrence Korb spoke of the 'defence budget's message to the world' and claims that Kissinger supported high defence spending for its symbolic and 'perceptual' impact on negotiations with the USSR rather than for its effect on defence capability. This same concern can be seen in many passages of the fiscal year 1981 defense report and it is clear that the administration and Congress believed that the US was perceived to be weak and that high defence spending would help to remedy that perception even if it did little or nothing to affect the real balance of forces in the short and medium term.

Brown referred to the 'hypothetical ability of the Soviets to destroy even 90 per cent or more of our ICBM warheads', and said that it was not the same thing as a first strike potential, nor would it amount to 'a major Soviet military advantage', but he argued if the US did not respond to it there may be 'perceptual problems'.[79] The nature of, what one may call, this 'perceptual balance' was elaborated in the section of the report which emphasised the need to retain an 'essential equivalence' in the nuclear balance, not because the USSR had or could achieve any real nuclear advantage, but because 'many countries make comparative judgements about our strength and that of the Soviets'. He argued that unless the US had new strategic programmes which could be 'recognised to be essentially equivalent . . . the Soviets could gain in the world, and we lose, not from war, but from changes in perceptions about the balance of nuclear power'.[80] This shift to a perceptual emphasis in congressional priority setting for defence was noted by the CBO which reported that from fiscal year 1981 Congress asked simply 'By how much should defence budget increase' and only then 'and how should those increases be allocated?'[81]

This is not to say that the defence debate of fiscal year 1981 ignored defence programmes or defence missions; these were discussed at length even if in a general and sometimes obscure way. However, this does not detract from the fact that the debate was principally about making an addition to the defence budget, and there was almost no discussion about the contribution that such spending would make to defence capability nor, as we have already seen, was it possible to relate capability to foreign policy goals. This fact was recognised by some members of the committee. Senator Domenici noted that there was a good deal less to the administration's defence budget than met the eye, and that it was a 'hollow shell of dollars' which covered the cost of growth of weapons but which provided no new capability. This point had been made in a rather different way in a CBO document of January 1980 which outlined the key issues in the defence budget. It noted that,

> Recent debate over defence spending, however, has been marked by a tendency to emphasize the budget authority target as an end in itself, rather than focusing on programmatic content.[82]

It went on to show that the administration had increased the defence request but had not initiated any new programmes on which to spend the money, yet, if the assessments of the Soviet threat were correct, new programmes were vital to improve the military capability of the United States. New strategic programmes should have been a very high priority given the widely held belief that Soviet capability had been increasing for several years, but the report concluded,

> The inescapable conclusion is that the bulk of the new funds in fiscal year 1981 will go to purchase items that are not classified as 'major procurement' . . . to strengthen the operating accounts of the military forces, or to support research and development or facilities construction not associated with major weapons systems.[83]

All these items are of course important to a military establishment, but the defence budget request did not specify these purposes. The fact that the administration had no equipment plans or programmes for its much vaunted Rapid Deployment Force and that it could not add in the short-term to an already very ambitious strategic investment programme, meant that the extra defence money voted to assuage public and congressional yearnings for a less complicated and more powerful past had to be poured into any part of the defence establishment capable of taking them. Although the increase in the defence budget was justified mainly in terms of the need for new equipment programmes the House Armed Services Committee was itself engaged in hearings on the defense industrial base that showed that the capacity to handle new programmes was simply not there.[84] However much the fiscal year 1981 defence budget may be intelligible in terms of post-Afghanistan hysteria it remains the apotheosis of responsible budgeting and priority setting.

CONCLUSION

The Budget and Impoundment Control Act of 1974 was never intended to reform executive budgeting, and the planning, programming and budgeting system used by the Department of Defense allows Congress to examine effectively only the annual defence increment. The Act does, however, impose a new framework on the intensely political committees that authorise and apporpriate funds and raise revenues in Congress, but it does not limit or remove any of the powers they possess or the procedures they operate. The new Budget Committees were deliberately created with limited constitutional powers *vis-à-vis* other committees and have shown existing committees an extensive generosity in recognising their jurisdictions and special interests. This, and the timetable problems created by the new system, have allowed the Armed Services Committees to continue to dominate the annual formulation of the congressional defence budget, although they and the Appropriations Committee still respond very strongly to the President's defence request. Those same committees continue to formulate the congressional budget piecemeal and have defended vigorously their special interests in the floor debates on the budget resolutions. Therefore, the formally centralised consideration of the budget does little beyond formalise and concentrate the traditional special-interest bargaining that typified the old budget system.

The established committees have changed very few of their budgeting practices, and the new Budget Committees continue to be dependent on their goodwill to operate. Even when these new committees tried independently to address the problem of setting spending priorities, especially that for defence, as in FY 1981, they discovered that there was no relationship between the defence policy objectives and military capability nor were they able to clarify that relationship from the 'expert' witnesses that were called before the committee. The executive's control of defence outlays, one year budgeting and the long lead-times associated with defence equipment procurement make it impossible for Congress to alter substantially the defence priority within the federal budget. In the face of these limitations Congress has indulged in 'perceptual' defence priority setting, thereby abandoning any claim to responsible budgeting.

FOOTNOTES

1. The concept of security 'in the greater than physical sense' is well covered in Robert W. Tucker, *The Radical Left and American Foreign Policy* (Baltimore, Johns Hopkins Press, 1971) *passim*.
2. The belief that the budget is not closely examined but proceeds through Congress by inertia is well established. See for example US Senate Budget Committee, *First Concurrent Resolution on the Budget – FY 1979*, (Report, 95th Congress, 2nd Session, 1978) p. 209, for the view of Senator Bellman and US Senate Budget Committee, *Can Congress Control the Power of the Purse?*, (Hearings, 95th Congress, 2nd Session, 1978) p. 51, for the view of the then Director of the Congressional Budget Office, Dr. Alice Rivlin.
3. See Burton B. Mayer, Jnr. 'Evolution of PPB in DoD', *Armed Forces Comptroller*, Vol. 18, no. 2, (Spring 1973) pp. 21–6.
4. See for example, General Accounting Office, *Models, Data and War: a Critique for the Foundation of Defence Analysis* (Washington, 12 Mar. 1980), ch. 3, 'The Modern Design for Defence Decision', pp. 32–48.

5. US House Budget Committee, *Five-Year Defense Planning* (Hearings, 95th Congress, 1st Session, 1977) p. 7.
6. US Department of Defense, *Summary of the DoD Planning Programing and Budgeting System* (Udated, issued Mar. 1980) p. 1.
7. Interview with Clyde O. Glaister, Director of Program and Financial Control, DoD, 1st April 1980.
8. *Five-Year Defense Planning*, op. cit., p. 30.
9. See the comments of General David C. Jones, USAF, Chairman of the Joint Chiefs of Staff, *United States Military Posture for FY 1982*, p. iv.
10. Interview, DoD Apr. 1980.
11. The outstanding example is the AV-8B aircraft, see Chapter 5 below.
12. See for example the American Enterprise Institute annual publication on the five year defence programme, especially those by Lawrence Korb for fiscal years 1978–82, 1979–83 and 1980–84.
13. US House Budget Comittee, *The Congressional Budget Process: a General Explanation* (Washington: Committee Print, 1981) p. 4.
14. See John Freejohn, *Porkbarrel Politics*, (Stanford UP, 1974) *passim*, for a description of concessions made to special interests in the formulation of the Public Works Bill and other legislation.
15. US House Budget Committee, *Congressional Control of Expenditure*, (Washington: Committee Print, 1977) p. 9.
16. Ibid., p. 3.
17. Ibid., p. 32.
18. *Can Congress Control the Power of the Purse?*, op. cit., p. 16.
19. *Congressional Control of Expenditure*, op. cit., p. 37. See also George Brite, *Authorizing Legislation Required Prior to Enactment of Appropriations* (Washington: Congressional Research Service, 1972) *passim*.
20. This point is made very clearly by Richard Fenno, *The Power of the Purse: Appropriations Politics in Congress* (Boston: Little Brown, 1966) pp. 7–8.
21. *Congressional Control of Expenditure*, op. cit., p. 41.
22. Ibid., p. 42.
23. See Fred P. Wacker (piece on unobligated balances).
24. *Five-Year Defence Planning*, op. cit., p. 39.
25. The point has been made many times but see Senator Bellmonn US – Senate Budget Committee, *First Concurrent Resolution on the Budget FY-1979* (Report, 95th Congress, 2nd Session, 1978) p. 209, and by the CBO in 'Reducing the Federal Budget: Strategies and Examples', (CBO, Feb. 1980) p. 5.
26. US House Budget Committee, *Budget Act Review*, (Hearings, 96th Congress, 1st Session, 1980) p. 41.
27. See Allen Schick, *The Impoundment Control Act of 1974: Legislative History and Implementation*, (Washington: Congressional Research Service, 1976) pp. 3–4.
28. The Congressional Budget and Impoundment Control Act, *Public Law 93–344*. 93rd Congress, H.R. 7130, 12 July 1974.
29. A review and assessment of the purposes of the new system is included in the authors' 'Innovations in Legislative Oversight of Defence Policy', *The Parliamentarian*, vol. LXI, no. 4. (Oct. 1980), pp. 215–29.

30. Among the many outline descriptions of the provisions of the act see George Gross, 'The Congressional Budget and Impoundment Control Act of 1974: a General Explanation', (Washington: House Budget Committee, 1975) p. 9.
31. Ibid., p. 7, and *Congressional Budget Process*, op. cit., p. 7. The CBO annual report is now submitted to the Budget Committees in January or February to be used in the markup of the first budget resolution.
32. The CBO has been diligent in fulfilling this role but very few committees have responded consistently to its advice.
33. Gross, op. cit., p. 6. Gross was the General Council to the House Budget Committee.
34. *Congressional Budget Process*, op. cit., pp. 1–2.
35. Ibid., p. 3.
36. *Power of the Purse,* op. cit., p. 5.
37. *Congressional Budget Process*, op. cit., p. 6.
38. This point was confirmed in several interviews with House Budget Committee staff in Apr. 1980 and Mar. 1981. The point is also made in Joel Havemann, *Congress and the Budget* (Indiana UP, 1978) *passim.*
39. *Budget Act Review*, op. cit., p. 19.
40. Allan Schick, *The First Years of the Congressional Process* (Washington: Congressional Research Service, 30 Jun. 1976) p. 7.
41. The reconciliation process, if supported by the Senate and the House, allows the budget committees to force authorisations committees to keep recommendations for new budget authority within the ceilings set in the most recent resolution.
42. *Second Concurrent Resolution on the Budget, FY-1980* (Conference Report, 96th Congress, 1st Session, 1979) p. 17.
43. See the Comments of Representative Ralf Regula in *Budget Act Review*, op. cit., pp. 257–9. The quotation is taken from p. 259.
44. See Havemann, op. cit., pp. 80–81.
45. Letter from Robert N. Giaimo, Chairman of the House Budget Committee to Thomas P. O'Neill, Jr., Speaker of the House, 2 Apr. 1980.
46. Letter from 10 House Committee chairmen to Thomas P. O'Neill, Jr., Speaker of the House, 27 Mar. 1980.
47. *Power of the Purse*, op. cit., p. 41.
48. Ibid., p. 22.
49. US House Budget Committee, *Views and Estimates of the Committees of the House on the Congressional Budget for Fiscal Year 1981*, (Committee Print, 96th Congress, 2nd Session, 1980) pp. 79–82.
50. See Lance T. LeLoupe, *The Fiscal Congress: Legislative Control of the Budget*, (Westport, Conn.: Greenwood Press, 1980) p. 15. LeLoupe describes the willingness of the Budget Committees to conceed spending requests as a *strategy*.
51. *Power of the Purse*, op. cit., p. 22.
52. Havemann, op. cit., p. 44, and p. 65.
53. This was confirmed in several interviews with House Armed Services Committee staff one of whom described the CBO defense staff as '21 year old Vasa graduates'.

54. In the 1977 Budget cycle the first and second concurrent resolutions were passed by 21 and 4 votes respectively.
55. Quoted in Aaron Wildavsky, *The Politics of the Budgetary Process*, 3rd ed (Boston: Little Brown, 1979) p. 258.
56. *Budget Act Review*, op. cit., p. 4.
57. Ibid., p. 51.
58. Ibid., p. 283.
59. S. Rept., No. 94-878 (1976) pp. 6–7.
60. US Senate Armed Services Committee, *Authorisations for DoD FY-1980*, (Report, 31 May 1980) p. 22.
61. *Congressional Budget Process*, op. cit., p. 6.
62. *US Senate Budget Committee, First Concurrent Resolution on the Budget FY-1981* (Hearings, 26 Feb.–2 Mar. 1980) p. 3.
63. Congressional Budget Office, 'International Political Assumptions in Defense Posture Statement', (CBO, 15 Mar. 1976) p. v.
64. 'Summary of the FY 1981 Defense Hearings Conducted by the Committee on the Budget, United States Senate', (Undated, issued by Senate Budget Committee Office, Apr. 190) p. 1.
65. Department of Defence, *Annual Report to Congress, FY 1981* (29 Jan. 1981) p. 26.
66. 'Summary', op. cit., p. 5.
67. Ibid., p. 13.
68. Senate Budget Committee, *First Concurrent Resolution FY-1981*, op. cit., pp. 184–5.
69. 'Summary', op. cit., p. 2.
70. Ibid., pp. 62–3.
71. 'An Interview with Zbigniew Brzezinski', *Wall Street Journal*, 15 Jan. 1980, p. 20.
72. Senate Budget Committee, *First Concurrent Resolution FY-1981*, op. cit., p. 219.
73. See Congressional Budget Office, 'Key Issues in Considering the Fiscal Year 1981 Defense Budget', (CBO, 23 Jan. 1980) p. 9, and 'Summary', op. cit., p. 9.
74. 'Summary', op. cit., p. 13.
75. See US Senate, *First Concurrent Resolution on the Budget FY-1981*,, (Conference Report, 96th Congress 2nd Session, 1980) p. 19.
76. Congressional Budget Office, 'Resources for Defense: A Review of Key Issues for FY82-84', (CBO Study, Jan. 1981) p. 1.
77. Senate Budget Committee, *First Concurrent Resolution FY-1981*, op. cit., p. 3 and p. 135.
78. See Lawrence J. Korb, 'The FY 1980–84 Defense Program: Issues and Trends', *AEI Foreign Policy and Defense Review*, vol. 1, no. 4, (June 1979) p. 27 for an assessment of changes on public attitudes in America towards defence spending.
79. *DoD Annual Report to Congress FY -1981*, op. cit., p. 6.
80. Ibid., pp. 68–9.
81. CBO, 'Resources for Defense', op. cit., p. 1.
82. CBO, 'Key Issues', op. cit., p. 1.
83. Ibid., p. 13.

84. See US House Armed Services Committee, *The Ailing Defense Industrial Base: Unready for Crisis*, (Committee Print, 96th Congress, 2nd Session, 1980), and US House Armed Services Committee, *Capability of U.S. Defense Industrial Base* (Hearings, 96th Congress, 2nd Session, 1980).

4 The Impact of Reform on Parliamentary Oversight of Defence Expenditure

This chapter assesses the success and failure of legislative reform in Britain after 1971 in so far as it relates to defence policy-making and resource allocations in general. Before any assessment of the impact of the new Parliamentary institutions and procedures on defence can be made it is of course necessary to outline the traditional role of the British Parliament in defence decision-making. Having outlined the role of the legislature in Britain it will then be possible to describe the ways in which the reforms of 1971 were *intended* to affect the defence decision-making process; and, finally, to indicate what in fact happened in practice before the experiment was finally curtailed in 1979.

DEFENCE DECISION-MAKING IN BRITAIN

Policy-making and budgeting for defence involves two processes. First of all it is necessary to fit commitments to resources on an 'inter-departmental' basis. This process is normally referred to as the debate over 'guns versus butter' – how much for defence compared with social expenditure? Secondly, it is necessary to deal with 'intra' defence allocations, or the allocations within the overall ceiling for defence spending to the three Services (RAF, Army and Navy) and the Procurement Executive (which has been responsible in Britain since 1971 for the purchase of major weapon and equipment systems). In Britain both these *strategic* decisions are (and they were before 1971), almost exclusively located within Whitehall or the executive branch. Parliament's role in this process, as in other expenditure issue-areas, is (as we saw in Chapter 1) limited primarily to *managerial* (scrutiny and information) and *legal* (audit) functions. This limited role for Parliament can be understood more fully if we outline in detail the defence policy process in Britain.

Both the 'inter-governmental' allocation of resources amongst alternative commitments, as well as the 'intra-departmental' allocation of defence resources amongst the Services and Procurement Executive in Britain are centralised. Parliament's role in defence budgeting is, and has always been, limited to the scrutiny of defence estimates and the legitimation of defence policies through the approval of estimates and the passing of the annual Appropriation Act.[1] In very general terms then we can argue that primary responsibility for 'inter-governmental' allocations (guns versus butter) rest with the Cabinet, assisted by the Treasury with its control over the Public Expenditure Survey Committee. The latter institution – PESC – entails a five year 'rolling' programme/review of the public expenditure consequences of existing policy commitments, against the best estimate/forecast of the future trends in the economy.[2] From this basis of future forecasting it is possible – in theory anyway – for the government to assess where its policies will lead and whether or not there is scope for additional expenditure in new or existing areas, or whether existing policies will have to be cut due to poor economic performance.

Feeding into this system is of course the 'intra-departmental' allocation decisions which for defence are the responsibility of the Secretary of State and the senior civil servants and servicemen in the Ministry of Defence and Procurement Executive.[3] The process of allocating with defence is normally enshrined within the Service and Procurement Executive generation of 'bids' for new expenditure programmes – known as ten year long-term costings (LTCs) – which are then set against the Treasury's best estimate of the likely defence allocation by the Central Staffs (civilian) within the MOD. If the allocation then arrived at is regarded as insufficient the individual Services then have scope to press their case for more within the Chiefs of Staff Committee (defence staff) and with the Secretary of State – who can ultimately take any such requests to Cabinet for preferential treatment if he thinks he can make a justifiable case. Parliament's role in this process has always been *post-hoc*, in the sense that it simply assesses the rectitude in 'value for money' terms of decisions already arrived at, without the ability to change any item within the government's defence budget. It is a *managerial* (scrutiny and information) and *legal* (audit), rather than *strategic* role.

The way in which 'inter-governmental' and 'intra-departmental' allocations come together has been summarised in some detail by Richard Burt and David Greenwood.[4] A short summary of these accounts will be presented, before a number of additional points are raised, which these two authorities have perhaps ignored and which are important in fully appreciating the limited role accorded to the legislature in Britain.

While it is difficult to pinpoint any one date to be the starting point for defence budgeting due to the sequential, parallel and continuous nature of the process – which is always approximately 16 months in advance of the existing financial year – Burt has taken the beginning of the PESC cycle as a convenient starting place. While it can be argued that this is hardly correct, for the moment this starting point will serve for illumination of the British defence policy-making and budgeting process:

(1) *December*
The Treasury sends its PESC instructions and forecasts to the MOD to guide the MODs budget request for the next but one April (16 months on) Budget. It is already preparing the final estimates for Parliamentary approval for the coming fiscal year in April.

(2) *January*
MOD Central Staff (Programme and Budget Division) gives the service departments and Procurement Executive tentative ceilings to guide them in their preparation of ten years LTC's. Since Service and Procurement Executive LTCs (bids) will always be above the tentative ceiling for Defence spending from the Treasury this begins the process of 'intra-departmental' allocation conflicts, as each *Service* fights to include its bids in the defence ceiling.

(3) *February/March*
Tentative LTC bids are sent to the Treasury for its consideration by the MOD (Programmes and Budget) staff, who also asked the Services to make cuts in their own bids and to defend only those they wish to retain as first priority. For information purposes the MOD (P & B) staff prepare an output budget in 12 functional headings (missions), with 550 Element Costings. This is the output (PPB system) budgeting process in Britain, but it tends to *follow* rather than lead or influence the input budgeting of the LTCs: it is therefore for

informational and presentational purposes to guide difficult decisions over 'marginal' bids later in the process.

(4) *April/May*
MOD (P & B) discuss alternative spending ceilings and bid allocations with Service departments, Treasury, FCO and Procurement Executive. Internally the centralised Operational Requirements and Defence Equipment Committees, as well as the Chiefs of Staff discuss the various alternatives available The Chiefs of Staff prepare their own report on the implications of alternative spending allocations. This is the crunch point for 'intra-departmental' allocation battles because the end result is the final MOD bid to be sent to the PEC in the Treasury.

(5) *June*
PESC bids are sent to the Treasury by each department, normally most spending departments are including additional bids above the tentative ceilings given to them in January/February and it is at this level that the 'inter-governmental' battle (guns versus butter) commences as the Permanent Secretaries fight over which department(s) will obtain either the marginal increases in expenditure which are available or the minimum cuts given the need to reduce expenditure. Clearly, the success of the MOD's Permanent Secretary in winning this 'inter-governmental' battle will have implications for 'intra-Departmental' bids above the initial tentative ceilings.

(6) *July/September*
The PESC Report is sent to Cabinet and the summer is spent in Ministers re-thrashing out the decisions and compromises reached by their officials. This means of course that Cabinet becomes the final court of appeal for departments either to try to win battles they have lost earlier in the process or to introduce new arguments to overturn or modify earlier decisions. Clearly, the necessity for departments to have a Minister who is able to defend his department and stand up to the Treasury is crucial because the Cabinet can overturn decisions arrived at in the PESC Report if it so wishes. But, while Cabinet is the court of final appeal, the scope for Cabinet innovation is limited by the incremental nature of the process: the Cabinet is not discussing fundamental policy changes normally but who gets the marginal increase in funds

available.[5] The battle is not over particular spending programmes but marginal adjustments to aggregate spending levels. The MOD will use any argument available to it – the Soviet menace, the NATO commitment, favourable Parliamentary Reports etc. – at this stage to defend its position and attempt to increase its allocation. The 'inter-governmental' budgetry allocation ends with the preparation of the Public Expenditure White Paper, which is presented on a five year forward basis for expenditure.

(7) *October*
The Cabinet decisions are then transmitted back to departments and the General Finance Division (GF) in MOD then begins the process of preparing the estimates, which are input based for presentation to Parliament for appropriation approval and scrutiny. The estimates are generally regarded as presentational and after October it is generally held that there is little scope for either 'inter-governmental', or 'intra-departmental' adjustments of defence expenditure. While it is the case that there is no scope for such alterations by appeals to Parliament (as occurs in the US when the Services appeal to Congress after Executive decisions) there is scope for some modification when discussions take place in the Winter over the problems of defence management in the context of inflation and cash limits.

(8) *November/December*
MOD (GF) sends the draft estimates to the Treasury and the final estimates are prepared in conjunction with the Annual Defence White Paper, which draws heavily on the functional/output budget format generated for presentational purposes by MOD (P & B) in the previous March. The Central Staff are by now involved in the next financial years bid preparation for PESC.

(9) *January/April*
The estimates and White Paper are presented to Parliament for debate and approval through the annual Appropriation Act.

(10) *'Post-Hoc' Review*
The Estimates Committee (1912–1970) normally scrutinised the annual estimates to assess 'value for money' of expenditure. Between 1971 and 1979 this role was fulfilled by

> the Defence and External Affairs Sub-Committee of the Expenditure Commitee and since 1979 by a Select Committee on Defence. Since 1861 the Public Accounts Committee, in conjunction with the Comptroller and Auditor-General's Department, has audited the accounts of the departments to check whether the money voted for particular functions has in fact been spent on those functions.

While this is a useful summary of the process for defence budgeting in Britain, as outlined by recent analysts (see Figure 4.1 for further presentational details), there are a number of points which have perhaps been underplayed or ignored and which ought to be emphasised for more inclusive account. Firstly, it has been argued by Greenwood that there are two budgeting processes taking place in the MOD along parallel lines - input budgeting (LTCs) and output budgeting (Element Costings on a mission basis).[6] But, as we have seen the output budget process comes *after* arguments over LTCs (bids) by the Service and Central Staff (P & B). Thus the output budgeting system in the MOD is for informational/presentational purposes; it does not guide decision-making or operate in parallel but acts as an aid to an input biased budget system which has always been in operation. This does not mean of course that Greenwood is wrong to argue that there is far more use made of cost-benefit analysis. Clearly these functions are performed by the Defence Operations Analysis Establishment at West Byfleet; by the new Operational Requirements and Defence Equipment Committees; and, have been reinforced by the creation of the Procurement Executive in 1971. It is, however, debatable whether these developments are sufficient to generate a truly planned approach to Britain's fundamental policy commitments for defence. This is another way of saying that Greenwood does not emphasise enough the fact that output-budgeting is at a sub-optimal level in the MOD. A fact testified to by a recent central co-ordinator of defence allocation decisions in the MOD, John Bourn, who has argued:[7]

> . . . these systems (output budgeting) have not in themselves been successful in either central or local government in the United Kingdom or elsewhere. We may have looked for too much. We may have made the mistake of believing that to institute new procedures would itself solve our problems. We have had to learn again that technique is no substitute for analysis, debate and dialogue.

	Year 1	Year 2
January		Decisions on estimates
February	Policy assumptions for 10-year costings issued	Printing estimates and submission to Parliament
March/ April		Defence debates
May	Completion of costings	**Interface with Public Expenditure Survey**
June	Analysis of costings	Public Expenditure Survey Committee's Report on 5-year Costing sent to Ministes
July	Short-term decisions based on costings	Ministerial consideration of, and decisions on, Public Expenditure Survey
August	Target for following year's estimate settled	
September October November	(1) Preparation of estimates (2) Identification of longer-term items for special study	Preparation of Government White Paper on Public Expenditure*
December	(1) Submission of estimates (2) Updating of 10-year costings	Preparation of Government White Paper on Public Expenditure*

SOURCE *Long Range Planning* (November 1970) p. 21.

FIGURE 4.1 *The annual cycle in UK long term defence planning and programming*

Such an admission indicates quite clearly that, whatever form of budgeting is taking place in Britain, it is far removed from the theories of PPB systems outlined in the 1950s and 1960s.

This conclusion is aposite because it leads us to a consideration of a second weakness in recent analyses of defence budgeting: the tendency to overstate the degree of centralisation and therefore overestimate the diminuition of the role of the separate Services (Army, Navy and RAF) in budgeting. This error is most glaringly made by Howard and Burt in their otherwise excellent accounts, but it is not made by Greenwood, who rightly emphasises the central role of the Service departments in the preparation of MOD PESC bids (LTCs).[8] We have already seen that the one major supposed instrument of central control – output-budgeting – has been a chimera and this must lead us to a realisation that the traditional Service dominated input budgeting process is still very much in operation in the MOD. This fact had been testified to be Michael Hobkirk, who has pointed to the relatively equal distribution of resources which the Services maintain for themselves (indicating 'buggins turn'?).[9] It should not surprise us either because the Services can be expected to want to retain a major say in defence budgeting, not only for defensive organisational reasons, but also because they are responsible for both professional advice to the government on defence matters and also for the running and administration of defence services in the field. While there may be arguments against those operationally responsible having a major say over defence budgeting allocations, it has generally been accepted in the UK that the Services have the right to a major say and the Chiefs of Staff committee and April report is testament to this role.[10] The central role of the Services is also indicated by the fact that though MOD (P & B) co-ordinates allocation decisions and sets the ceilings in conjuction with the Treasury, the actual bids (LTCs) are prepared by the Procurement Executive and the three Service departments. The P & B division is therefore merely co-ordinating and not dominating the defence budget process centrally. Nor could it do so with a staff of six. Finally, while it might appear that centralisaton is on the increase in the MOD budgeting process it is as well to bear in mind that when the MOD (P & B) division is bargaining with the Treasury over financial ceilings it is doing so in order to accommodate the bids and preferences emanating from the Services, not from the MOD civilian Central Staffs as such.

A third omission, notably from Burt's work, has been the analysis of fundamental policy decisions which guide annual and medium term budgeting decisions. Burt's analysis is overly concerned with the process of financial management and control and as such overstates the dominant role of the Treasury and MOD Central Staffs in managing and controlling the defence effort in expenditure terms. Now while it is fair to argue, as Burt does,[11] that financial necessity has often generated policy reviews in Britain, this should not cloud us to the appreciation of the fact that the PESC system for defence is also directed by fundamental policy decisions taken by governments – often in the absence of immediate financial crises. An example of this would be in the 1974/75 Defence Review implemented by the Labour government due to its commitment to changing the balance between social and defence expenditure prior to taking office. A similar, if different commitment, has also been undertaken by the Thatcher government with its decision to spend more on defence even at a time of cutting expenditure in other areas.[12] The point to be made here is that while the defence budgeting process in Britain is incremental in most respects this is not to say that fundamental policy reviews do not occur, nor that they are not important. Since 1945 there have been a number of Defence Reviews, as well as policy changes indicated in the Defence White Papers, which are really the starting point for the defence budgeting process in Britain and which guide both the MOD and Treasury in its PESC and LTC deliberations. In this sense too much can be made of the decisions taken by Permanent Secretaries in PESC because, if they do their job correctly, the decisions taken ought to reflect the preferences specified by Ministers. In the defence field, particularly between 1957 and 1977, Ministers have generally been fairly clear that the defence commitment ought to be reduced and in the respect the Treasury and MOD have reflected this consensus.[13] (See Figure 4.2 and Table 4.1 for recent trends including increases after 1977.)

The defence budgeting system cannot therefore be understood merely by analysing the institutional processes and relationships within PESC; to understand the driving force behind these processes we need to understand the social/economic and political variables which impinge on governments. Thus in understanding who or what shapes the defence budget in Britain, we need to consider what causes governments to shift priorities. While it is true that ideological commitments are important, so also are strategic assumptions about 'threats' (for example the increased 'Soviet threat' which encouraged even a Labour government to increase defence spending by 3% in real terms in 1977, and the Thatcher administration to replace Polaris). Clearly, these perceptions of a 'threat' have always been apparent in Service 'bids', but it is the acceptance of this position by the government – which give the Services additional expenditure – which is crucial. There are also social and economic, as well as political, considerations of importance. The changing nature of economic circumstances will also have an impact on the defence effort. The Heath government used the production of more naval ships than originally intended as a counter-cyclical method of reducing high unemployment in the early 1970s,[14] which indicated the interrelationship between social and economic problems and an increased defence effort which had little to do with the formal PESC and LTC system. Finally, changes in the technology available within the defence field will also play a crucial role in shaping the defence effort and budgetary decisions, either about overall shares of expenditure or the volume of goods to be produced.

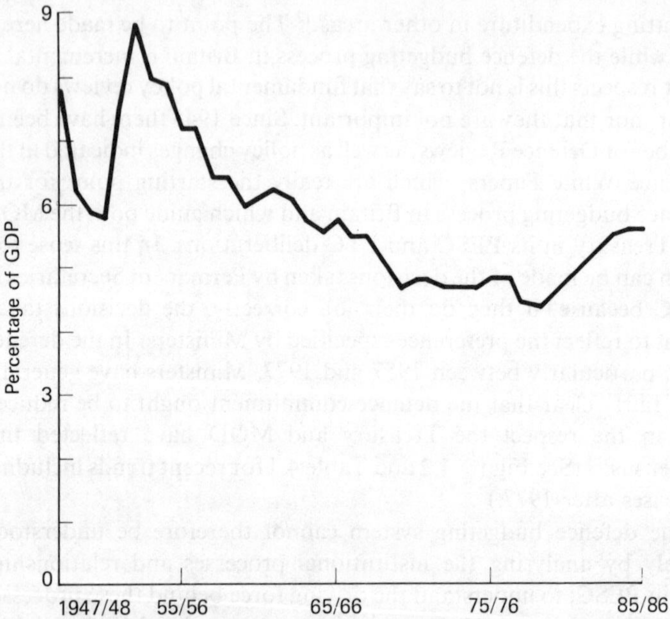

SOURCE Malcolm Chalmers, *The Cost of Britain's Defence* (Peace Studies Paper No. 10, University of Bradford, 1984) p. 55.

FIGURE 4.2. *UK defence burden (1947/48–1985/86) (UK defence spending as percentage of Gross Domestic Product at Market prices)*

This factor is an important one because most commentators fail to appreciate the continuing bargaining over 'inter' and 'intra' defence allocations which is apparent throughout the budgetary cycle. Most commentators assume that there is no scope for manoeuvre after the Cabinet's decisions on the Public Expenditure White Paper in September. This of course ignores the impact of defence management problems, associated with inflation and cash limits, in the British system.[15] At the beginning of the annual budgeting exercise the MOD (P & B) Division is concerned to win acceptance from the Treasury that cash limits (imposed since 1975/76) on annual expenditure are not sacrosanct. In other words it is important for all departments to ensure that the limits imposed can be adjusted if problems arise. This problem is particularly acute for the MOD because, while it must spend money allocated for anyone year in that year, there is considerble slippage in defence programmes due to industrial/ management problems and to the exigencies associated with

TABLE 4.1 *UK defence burden (1945–86)*

Financial year	*Defence spending (£ million, current prices)*	*Defence spending (as % GDP market prices)*	*Defence spending (as % GDP factor cost)*
1945/46	4 410	a	...
1946/47	1 653	16.2	18.5
1947/48	854	7.8	8.9
1948/49	753	6.3	7.2
1949/50	741	5.9	6.7
1950/51	777	5.8	6.6
1951/52	1 110	7.5	8.6
1952/53	1 404	8.8	10.0
1953/54	1 364	8.0	9.0
1954/55	1 436	7.9	8.9
1955/56	1 405	7.2	8.2
1956/57	1 525	7.2	8.2
1957/58	1 430	6.4	7.3
1958/59	1 468	6.4	7.2
1959/60	1 476	6.0	6.8
1960/61	1 596	6.1	6.9
1961/62	1 689	6.2	6.9
1962/63	1 767	6.1	6.9
1963/64	1 792	5.8	6.5
1964/65	1 909	5.6	6.4
1965/66	2 056	5.7	6.5
1966/67	2 115	5.5	6.3
1967/68	2 254	5.5	6.4
1968/69	2 232	5.1	5.9
1969/70	2 204	4.7	5.5
1970/71	2 503	4.8	5.6
1971/72	2 828	4.8	5.5
1972/73	3 092	4.7	5.3
1973/74	3 484	4.7	5.3
1974/75	4 164	4.7	5.2
1975/76	5 346	4.8	5.4
1976/77	6 158	4.8	5.4
1977/78	6 787	4.5	5.1
1978/79	7 455	4.4	5.0
1979/80	9 178	4.5	5.3
1980/81	11 180	4.8	5.6
1981/82	12 606	5.0	5.9
1982/83	14 411	5.3	6.2
1983/84	15 987	5.5	6.5
1984/85	17 290	5.6	6.6
1985/86	18 330	5.6	6.7

SOURCE Malcolm Chalmers, *The Cost of Britain's Defence* (Peace Studies Paper No. 10, University of Bradford) p. 72.

operating on technological frontiers which the MOD cannot control. This means that there is a continuous potentiality for 'underspend' or 'overspend' in particular years and the MOD has been involved in a battle with the Treasury to win acceptance that it can carry over money voted for a particular function but not spent in the year for which it was voted.[16]

The MOD has however other financial management problems related to cash limits and inflation and high technology which appear *after* the September White Paper process has been finalised. The PESC process is conducted at constant price levels and, after deliberation by Cabinet (when the annual Estimates are prepared by the GF division), these constant prices (volume of goods and services desired) confront current prices or economic reality. It is at this point that cash limits become crucial because if cash limits are set at 14% (as in 1979/80) and inflation is running at 20%+ (as in 1979/80) then unless cash limits are extended the volume production of equipment must be reduced or specific programmes (accepted by the Cabinet from LTC bids) may have to be curtailed. This problem is exacerbated of course when wage settlements for the armed forces and civilian staffs outstrip cash limit and when high technology costs exceed average inflation levels.[17] Thus when the GF division confronts the trade-off between constant and current price levels there is a conflict and dialogue taking place with Treasury as the MOD tries to win supplementary estimates above those agreed within the Cabinet to accommodate inflation. Clearly, while this task will have been previewed earlier in the year, the real crunch (with definite consequences for both 'intra-departmental' and 'inter-governmental' defence allocations) occur after the Cabinet's budgeting decisions in the summer. As John Bourn has argued, however, this may well undermine efficient planning of defence because when (as has been normal in recent years) cuts have to be made to accommodate rising inflation – whatever the modification allowed in cash limits – these cuts, in coming at the end of the financial year, tend to fall on what *can be* rather than upon what is *most desirable* to cut.[18] Clearly, when taking this perspective on British defence budgeting it would appear to resemble more the 'crude axe blows' outlined by Martin, than the rational planning process outlined by Greenwood.[19]

DEFENCE AND PARLIAMENT PRIOR TO 1971

Whatever the respective merits of the case are in relation to the rationality or irrationality of Whithall defence decision-making it is clear that most of the major decisions on defence in Britain were, and are, taken within the executive branch well before the annual Defence White Paper and Defence Estimates are prepared in the Winter of each year, for Parliamentary approval. This meant that Parliament's role was severely circumscribed in fact if not in theory before 1971. Theoretically Parliament controlled defence spending through its power to vote for or against the defence estimates and the Finance Bill which raised the revenue for all government expenditure. But, as we saw earlier, this role has been a myth in modern times due to the discipline of party politics in a legislature dominated by two major parties. Parliament had a formal role in controlling defence decision-making but in practice this role was limited to scrutiny, the provision of information and the audit of the accounts of the Ministry of Defence and Service departments. Interestingly enough however, while it is true that Parliament's role in controlling the executive has been limited, Parliament's scrutiny of defence was historically more extensive than had been the case in other areas of government policy-making. In order to understand why this was so it is necessary to look first at the formal scrutiny and audit powers of Parliament (in particular the House of Commons) and how these were used in practice in relation to overseeing defence expenditure and policy-making.

Parliament discharged its formal powers of defence policy and expenditure control and scrutiny through its ability to debate and pass the annual departmental estimates of the Ministry of Defence and the Service departments and any subsequent supplementary estimates which were required. On top of this defence issues were raised in the House of Commons through the debate on the annual Defence White Paper and through the normal process of question time and through the Select Committee structure of the House. The two most influential and important Select Committees for defence issues were the Public Accounts Committee (which still operates) and the Estimates Committee. As we saw in Chapter 1, both the PAC and the Estimates Committee had responsibility for government-wide scrutiny of expenditure and administration. Defence however was of particular concern for both these committees in the period after 1945 and on balance defence issues were dealt with far more systematically in Parliament after 1945 than any other topic. This might at first appear strange when one realises that there was something of all party consensus on the broad ends of post-war defence policy. After 1945 the front-bench spokesmen of both the Labour and Conservative parties were agreed on the need to maintain and develop a nuclear capability; to strengthen Britain's NATO commitment; to maintain Britain's world role; to reduce defence expenditure at a time of rising GDP; and, to move from a conscript to an all volunteer army.[20] Disagreement with these policies certainly existed but this disagreement was largely confined to minority/extreme viewpoints within each of the parties (the right-wing desire to maintain Empire and the left-wing desire to move towards unilateral disarmament) and did not seriously question the dominance of the leadership over defence policies in this period.

Only once, was there an 'unholy alliance' of Labour and Conservative MPs against the frontbench consensus agreement on policy. The issue here was over whether, under Duncan Sandys and Macmillan, the traditional conventional roles of the armed forces should be downgraded after 1957/58 in favour of emphasis on nuclear capabilities and the strategic concept of 'massive retaliation'. The desire to maintain a larger conventional capability – particularly in the Army – brought together a number of Conservative and Labour MPs to argue against the Conservative government's and the Labour Opposition's frontbench policy agreement. It may well have been party due to this pressure that the armed forces in Britain were able to overturn much of the Sandys doctrine in the early 1960s.[21]

Despite this atypical influence, the general picture in Parliament in this period was one of Conservative and Labour leaders disagreeing over means and not ends (the size of the defence effort not its rationale or goals). This general consenus was also mirrored by the fact that the backbench defence party committees of the House of Commons were also normally staffed by MPs who had experience of the armed forces and were generally concerned to defend their interests whenever possible.[22] But if this was the case then why should it be that the PAC and the Estimates Committee should devote so much of their respective time and effort to auditing and scrutinising the defence effort and drawing fairly critical conclusions from their deliberations? The answer to this seeming conundrum lies in the structural problems facing the British economy and defence in this period and is best understood if we look at the failure of the government in this period to co-ordinate the defence effort in a changed world environment or to resolve the problems of inflation, technological sophistication and declining economic performance.

Since 1945 the speed of technological change has risen at an alarming rate and so has the cost of defence equipment as a result. This is known as the 'relative price effect' and relates to the fact that the cost of services in the public sector rise at a rate proportionately higher than inflationary costs in the private sector. A problem which is multiplied several times over in the defence field which is almost wholly publicly financed and requires increasingly technologically sophisticated weapon systems to compete and maintain any semblance of parity in destructive/defensive capability.[23] Thus, because the defence effort is always conducted on the frontiers of advanced technology, future costs forecasting is problematic and there is always a tendency for costs to escalate and the 'lead' time for production to extend as technology develops and as operational requirements and specifications change.

In the 1950s and early 1960s Britain experienced these problems to an alarming extent and a number of projects were cancelled outright – Blue Streak, Skybolt, Blue Water and TSR-2 and other projected aircraft – and cost over-runs became glaring apparent (the cost of Seaslug missle rose from £4½ million to £70 million).[24] It is not surprising therefore that these problems in government contracting and weapons procurement should generate interest and concern in Parliament, notwithstanding the general support for the existing defence effort.

In particular, then, the Public Account Committee took an especial interest in defence problems after 1945 in an attempt to control cost over-runs and time delays in weapons procurement. Nor was this surprising given the PACs brief to audit the accounts of government departments and to check for efficiency in administration. Nor should it be surprising to learn that the PAC discovered a number of cases in which existing departmental arrangements were inadequate for both procurement contracting and financial discipline in project management. In a 1955/56 Report, glaring cost underestimations were revealed by the PAC on proposals for the Swift Aircraft which was eventually curtailed.[25] In perhaps the most celebrated case of all the PAC discovered in 1963 that the Ferranti Company was making excessive profits from open-ended contracts on Bloodhound missiles; resulting in the Company having to return excessive profits to the Exchequer.[26] In 1967/68 a critical report from the PAC indicated that the costing of the Spey Engine from Rolls-Royce for newly purchased Phantom jets were financially lax.[27] Nor was this all because these were only the more celebrated cases of PAC audit of defence in Britain. The PAC has over the post-war years spent a considerable amount of its time exposing lower level financial weaknesses in defence contracting and in other fields of government activity.[28]

This interest in solving inflationary problems of procurement also spilled over into other Select Committee activities in the period 1945–71. As we saw the PAC scrutiny of expenditure and policy has always been 'after the fact' of government spending and, therefore, unable to control or influence what the government is intending to achieve. For this reason in 1912 the Estimates Committee was given the brief of scrutinising the existing activities of government Departments as reflected in the value for money of existing administrative relationships. After 1945 therefore the Estimates Committee was itself concerned to look in detail at procurement issues. In the same way as the PAC the Estimates Committee was particularly effective in revealing the inadequacies of the procurement and research and development process for defence in Britain. Its report in 1956/57 on *Supply of Military Aircraft* was a classic statement of the inadequacy of the relationship between the Ministry of Supply and Ministry of Aviation for procurement of the Swift Aircraft.[29] Procurement issues were again studied by the Estimates Committee in 1955/56, in *Naval Research and Development*; in 1964/65, in *Electrical and Electronic Equipment for the Services*; in 1955/56, *Food Supplies for the Armed Services*; in 1951/52, *Royal Ordinance Factories*; and, in 1964/65, *Non-War like Stores for the Services*.[30] In most of these reports the Estimates Committee called for enhanced co-ordination of the Service effort and internal management reforms. These demands, which were somewhat different to the demand for financial rectitude in contracting emanating from the PAC, confronted existing bureaucratic and Service practices and this probably explains why (unlike the successful impact experienced over research and development contracting) these proposals were only half-heartedly accepted.

The interest in procurement and cost and time problems in research and development was not confined only to the PAC and Estimates Committee in Parliament. Given the horrendous problems experienced in procurement in the 1950s it was not surprising that this would lead to internal Whitehall demands for reform. In 1961/62 a series of changes (known as the Gibbs/Zuckermann reforms) which were parri passu with broad administrative reforms aimed at organisational centralisation in 1963/64, were introduced into research and development for defence. The broad thrust of these reforms were aimed at increased cost-effectiveness, the earlier and more comprehensive specification of operation requirements and a move towards greater communality of Service designs in procurement. There is little doubt that these reforms contributed to, without solving completely, the tendency to fewer time and cost over-runs in the late 1960s.[31] There is also no doubt that these reforms caused concern in Parliament, coming as they did at the same time as the 1961 Plowden reforms of financial management and the 1963/64 central organisational changes in defence. As a result the Select Committee on Science and Technology, which had been created in 1966, decided to look into the broad area of defence research and development. The reasons for this were not simply because there had been changes in the defence organisation but also because defence research and development dominated all research and development in Britain. The Select Committee Report, which appeared in 1968/69, was highly critical of the Gibbs/Zuckerman reforms and of the later Downey Reforms of procurement management. In general the Select Committee re-emphasised the earlier concerns of the PAC and Estimates Committee that there were too many committees and an inflexibility of procedure which militated against speed and financial rectitude. In particular the Committee felt that there was an inadequacy of independent advice to the government establishments; and a total inadequacy to give financial control to project managers who already had technical control over programmes. In this respect the Committee mirrored the similar concern to adopt 'accountable management' which was the hallmark of the 1968/69 Fulton Report on the civil service and of the later 1971 Rayner Report on procurement.[32]

Though the government did not accept the full recommendations of the Select Committee on Science and Technology there was a partial acceptance of the idea of project managers being given more financial responsibility. This greater autonomy was not however to undermine 'line management' responsibility through the traditional financial structure with its apex in the office of the Permanent Secretary's office. Nevertheless within two years of this report, and taken together with the Rayner Report, *Organisation for Defence Procurement and Civil Aerospace* (Cmnd 4641, 1981), the government was to accept the need for a far more co-ordinated and relatively autonomous and centralised procurement organisation within the Ministry of Defence with the creation of the Procurement Executive.[33] This fact alone indicates that, while it would be an overstatement to contend that this was solely the work of Parliament, the work of the PAC, Estimates Committee and Select Committee on Science and Technology certainly contributed to and supported the creation of the Procurement Executive: it assisted a development that was already beginning to be seen to be necessary within government circles.

In this way we can see the success of the scrutiny and information (*managerial*) role that Parliament fulfilled up to 1971. Parliament was able to pinpoint glaring administrative shortcomings and contribute to (if not make) decisions which were aimed at rationalising inefficiencies in administration and management systems. Clearly, while this was not a major policy-making role but more an administrative watchdog role, it was reflected is much of the general, non defence related, work that the Estimates Committee was involved with between 1945 and 1971.

It is worth re-emphasising, however, that while the Estimates Committee was involved in scrutinising many areas of government activity, defence was the field in which it undertook its most extensive and continuous work. Johnson has argued that between 1948 and 1964/65 the Estimates Committee published 34 defence related reports, and after 1964/65 a further two full reports and one uncompleted study were undertaken by the Committee.[34] (See Table 4.2 for details). Obviously the reason for this interest related to the problems of technological change and the perception of research and development cost over-runs, but there were other reasons why defence should be of particular concern to Parliament after 1945. First of all, although Britain had come out of the Second World War on the side of the victors in truth this had only been achieved at considerable cost to the nation in terms of capital assets and economic dislocation.[35] With hindsight it appears true today that the nation never fully recovered from this set back and, for those who had eyes to see, this was becoming painfully apparent in the 1950s and 1960s as the cost of weapons systems rose and the nation's ability to afford these and the worldwide commitments (NATO, CENTO and SEATO)[36] which Britain had entered into in the post-war period became intolerable. The Estimates Committee therefore found itself obliged to consider the growing incompatibility between the roles and resources which were available to Britain and the policy commitments entered into. Thus in this period five enquiries were conducted into the need for and consequences of *Rearmament* over Korea; two reports remarked upon the costs of *Overseas Military Expenditure*; and, relatedly, reports were published dealing with such things as *Diplomatic Buildings Overseas*; and *The Sale of Military Equipment Abroad.*[37]

At the same time, the concern to indicate that at the administrative

TABLE 4.2 *The defence related reports of the Select Committee of Estimates (1945–71)*

1947/48	The Use of Royal Ordinance Factories and Royal Naval Establishments in connection with the Production and Export Drive (7th Report, HC 200)
1948/49	The Defence Estimates (2nd Report, HC 86-1, 317)
	Government Hospitality, Departmental Entertainment, and official Entertainment in the Armed Forces (9th Report, HC 237)
	The Defence Estimates (17th Report, HC 313)
1950	Storage and Maintenance in the Defence Services (2nd Report, HC 109)
	Rearmament (3rd Report, HC 178)
	His Majesty's Dockyards (8th and 9th Reports, HC 245–59)
	Rearmament (10th Report, HC 260)
1951/52	Rearmament (2nd Report, HC 114)
	Rearmament (10th Report, HC 288)
	The Royal Ordinance Factories (12th Report, HC 327)
1952/53	Call-up, Posting and Movement of National Servicemen (3rd Report, HC 132)
	Rearmament (7th Report, HC 178)
1953/54	Royal Air Force Non-Flying Establishments (8th Report, HC 291)
1955/56	Works and Buildings of the Service Departments (Army) (3rd Report, HC 198)
	Food Supplies of the Armed Services (6th Report, HC 322)
	Naval Research and Development (7th Report, HC 345)
1956/57	The Supply of Military Aircraft (2nd Report, HC 34)
1957/58	The Reserve Fleet (3rd Report, HC 237)
	Land Branches of the Service Departments (4th Report, HC 238)
1958/59	Sale of Military Equipment Abroad (2nd Report, HC 229)
	Medical Services of the Armed Forces (4th Report, HC 253)
1959/60	The Admiralty Headquarters Organization (1st Report, HC 249)
1961/62	Trooping (1st Report, HC 49)
	Form of the Estimates of the Defence Departments (5th Report, HC 198)
	The War Office (8th Report, HC 241)
	Her Majesty's Dockyards (9th Report, HC 263)
1962/63	The Admiralty Headquarters Organization (5th Report, HC 148)
	Military Expenditure Overseas (10th Report, HC 282)
1963/64	The Form of the Estimates on the Defence Departments (4th Report, HC 119)
	Military Expenditure Overseas (9th Report, HC 302)
	Service Colleges (8th Report, HC 296)
1964/65	Electrical and Electronic Equipment for the Services (7th Report, HC 358)
	Non-Warlike Stores of the Services (8th Report, HC 359)
1966/67	The Movement of Service Personnel and Stores (7th Report, HC 365)
	Diplomatic Buildings Overseas (14th Report, HC 666)
1969/70	Recruitment for the Armed Services (Uncomplete Report, HC 53 i–xxii and HC 300)

and Service levels there was a mismatch between policy goals and the availability of resources (the Estimates Committee could not specify that the policy was wrong and needed changing; it could only do this indirectly by revealing the disparity between the two) was matched by a consequent concern to improve Service efficiency overall so that, even if policy was not changed, then the Services would be operating with muscle rather than fat in operational terms. Thus a series of reports were published dealing with Service efficiency and their organisational structures: these included (1950/51 and 1961/62) *Dockyards*; (1957/58) the *Reserve Fleet*; (1959/60 and 1962/63) *Admiralty Headquarters*; and (1961/62) *War Office*.[38]

Eventually these studies spilled over into a final area of concern at this time. By the middle of the 1950s it became apparent that not only was there tremendous conflict within the Services over resource allocation as the defence budget was being reduced by Macmillan and Sandys,[39] but that there was a total lack of central co-ordination of the defence effort. This failure of the Ministry of Defence to control the relatively autonomous Services Departments was manifested in the failure to budget effectively for the future, and by an over-reliance on updated 'input' biased budgeting systems which allowed for Service independence. The eventual outcome of this process was to be the downgrading of the three Service Departments in 1964 under the central control of the Ministry of Defence and the application from 1958 of forward budgeting techniques, which were to be the forerunners of the general Plowden – PESC reforms in Whitehall in the early 1960s.[40]

While the Estimates Committee did not bring about these change it was apparent in many of its reports in the 1950s that there was a desire to indicate the debilitating effects of Service autonomy on relatively minor problems and functions, which contributed to excessive expenditure and an inability to co-ordinate the defence effort. Such reports as the (1950) *Storage and Maintenance of the Defence Services*; the (1956/57) *Stores and Ordinance Depots of the Service Departments*; the (1957/58) *Land Branches of the Service Departments*; the (1958/59) *Medical Services of the Armed Forces*; the (1961/62) *Trooping*; the (1963/674) *Service Colleges*; the (1964/65) *Non-Warlike Stores of the Services*; and, the (1966/67) *Movement of Service Personnel and Store*, while not openly espousing a change in policy underlined continually the duplication (not to say triplication) of effort and failure of co-ordination in the Services.[41] Clearly these reports contributed to the environment which was eventually to lead to centralisation of policy-making and resource allocation within the Ministry of Defence. The Estimates Committee in these reports, and in its reports on *The Form of the Defence Estimates* (1963/74), also supported the growing demand for forward defence budgeting on a five to ten year basis using quantification, and computer systems.[42]

It would be wrong however to conclude from this that the Estimates Committee, and therefore Parliament indirectly, had a major role in policy-making. This would be (to quote Denis Healey's famous barb against the Select Committee on Science and Technology assumption that it had been influential) to behave '. . . Like cocks who think that by their crowing they have made the sunrise'.[43] While there were some successes for the PAC and Estimates Committee and the Science and Technology Committees it is probably true to say that they only had an influence when the environment was already conducive to change. When the environment was not conducive the Committee may have eventually contributed to a change of attitude but it was unlikely that it was ever able to force the pace of change behind the proposals they espoused. A number of examples will underline this point. First of all, there were successes for the PAC, Estimates and Science and Technology Committees in the administration of procurement. Having said this it was also the case that the problems of time and cost over-run were so glaringly obvious to the government anyway that it was inevitably that something would have to be done in the future. Interestingly enough it was not until after the Whitehall conducted Gibbs/ Zuckermann and Downey, Fulton and Rayner Reports that fundamental changes were implemented in the administration of procurement. Although it would perhaps be unfair to the PAC – which has always had a tremendous influence with the Accounting Officers in individual Departments – to conclude that it did not have a fundamental impact on contracting practice after the Ferranti scandal, in general terms the impact of Parliamentary Committees even in this field was on balance indicative of a general concern rather than the instigator of it.[44]

Johnson has drawn a similar conclusion concerning the role of the Estimates Committee in influencing the move to defence organisational centralisation in 1964: it prepared the ground and encouraged the process it did not instigate the reform as such.[45] Similar conclusions can also be made about the impact of the reports concerned about overseas military expenditure and the demand for the provision of more information for Parliament in the Defence White Papers: it was Denis Healey's own proclivity for this problem and for the dissemination of more information which explains why Parliament was better informed after 1964 and why the Labour government began to question the overall lack of balance between commitments and resources.[46] Perhaps the ultimate indicator of the underlying weakness of the Estimates Committee role was shown by in the way in which its recommendations for changes in the naval dockyards in 1950/51 were totally rejected by the Admiralty. Johnson has argued that the fact that most of these proposals were eventually accepted in 1961/62 is indicative of the success for the Committee in shaping long-term thinking.[47] It can however be seen in a very different light: it indicates that even when the Committee was in a position to see glaring anomolies it was unble to force the logic of its insight of a bureaucratic actor (in this case the Admiralty) which was in a position to ignore this advice. The fact that the decision was eventually taken to introduce similar reforms a decade later clearly indicates that it was taken because other factors had changed (Economic circumstances, global commitments and Cabinet and Ministerial preferences) not because the Estimates Committee had any real impact.

Overall then one must conclude that Parliament's role up to 1971 was fairly negligible in terms of influencing policy choices and of scrutinising the activities of the executive. This is not to argue that the PAC, backed by the Comptroller and Auditor-General and his staff, failed to fulfil their legal/auditing role effectively. As we saw, this role was most effectively discharged and revealed a number of glaring anomalies and administrative practices in defence. It is however in terms of *strategic* and *managerial* roles that Parliament was seen to be deficient.

First of all, despite its theoretical power of the purse, Parliament was not consulted on whether or not Britain should develop an Atomic weapon in the 1940s; it was not consulted over the commitments to NATO in 1955; it was not consulted over the Suez invasion; and it was not consulted in detail over the complete shift in emphasis in 1953 and again in 1957 when massive nuclear retaliation was used as an excuse to restructure in a radical way the conventional force posture of the Services. A similar lack of detailed Parliamentary consideration of options and scenarios was the order of the day in the 1960s as the Labour government undertook an almost continuous review of defence policy and ultimately decided to concentrate on a NATO role with a strong nuclear presence, at the expense of the traditional East of Suez posture.[48] Parliament's role was merely to support or reject these policies in the lobbies of the House of Commons and neither the Estimates Committee nor the PAC or the other Select Committees introduced in the 1960s made any discernible difference to executive dominance of policy-making and resource allocation. What is perhaps more damning is the fact that the Estimates Committee never really attempted to discuss the options that faced Britain and confined itself to relatively esoteric studies of particular Service or organisational problems.

Of course it would be unfair to be too hard on the Committee and Parliament as such because the remit of the Committee precluded it from studying policy. Furthermore, as Johnson has argued, when it did try, when it was first re-formed after 1945, to look at the Defence Estimates in total and the overall impact of Rearmament, it simply lacked the time, the expertise, the information, the staff and the technical capacity to discharge an effective alternative policy scenario role.[49] In particular the Committee was forced to adopt a bipartisan approach because it was drawn from MPs from all shades of opinion and nothing would have been achieved other than contention if policy had been continually debated. Furthermore, the Committee was never given the long-term costings of alternative programmes and the detailed 'threat' perception documents or Service equipment 'bids' which are fundamental to an adequate analysis of defence policy. Not even the fact of an annual Defence White Paper or, later, the agreement to introduce 'output'/functional budget figures in this document, were sufficient to overcome this paucity of Parliamentary information. Without this information, and given all the time in the world, it is doubtful whether Parliament could have effectively questioned the government's policy commitments.[50] In particular Parliament simply did not have the framework for judging the efficacy of defence spending in relation to other domestic expenditure. For this reason a strategic role was never attempted and it is doubtful whether it was in fact thought desirable until into the later 1960s.[51]

Perhaps the major criticism that can be made of Parliament and the Estimates Committee however relates to its failure to discharge its scrutiny role effectively. In general terms this criticism can be made more forcefully of the impact of the Estimates Committee in all other policy areas other than defence, but even if defence was the most effectively scrutinised area of government activity it still suffered from a number of weaknesses. Most important of all, given the secrecy problems surrounding defence issues the Estimates Committee continually confronted a problem of being unable to obtain classified information. This problem was partly overcome by the practice of 'sidelining' (providing the information on a confidential nature as long as it was not published), but this militated against a full disclosure of information to all but a select band of

Parliamentarians and always on the government and Services terms.[52] Secondly, if the information provided militated against comprehensive analysis, the recommendations which were eventually made to the government were rarely accepted. Obviously the government and Service departments could argue that the Estimates Committee lacked adequate information and so their recommendations were inadequate. In general terms however the failure to accept all but the most anodine or glaringly obvious recommendations and the tendency for the Service Departments to defend their vested interests and autonomy against all-comers were pervasive and intracticable problems for Parliament.

One reason for this failure was the fact that scrutiny led to no punishment for the Services unless they were prepared to punish themselves. The Estimates Committee had no teeth because it failed – except in one or two occasions – to follow up its own reports and discover whether anything had been done. Unfortunately even when the Committee did undertake retrospective scrutiny of its own recommendations it did not always achieve very much. This was clearly the case with attempts to force the Admiralty and War Office to rationalise their headquarters arrangements and the naval dockyards.[53] Finally, the Committee failed itself to be as forceful as it might have been. Johnson argued that the Committee pushed against the bounds of the remit given it and on occasions it came very close to questioning policy.[54] Undoubtedly there is some truth in this but in general terms the Committee was content to eschew contention and concentrate on welfare and related mundane, technical issue affecting the services. Thus instead of questioning the fundamental mismatch between resources and overseas commitments the reports on Overseas Military Expenditure concentrated on such rivetting issues as accommodation, hospitals, amenities and stores overseas. A desire to eschew contention was also indicated in the mundane nature of many other technical studies: *Electrical and Electronic Equipment for the Services*; *Food Supplies for the Armed Services*; *Non-Warlike Stores for the Services*; and, *Movement of Service Personnel and Stores*. At a time when Britain was indulging in a fundamental reappraisal of its world role and the reshaping and rearming of its force structure it is incredible that Parliament should have been concerning itself with such pressing problems as whether or not food provisions should be co-ordinated or hived-off to private enterprise!

Overall then Parliament, through its Select Committees, was able up to 1971 to argue that it had provided itself with a fairly consistent scrutiny of defence administration and organisation and that it was now provided with far more detailed information of how the defence establishment was organised than had been the case hithertofore. It could not be argued however that Parliament was able either to question policy or resource allocation decisions effectively, nor was it able to claim that if fully scrutinised defence activities – mainly because its recommendations had little discernible impact. Johnson has perhaps put the matter adequately when he argues that the PAC had an impact because it could always blame the Permanent Secretary, as Chief Accounting Officer, for any laxity in financial administration, but the Estimates and other Select Committees could not pin decisions on anyone because they could not question Ministers or delve in the rarified air of policy.[55] Unfortunately, while there was little impact on government Departments, this problem was compounded by the fact that while the Select Committees gave to Parliament more information than had ever been the case in the past, the House of Commons and MPs themselves were unwilling to make effective use of this information. Reports from the Committees were rarely read or debated and when debates did take place they were poorly attended and inevitably dominated by those committee members who had been responsible for the reports. This problem was not overcome even after 1960 when the government allowed for one debate on the PAC Report and two debates per session on Estimate Committee reports.[56]

As a consequence the Service departments realised they could safely ignore the recommendations of the Estimates Committee and the government was able to place obstacles in the way of Committee studies by refusing to allow technical specialists to serve and also by withholding permission for the Select Committees to travel overseas to take evidence.[57] But, and this is testament to the concern felt in Parliament in the 1960s and pressure for reform that was experienced after 1966, the continued amateurism of the Estimates Committee was soon to be questioned. By 1964/65 the Procedure Committee of the House was accepting the case for overseas visits to be a statutory right and also for technical and specialist advisers to be appointed to particular studies on an *ad-hoc* basis.[58] Both of these issues were of particular concern in so far as defence issues were concerned. Given that defence operates on the technological frontier and strategic and operational considerations are immensely complicated and esoteric and beyond the reach of the ordinary 'lay' (generalist) MP specialist advice is crucial. This realisation eventually contributed to the desire by the Procedure Committee to recommend the creation of specialist subject sub-committees for the Estimates Committee, of which one would be for Defence and Overseas Affairs.[59] It was intended of course that this would end the amateurism of the Estimates Committee, give it the same technical back-up that the PAC was able to muster and ensure the continuous scrutiny of specific areas of government activity. Indeed in 1964/65 the Procedure Committee wanted to go even further than this by replacing the Estimates Committee with an Expenditure Committee to look at expenditure policy in detail. The Labour government would not countenance this development and opted for a limited experiment in subject specific and department related *ad-hoc* Select Committees after 1966.[60]

Interestingly enough there is some evidence that Labour was concerned abut institutionalising a permanent defence related committee. While a senior defence civil servant has argued that defence is peculiar in that is requires a ten year forward projection of policy and expenditure to account adequately for inflation and technological sophistication, this implies that Parliament (limited to an annual review of cash for a particular year's defence expenditure) is most obviously in need of a permanent, expert scrutinising committee.[61] But the Labour government in 1967/68 abolished the Estimates Specialist Sub-Committees on the grounds that the subjects were adequately scrutinised in the new subject Select Committees. This of course was a nonsense because there was no defence related Select Committee. As a consequence there were demands throughout 1969 for a defence-specific committee to be set up, but all of these requests were turned down by the government.[62] This unsatisfactory arrangement probably explains – along with the downgrading of the role of the Estimates Committee after 1966 – why no defence related Reports appeared from this committee in 1965/66, 1967/68 and 1968/69. This attempt to weaken Parliamentary scrutiny of defence by the government and the Services (interestingly enough even Crossman while Leader of the House had argued that the most difficult hurdle for reformers would be creating a defence related committee)[63] probably contributed to the environment in which the inadequacies of Parliamentary scrutiny became more glaringly apparent and assisted Parliament in its decision to reform the Procedure Committee to look into the need for further reform of oversight procedures. As we saw earlier, the eventual 1968/69 report – although modified in some details – was to serve as the basic framework which resulted in the old Estimates Committee being replaced by the Select Committee on Expenditure, which was able to question Ministers, policy and expenditure allocations, and which also had a specialist sub-committee for Defence and External Affairs. The question we must now ask is how successful was this new innovation in overcoming the constraints of an executive dominated Parliament and extending legislative oversight of defence further than that achieved by the old Estimates Committee?

THE IMPACT AND ROLE OF THE SELECT COMMITTEE ON EXPENDITURE AND ITS DEFENCE AND EXTERNAL AFFAIRS SUB-COMMITTEE(1971–79)

The first thing to say is that it is a very difficult task to assess the success and failure of the Select Committee on Expenditure (SCOE) and its Defence and External Affairs Committee (DEASC) between 1971 and 1979 because it is not at all clear what these two bodies were supposed to be achieving. There was in other words a conflict over the role that reformers wanted to see Parliament fulfilling after 1970 which we discussed in Chapter 1.[64] It is clear from this earlier discussion that there are at least three roles that Parliament might perform; each of these roles can be seen to conform with a particular group or faction of Parliamentary reformers' aspirations at the end of the 1960s.

As we saw Parliament might be given a role, like the American Congress, in policy-making and *strategic* resource allocation. If Parliament were to fulfil this role in Britain it would imply for defence policy-making that the legislature would have either a share in, or veto over, at least two different types of decisions which it was normally precluded from before 1971. These two roles would involve, (i) decisions relating to '*inter*-governmental' (guns versus butter) allocations of exenditure ceilings for defence and domestic spending departments; plus, (ii) allocation decisions *intra* (as between the three Services and the Procurement Executive, or as between different roles – NATO, East of Suez, Nuclear, Home Defence etc.) the Defence establishment. Clearly the old Estimates Committee had never approached either of these two roles because of its inability to consider policy issues and because it lacked the mechanism to compare and contrast the relative claims of different spending requests between social and defence needs or within the Ministry of Defence. To fulfil his role the legislature would require a committee structure which mirrored the Whitehall PESC system, had the full PESC information on input and output budget figures, departmental spending 'bids', and a remit which allowed it to consider government spending priorities and to consider alternatives to this. In terms of the factions within the debate over Parliamentary reform this approach can be seen as the 'maximalist' position adopted by people like John Mackintosh who wanted to check executive pre-eminence.[65]

But Parliament might be conceived as fulfilling not a *strategic* but a *managerial* role, which involves the continuous scrutiny of executive actions, the provision of information and public debate and possible censure, without implying an ultimate power-sharing or Parliamentary veto of government actions. In so far as defence was concerned such a role would not require the relative merits of defence and other spending programmes being considered by Parliamentary committees in any detail but merely an extension of the scrutiny role which the Estimates Committee had undertaken previously for defence organisation and administration. This role would imply that the old Estimates Committee role had been sound but that it lacked continuity and specialism and would require perhaps the introduction of a specialist subject or department related committee to maintain a continuous check on a particular area of government activity. It would also follow – given the information, expertise and technical weaknesses experienced by the Estimates Committee – that such a new committee might be given a broader remit to look at policy and the information and assistance to allow it to discharge its scrutiny role more effectively. This view of reform accorded in late 1960s with the 'moderate' reforming school in Parliament, to which a large number of MPs subscribed. Another variant of this school – a 'minimalist' approach perhaps – was that while the old Estimates Committee had problems it did not require fundamental modification but merely more technical assistance so that it could provide more information for Parliamentary debates without giving Parliament any additional powers over the executive.[66] This would also involve a strengthening of the information available to allow Parliament to discharge its third, *legal* (audit) role through the PAC – this was not contentious however as most reformer were content that this role at least was satisfactorily discharged by Parliament.

It should be apparent therefore that there is something of a problem in assessing the success and failure of the 1971 reform because there was no fundamental agreement on what role Parliament ought to be fulfilling through its new Select Committee on

Expenditure. This problem is compounded if one looks at the remit structure and practice of the committee which was in fact instituted in 1971.

The 1968/69 Procedure Committee had recommended that the annual and piecemeal scrutiny of estimates and specific policies and departmental responsibilities should be replaced by the publication of an annual white paper on public expenditure which contained five-year-forward projections. This white paper would be followed by a two-day debate and an Expenditure Committee would review the overall allocation of resources amongst all uses – in other words strategically look at the government spending and policy priorities and critically appraise these in detail. To assist detailed scrutiny it was intended that SCOE would have one general sub-committee which would co-ordinate the findings and studies of eight sub-committees each having nine Members.[67]

The Conservative Government, however, while accepting the bias of these recommendations, and while not changing the remit of SCOE, made it difficult for it to discharge its role effectively because it reduced the scope of the committee limiting this to five sub-committees to eight Members only with one general sub-committee. The consequence of this was that some subject areas (like transport) were dealt with across a number of sub-committees without any necessary department-related competence.[68] This unwillingness to encourage primarily departmental scrutiny was witnessed clearly in the defence field where the sub-committee was given responsibility for both defence and external affairs issues.

Unfortunately, this responsibility for defence and external affairs imposed a crucial burden on an effective expenditure scrutiny role from the beginning because, in order to scrutinise expenditure policies and priorities, it is important that parliamentary committees are able to check and query those departments responsible for formulating spending decisions. But when a committee is responsible for policies emanating from the Ministry of Defence, the Treasury, the Department of Trade, the Property Services Agency, and the Foreign and Commonwealth Office, such a committee is given a scrutiny task that it is hardly likely to be able to discharge fully due to complexity and pressure of work. Furthermore, DEASC was provided with only limited staff back-up of one parliamentary clerk, with clerical assistance, and, initially, one (though it later became two and then three) specialist adviser with two auditors seconded from the Exchequer and Audit Department.[69] It is not surprising therefore that DEASC had difficulty in fully discharging it responsibility for scrutiny of defence and external affair, but this weakness was compounded immediately by an attitudinal and structural weakness in the nature of SCOE itself.

We have argued that there were contradictory and divergent pressures behind the demand for reform of Parliament and as a result SCOE was given a role which it could not fulfil either institutionally or because of the attitude of MPs. The institutional weaknesses of SCOE relate to the fact that though a general sub-committee was created to bring together the studies of the various sub-committees, these sub-committees were unable to scrutinise departmental expenditure policies in detail because of lack of staff and time; and, secondly, the general sub-committee failed to develop into the co-ordinating body which had been intended due to opposition to this dominant role by the other sub-committees (which did not want to become second-tier committees) and because the general sub-committee was unable to obtain the forecasting models and related information from the Treasury which would have been necessary for it to discharge its stragegic responsibilities fully.[70]

The attitudinal difficulty arose due to the self-ascribed role of MPs in defending 'pet' projects rather than taking on the neo-civil servant role implied in the brief given to SCOE . . . 'to examine in as much detail as possible the implications in terms of public expenditure of the policy objectives chosen by Ministers'.[71] As Robinson has argued SCOE never effectively approached this role because each of the sub-committees decided to pursue its own priorities in its area of competence, such that the overall priority-setting role desired by the 'maximalists' gave way to an enhanced Estimates Committee role of scrutinising the value for money of particular policies and programmes in expenditure terms.[72]

This limited scrutiny role and emphasis only on particular policies was clearly apparent in DEASC from its inception. To cope with the 'maximalist' position implied in the 1968/69 Procedure Committee Report DEASC would have had to obtain all available information within the Ministry of Defence related to its forward plans, with all options available for the ten-year planning period on which this department operates.

Taking these central pieces of information the sub-committee would then have had to ask the Foreign and Commonwealth Office for its assessment of 'threat' to the UK and its judgment of foreseeable foreign policy commitments, and then mesh these with both defence capabilities/potentialities/options and the Treasury's best assessment of the medium to long term future of the economy.

This, however, would be the first stage of this exercise since this activity would only allow DEASC to decide if the decisions taken by civil servants and Ministers in Whitehall were correct on the basis of the figures and assumptions available to them. But the role implied in the creation of DEASC and SCOE was the DEASC would then ask outside experts for alternative forecasts of the technological, strategic, and economic future and present to the full committee alternative defence expenditure scenarios in the light of these alternative figure and assumptions.

Nor would this be the end of the matter because SCOE would then have been expected to take all these alternatives and mesh these with similar exercises undertaken by the other sub-committees to arrive at a range of alternative resource allocation patterns to those presented by the Government to inform debate and public awareness. This was all to be achieved by 47 MPs (with 9 members on DEASC), fitting this activity in with their other parliamentary and constituency responsibilities, serviced by one parliamentary clerk per committee with minimal administrative back-up and part-time specialist advisers!

It is hardly surprising therefore that DEASC and other sub-committees contented themselves with doing what was possible within the time and staff limits they found themselves: they pursued an enlarged manageral Estimates Committee role of scrutinising particular packages rather than budgetary priorities per se. However DEASC did come to question fundamental policy and expenditure–allocation decisions of the Government before it was abolished in 1979, and in this way tended to go further than all of the sub-committees other than the general sub-committees.[73] Despite this move to update and provide a more comprehensive scrutiny role to that discharged through the old Estimates Committee there were a number of difficulties which limited the effectiveness of DEASC in achieving this more limited role even though, on occasions, it was able to approach policy issues and was able to study more contentious issues than had been the case before.

From the outset DEASC's role – like that of SCOE as a whole – was circumscribed by the advice it received. According to the specialist adviser on DEASC, Brigadier Kenneth Hunt, the committee took the 'stated' defence expenditure level as a 'given' and concentrated on 'value for money' considerations[74] – in other words it copied the old Estimates Committee scrutiny role. It was decided also to keep out of 'political' (general policy) areas which would lead to the civil servants resisting the dissemination of information which was regarded as politically sensitive – this of course limited DEASC to the study of largely technical topics and issues of which the MPs or specialist adviser had some detailed knowledge, such as the assessment of the 'value for money' of weapon procurement systems; the availability of logistic support for the front line; the nature and efficiency of the reserves; and the quality of accommodation for servicemen. This was clearly a very different role from that envisaged by the 1968/69 Procedure Committee Report and was only possible because the membership of the sub-committee was 'non-ideological': few of the members of DEASC were technically competent in defence matters (although most of them had been servicemen and were generally pro-defence whether they came from the Labour or the Conservative side of the House)[75] and this meant that apart from the most active members of the committee (David Owen and John Gilbert between 1971 and 1974, and John Roper and Geoffrey Finsberg after 1974) most of the membership consisted of backbench MPs who were generally prepared not to take on issues which the MOD, or the specialist adviser, said were sensitive. The committee also strove to adopt a 'bipartisan' approach which led it to pursue non-contentious issues in a political sense.[76]

As a result the recommendations and work of DEASC fell into five categories which can be labelled respectively: scrutiny of value for money and efficiency: support for the services; questioning of overall priorities; social welfarism; and generalised support for the defence effort/public relations.

Interestingly enough, although the recommendations from DEASC were not generally taken up by MOD or other Whitehall departments the sub-committee had the reputation of being hard-working and one of the more popular committees. This fact probably owes something to the limited aspirations of the backbenchers sitting on DEASC as well as the fact that they were, given their general pro-defence/services attitude, seeking to publicise the parlous state of Britain's defence and attempting to do something to assist the serviceman and the individual services whenever possible. (See Table 4.3 and Figure 4.3 for the trends in Defence Expenditure since 1945.)

As a result these two categories of work – social welfare and public relations recommendations – experienced the highest degree of success rate. Unfortunately, while this may well have been the case it

TABLE 4.3 *UK defence spending (1945–86)*

Financial year	*Defence spending (£ million current prices)*	*Defence spending (£ million 1981–82 cost terms)*
1945/46	4 410	47 653
1946/47	1 653	17 694
1947/48	854	8 851
1948/49	753	7 416
1949/50	741	7 114
1950/51	777	7 260
1951/52	1 110	9 605
1952/53	1 404	11 351
1953/54	1 364	10 761
1954/55	1 436	11 061
1955/56	1 405	10 367
1956/57	1 525	10 633
1957/58	1 430	9 618
1958/59	1 468	9 563
1959/60	1 476	9 506
1960/61	1 596	10 080
1961/62	1 689	10 297
1962/63	1 767	10 464
1963/64	1 792	10 345
1964/65	1 909	10 539
1965/66	2 056	10 851
1966/67	2 115	10 716
1967/68	2 254	11 100
1968/69	2 232	10 471
1969/70	2 204	9 834
1970/71	2 503	10 320
1971/72	2 828	10 675
1972/73	3 092	10 796
1973/74	3 484	11 380
1974/75	4 164	11 329
1975/76	5 346	11 664
1976/77	6 158	11 858
1977/78	6 821	11 554
1978/79	7 496	11 478
1979/80	9 227	12 056
1980/81	11 180	12 374
1981/82	12 606	12 606
1982/83	14 411	13 406
1983/84	15 987	14 163
1984/85	17 290	14 588
1985/86	18 330	14 871

SOURCE Malcolm Chalmers, *The Cost of Britain's Defence* (Peace Studies Paper No.10, University of Bradford), p. 74.

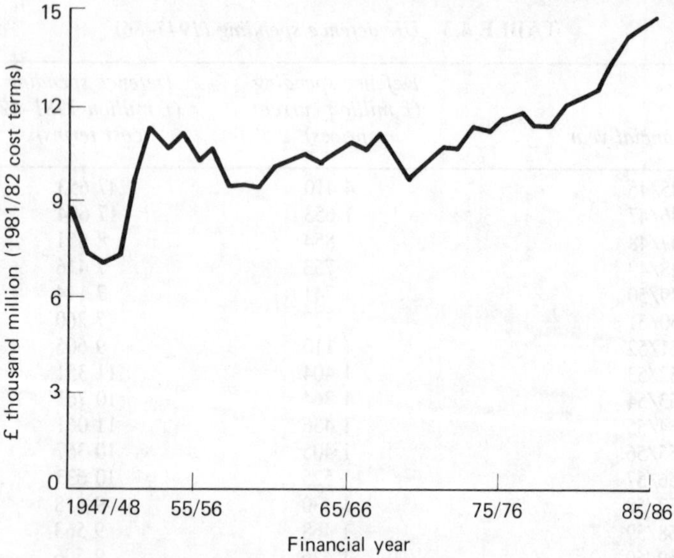

SOURCE Malcolm Chalmers, *The Cost of Britain's Defence* (Peace Studies Paper No. 10, University of Bradford) p. 56.

FIGURE 4.3 *UK defence spending (1947/48–85/86)*

is clear that those recommendations ('value for money' and alternative priority setting) which came closest to the 'maximalist' roles intended for the committee experienced the worst record of successful implementation and the highest quotient of hostility between DEASC and the civilian side of MOD.[77]

Taking the two categories of work which recorded the most success in implementation of recommendations – social welfare issues and public relations – it is clear that DEASC was able to influence government policy because its recommendations either accorded with what the Government was attempting to do, or the issue raised were of marginal impact on existing bureaucratic/service operating procedures. The reinforcing role of DEASC was seen most clearly in the public relations work of the committee. Report, such as *Defence after the Review* and *The Cumulative Effects of Defence Cuts*[78] were clearly aimed at educating the public and Parliament to the consequences of the constant cuts in defence under both the Heath and Labour Governments of the 1970s.

If DEASC was successful by reinforcing existing MOD/service goals, it was also able to influence government policies in cases where the impact of DEASC recommendations was of marginal consequence in expenditure and organisational terms. In particular those recommendations – such as improvements in married quarters in Gibraltar; the modernisation of barracks and changes in rates for occupancy; and improved briefings for servicemen and their families travelling abroad – which can be seen as having a social welfare impact were generally within this category.[79]

Unfortunately, this was not the 'maximalist' role that the Procedure Committee had intended DEASC to fulfil and in those areas which SCOE and DEASC were supposed to operate, the MOD was most reluctant to act. Recommendations of a 'political' rather than of a 'technical' nature such as those which questioned overall governmental priorities were quickly rejected or ignored. Into this category fall recommendations for the Government to review once more the need for MRCA/ADV;[80] make no more cuts after the defence review of 1975;[81] review the decision to withdraw the frigate guardship from Hong Kong and reduce the garrison there and in Cyprus;[82] and to spend more on logistical support for the front line.[83]

These recommendations were rejected either because they questioned existing service/MOD practices or governmental resource allocation priorities, or would have required additional expenditure not available at that time. On some occasions, however, DEASC was able to make MOD and Ministers think about operating procedures and priorities, but it was generally the case that DEASC was only able to do this when the Government, or civil service or services did not have a strongly held alternative view.

In this light, while the record of DEASC influencing policy over 'value for money' and 'service defence' issues was poor, there were a few occasions on which DEASC was able to influence government policy because it was in advance of government or bureaucratic thinking, or because it was supporting a claim by one of the services which the Government and MOD were willing to countenance due to the strength of argument presented.

Without any doubt the DEASC recommendations on reverse and reinforcements,[84] which influenced the Shapland Report on the fundamental reorganisation of the reserves were of this nature.[85] This was a classic case of the specialist adviser influencing MOD/service thinking and creating an environment in which the specialist adviser was able to push the committee into an area in which it might make useful recommendations.

Unfortunately this case also pinpoints the weakness of the 1970/71 reform in Parliament: it was heavily dependent on the quality and knowledge of the specialist advisers and yet even with this expertise could only rarely influence the Government and civil service to make policy changes – few of which were radical.

Similar conclusions can be drawn when one looks at the final category of recommendations from DEASC – value for money. Without any doubt the vast majority of recommendations between 1971 and 1979 fell into this category, indicating that DEASC was little more than an enhanced estimates committee for defence. Unfortunately as the old estimates committee had experienced in the past,[86] attempts to increase efficiency in Whitehall immediately run up against the defence of existing practices and bureaucratic operating procedures. It is unfortunately, therefore, the area in which the civil service is most loath to make adjustments since any changes become, by their very nature, either a recognition that the civil servants have been making mistakes in the past or require the disturbance of working relationships which have taken decades to develop. It is not surprising therefore that such recommendations were generally rejected.[87]

Despite this poor record, there were a few cases in which DEASC was able to influence the Government and MOD. The MOD agreed to provide more information to Parliament in the defence white paper (the 1980 version appearing in two parts)[88] and it did provide DEASC with progress reports on recommendations every October. MOD also concurred with DEASC in its call for the creation of a computer system for all the services, rather than each one having its own system as in the past.[89] The MOD did institute an independent study into the possibility of tri-service training although little came of this in the end.[90] One word of caution is perhaps necessary here because, while on the face of it DEASC had little impact in this field, a number of civil servants expressed the opinion that sometimes the views of the civil servants were affected by DEASC recommendations such that after a short time recommendations initially rejected become live options in internal department discussions.[91]

One should not, however, make too much of this informal/indirect pressure by Parliament which, while undoubtedly real, is counter-balanced by the informal influence flowing from the civil service and services to the MPs sitting on parliamentary committees. In other words many of the initial DEASC recommendations may well have appeared only because the civil servants or services were using the committee as a vehicle for continuing intra-Whitehall battles.[92]

CONCLUSIONS

In general terms then we can argue that DEASC, while a popular committee for those who served on it, failed to fulfil either the goals it set for itself (to scrutinise value for money more effectively) or the more grandiose aspirations of the maximalists on the 1968/69 Procedure Committee (the control of executive policy-making). Undoubtedly, DEASC's greatest successes were achieved through providing more information for Parliament and the public and in defending both the services and defence as a whole in a period of cuts in public expenditure. Overall, however, the committee appeared to have had little impact in those areas of scrutiny and control of the Executive which generated the demand for the parliamentary reforms in the first place – perhaps the perfect example of this was the complete failure of DEASC to notice the £1 billion programme being undertaken on the Chevaline enhancement of Polaris.[93]

Although we can conclude therefore that Parliament was certainly better and more continuously informed after 1971 – and some indication of the coverage of defence issues in the 1970s as compared with the work of the Estimates Committee can be gleaned from comparing the topics studied in Tables 4.2 and 4.4 – it was still the case that Johnson's conclusion concerning the impact and efficacy of Parliamentary Select Committees (written in 1964) was as true in 1979 as it had been earlier. Johnson argued that unless the government was prepared to diminish its own authority and allow Parliament an enhanced role, sharing power in policy-making, then attempts to extend Parliamentary policy influence would be bound to fail.[94] Obviously the reasons for this are related to executive dominance of information and voting strengths in the House of Commons, and in the defence field to the excessive secrecy of the defence establishment. There are also a number of additional problems however which relate to the role of the executive and the position taken by MPs themselves (particularly in DEASC) about their own role which further militated against either a more effective *strategic* or *managerial* role between 1971 and 1979.

We can understand why DEASC failed to fulfil either of the two roles which reformers intended for it by first of all indicating what information would have been necessary for it to discharge its role of strategically influencing the executive (Cabinet, Treasury and MOD). To make any sense of public expenditure policy priorities both DEASC and SCOE would have required the Treasury PESC figures

TABLE 4.4 *Defence related reports from the Select Committee on Expenditure (Defence and External Affairs Sub-Committee): 1971–79*

1970/71	Expenditure Committee (Defence) (Minutes of Evidence to 26th October 1971) (HC 628)
1971/72	Second Report from the Expenditure Committee (Defence) (HC 141) Ninth Report from the Expenditure Committee (Defence) (HC 516)
1972/73	Gibraltar (HC 147) Visit to Ottawa and Washington (HC 296) Nuclear Weapons Programme (HC 399)
1973/74	Accommodation and Staffing in Ottawa and Washington (HC 29) The Future of the Main Battle Tank and Helicopter Borne Anti-Tank MRCA (HC 99) Review of Previous Defence Recommendations (HC 167) Defence Expenditure (HC 169) Defence Medical Services (HC 168)
1974	The Cruiser Programme (HC 175) Defence Cuts (HC 308) Service Married Quarters in Gibraltar (HC 309)
1974/75	Central Management of the Services (HC 220) The Defence Review Proposals (HC 259) Review of Previous Defence Recommendations (HC 471) British Forces Germany (HC 472) Diplomatic Manpower and Property Overseas (HC 473)
1975/76	HM Naval Base and HM Dockyard Devonport (Evidence only) (HC 139) Defence (HC 155) Defence Cuts (HC 236) Hong Kong and Cyprus (HC 270) Defence Policy after the Review (HC 431) Guided Weapons (HC 597) Diplomatic Manpower and Property Overseas (1976 Review) (HC 604) Cuts in Defence Expenditure (MOD) (HC 692) Visit to Canada and the US (HC 696) Defence Medical Services (HC 695)
1976/77	Previous Recommendations FCO, Treasury and MOD (HC 34) Cumulative Effects of Cuts in Defence Expenditure (HC 254) Progress towards the implementation of the final act of the Conference on Security and Co-operation in Europe (HC 392) Reserves and Reinforcements (HC 393)
1977/78	CPRS Review of Overseas Representation (HC 54) Joint Training of Servicemen (HC 86) The Chieftain Tank Engine (HC 485) British Embassy Bonn (HC 562) British Forces Germany (HC 563) Selected Public Expenditure Programmes (DEASC) (HC 600) MOD Management Review (Minutes to Evidence only) (HC 566)
1978/79	Statement on Defence Estimates (Evidence only) (HC 309) Logistic Support for the Front Line (HC 259) The Future of the United Kingdom's Nuclear Weapons Policy (HC 348)

and its medium term economic forecasts and models – these were not available to either SCOE or DEASC which, lacking the staff to compile their own forecast (unlike the CBO in the US), were forced to pursue alternative and more limited goals.[95] Added to this, DEASC would have required a vast array of information from within the MOD and Service departments to fulfil even its more limited individual *strategic* role. To question, let alone provide alternatives to the MOD PESC bids (which is what was intended in theory), DEASC would have required details of LTCs and all Service bids; the Ledger/Target headings for each of the Services and the Vote Book which is controlled by civil service managers for internal accounting purposes (but which provides information on the estimated amounts for particular functions and the priority ordering of these functions); the Joint Chiefs of Staff April Report; the MOD (P & B) division studies of alternative spending scenarios prior to the PESC bid; the reports from individual project managers on time and cost, as well as volume, problems in production; the FCO 'threat' perception documents; a presentation of the range of 'costed options' available to fulfil specific missions and mission functions; internal review documents such as PARs and the Rayner studies;[96] and, a complete change in the information presented to Parliament in the annual Defence White Paper and supply estimates. The latter present only the most limited and anodine statements of the reasons for particular expenditure requests and are far less informative than they used to be; while the former annual document which is supposed to extend Parliamentary knowledge is almost wholly presented in output/functional terms, on the basis of the element costings. While this provides useful information on the cost of particular missions it is relatively useless information if Parliament is to fulfil a priority setting role because the element costing process does not act as a central input into the budgetary decision-making process. As we have argued, however, the relevant information on the budgetary process – apart from a short summary of the LTCs which was withdrawn by the incoming Labour government in 1974 – was never given to Parliament. It is hardly surprising therefore that DEASC's role should have been limited to scrutiny of decisions already taken and in an unsystematic, if more detailed, manner than hithertofore. Interestingly enough, while the explanation for this obviously rests with the defence of executive privileges by government and the civil servants and Service Heads, part of the explanation for this failure also rests with both the specialist advice received by the sub-committee and the nature of British Parliamentary procedures and attitudes.

Without any doubt the British civil service and the British Armed Forces are excessively, if not paranoically, secretive about their activities and roles in defence budgeting when compared with the United States. Indeed, the inability of MOD to give DEASC – a Parliamentary committee – information which was freely available to journalists or in NATO documents in Western Europe and the United States is ample testament to this paranoid secretiveness.[97] Indeed, under the Labour administration – particularly under Fred Mulley – this secretiveness took on an even more extreme form as the natural proclivity to operate behind closed doors by the senior Civil Servants in Britain was heightened by a right-wing Labour Minister's fear of giving information to the left-wing opposition within his own party. This fear of course took the vetting of DEASC members further than the natural sensitivity towards MPs being provided with information coded SECRET by the civil service. This vetting of MPs, which was undertaken in collaboration with the MOD, Cabinet Office, Whips Office, Chief Clerk's Office in the Commons, as well as by the chairman of SCOE was yet a further reason for the relatively non-contentious role of DEASC.[98] Indeed, there were Parliamentary questions at one stage in DEASC's work over the apparent demotion of one Parliamentary clerk, who assisted the sub-comittee and attempted to obtain the information for DEASC which we have argued was necessary for it to fulfil its role.[99] Given this resistance to providing relevant information – which even extended to refusing permission for academic and Service personnel to appear before DEASC to be asked questions and conflict over sidelining of information[100] – sufficient explanation of why the sub-committee failed to fulfil its highest aspirations is provided. In a microcosm, the problem for legislative oversight in Britain is that (unlike the Congress) Parliament neither has the powers to change budget allocations, nor the information or research support to provide the legislature with the information to discharge a controlling role. The parliamentary committees in Britain are totally dependent – and particularly in defence – on information from, and the 'goodwill' of, Whitehall. Even the specialist advisers provided for the DEASC were of former Service backgrounds and themselves dependent on MOD information, there being no British equivalent of Rand, Brookings or the Ford Foundation for providing alternative information sources.

While this reliance on Whitehall for information explains much in the failure of DEASC, MPs in Britain are also likely to compound this weakness by their own abject attitude to reform and their own Parliamentary role. As already indicated, backbench MPs in Britain were unprepared to take on the work required to fulfil the quasi-civil service role intended by some refomers for them in the SCOE reform. MPs, while being heavily committed to constituency, business and party roles, are however likely to prefer to be involved in discussing issues of media prominence or of personnel interest rather than working diligently over financial management problems which are complex, time consuming and unglamourous. As a consequence MPs'own attitudes contributed to the decision to limit SCOE and DEASC's role to a more limited rather than controlling role over the Executive. At the same time the need for DEASC to find bipartisan support for studies and report also tended to force the sub-committee into relatively non-contentious areas.[101] Relatedly of course were the problems associated with the failure to provide the sub-committees with adequate research and staff back up and the opposition within senior echelons of Parlament (The Clerks Office and amongst MPs) to an enhanced Parliamentary role *vis-à-vis* the Executive.[102]

Not surprisingly therefore Parliamentary control of defence budgeting was not particularly extended by either the activities of SCOE or DEASC. This was mainly because at no time did either of these committees ever obtain the important information related to the defence budgeting process which we have outlined earlier.[103] DEASC's role was effective in providing more information about defence matters and some choices, but it failed to fulfil the brief given to it in Standing Order 87 to review public expenditure priorities and provide alternatives. Ironically, the Thatcher government of May 1979, responding to a 1978/79 Procedure Committee report assessing the limited success of SCOE, accepted the argument for a further innovation in 1979.[104] This innovation has seen the curtailment of SCOE and it sub-committees and their replacement with 14 new Departmental related committees – one of which is the Select Committee on Defence (SCOD).[105] On the face of it, the creation of a departmentally related committee ought to provide the scope for an even more in-depth and continuous perusal of defence budgeting along the lines of the managerial role adopted by both DEASC and the Estimates Committee. In practice however this new departure appears as a retrograde step because, added to the limitations already enumerated of lack of independent information and dependence on MOD 'goodwill', are the structural weaknesses of this new reform.

Under the new system of department-specific committees there is no institutional structure at all in Parliament for the bringing together of all departmental decisions to allow Parliament to assess strategically inter-governmental allocations in the manner of the Congressional budget system. Ironically, this was what SCOE was supposed to do, but this capability to parallel the Treasury PESC system has been replaced by a single *independent* committee responsible for Treasury and Civil Service issues. Added to this retrograde step has been the decision to divide DEASC responsibilities between autonomous Defence and Foreign Relations Committees, which are hardly likely to be able to bring together the 'threat' and strategic perceptions of the FCO and the defence capabilities of the MOD if they do not now operate in tandem. It is likely therefore that SCOD will find that it is able neither to influence broad policy (the aim of the new reform) nor the provision of alternative defence policy and expenditure options (the aim of the old reform) but will be limited to the detailed scrutiny of weapons procurement programmes and *ad-hoc* issues – the role formerly undertaken by the old Estimates Committee and to which DEASC found itself effectively confined between 1971 and 1979. As we shall see in later chapters – when we consider Parliamentary oversight of procurement and manpower issues – this is worrying for legislative oversight in Britain because while this more limited role has obviously extended Parliamentary and academc knowledge of Defence policy issues and organisation it has not allowed for enhanced public influence over what remains effectively an executive and Service dominated process.

NOTES

1. Richard Burt, *Defence Budgeting: the British and American Cases* (London: International Institute for Strategic Studies, 1970) p. 5.
2. Maurice Wright, 'From planning to control: PESC in the 1970's, in *Public Spending Decisions*, ed. Maurice Wright (London: Allen & Unwin, 1980) pp. 88–119.
3. On the role of the MOD see: Michael Howard, *The Central Organisation of Defence* (London: RUSI, 1970): David Greenwood, *Budgeting for Defence* (London: RUSI, 1972); and, Burt, ibid. On the role of the Procurement Executive see: Clive Ponting, 'The Reorganisation of Defence Procurement' (paper presented to the Centennial Seminar, Dept. of External Studies, Oxford University, March 1980).

4. Ibid. This account, which relies heavily on Burt and Greenwood has been supplemented by interviews with civil servants within the MOD and FCO to take account of changes in the 1970s.
5. For a discussion of marginal/incremental conflicts see: Hugh Heclo and Aaron Wildavsky, *The Private Government of Public Money* (Los Angeles: University of California, 1974) pp. 198–262.
6. Greenwood, op. cit., pp. 39–40.
7. John Bourn, 'The Planning, Administration and Control of Defence Expenditure' (paper presented to the Centennial Seminar, Dept. of External Studies, University of Oxford, March 1980) p. 7. Mr Bourn was Assistant Under Secretary (Programmes and Budget) MOD. For further details of the failure of PPB in Britain see Peter Else and G. P. Marshall, *The Management of Public Expenditure* (London: Policy Studies Institute, No. 580, March 1979); and, Keith Hartley, 'Programme Budgeting and the Economics of Defence', *Public Administation* (Spring 1974) pp. 55–72.
8. Greenwood, op. cit., pp. 41–2.
9. Michael Hobkirk, 'The Organisation of Defence Policy-Making in the UK and USA', in *The Management of Defence* ed. Lawrence Martin (London: Macmillan, 1976) pp. 12–13.
10. For this basic argument see: Sir Leo Pliatsky, 'Paying for Defence: the Defence Budget and the Public Expenditure System' (paper presented to the Centennial Seminar, Dept. of External Studies, University of Oxford, March 1980).
11. Burt, op. cit., pp. 32–4.
12. Pliatsky, op. cit., pp. 14–15.
13. For an introduction to the process of policy rethink see: Lawrence Martin, *British Defence Policy: the Long Recessional* (London: IISS, Adelphi Paper 61, 1969); and, David Greenwood, 'Constraints and Choice in the Evolution of the British Defence Budget', *British Journal of International Studies*, vol. 2 (1976) pp. 5–26.
14. Pliatsky, op. cit., p. 11.
15. On the introduction of cash limits see: Maurice Wright, op. cit., pp. 101–3.
16. On this problem see eighth report from the Expenditure Committee, *Defence Expenditure* (Session 1977/78, H.C. 600-i), paras 6–15 and Minutes of Evidence, pp. 1–50.
17. Bourn, op. cit., pp. 4–7.
18. Ibid., p. 7.
19. Greenwood, op. cit., pp. 92–4.
20. William P. Snyder, *The Politics of British Defence Policy* (Ohio State University Press, 1964) pp. 48–53; and, David Greenwood 'Defence and National Priorities Since 1945', in J. Bayliss (ed.), *British Policy in a Changing World* (London: Croom Helm, 1977) pp. 174–207.
21. J. Bayliss, 'Defence Decision-Making in Britain and the Determinants of Defence Policy', *Royal United Services Institute Journal*, vol. 120 (March 1975) p. 45.
22. Snyder, op. cit., pp. 66–9.
23. See Bourn and Pliatsky, op. cit. on this problem.

24. For an overview and case study of the TSR-2 cancellation see G. Williams, *Crisis in Procurement* (London: RUSI, 1969).
25. On this role see Colin Turpin, *Government Contracts* (Harmondsworth, Middlesex: Penguin, 1972) pp. 42–6.
26. Ibid., pp. 39 and 42–6.
27. Ibid., pp. 45–6.
28. Hartley, op. cit., pp. 67–8.
29. Nevil Johnson, *Parliament and Administration* (London: Allen & Unwin, 1964) pp. 66–7.
30. Ibid.
31. Howard, op. cit., pp. 12–13.
32. Michael Dillon, 'Recurring Dilemmas and Decision-Making for Defence' in Bayliss (ed.), op. cit., pp. 215–19.
33. See Clive Ponting for an overview, op. cit.; and, Dillon, ibid., pp. 213–19.
34. Johnson, op. cit., pp. 62–3.
35. On the problems of the post-war economy see Sidney Pollard, *The Development of the British Economy, 1914–1967* (London: Edward Arnold, 1973) pp. 330–9.
36. Greenwood (1974), op. cit., pp. 174–207.
37. Johnson, op. cit., pp. 62–4.
38. Ibid., pp. 64–5.
39. Snyder, op. cit., pp. 103–49.
40. Burt, op. cit., pp. 32–4.
41. Johnson, op. cit., p. 63.
42. Ibid., p. 63.
43. This was quoted in Tam Dalyell, 'Westminster Scene', *New Scientist* (30 October 1969) p. 252.
44. Johnson, op. cit., pp. 132–3.
45. Ibid., pp. 63–4 & 132.
46. Greenwood, op. cit., pp. 199–204.
47. Johnson, op. cit., pp. 64–5.
48. Snyder, op. cit, pp. 65–6.
49. Johnson, op. cit., p. 62.
50. Hartley, op. cit., pp. 56–9.
51. Johnson, op. cit., pp. 158–66.
52. Ibid., p. 62.
53. Ibid., pp. 63–6 and 136.
54. Ibid., p. 66.
55. Ibid., pp. 135–8.
56. Ibid., pp. 139–41.
57. Martin Partington, 'Parliamentary Committees: Recent Developments', *Parliamentary Affairs*, vol. 23, no. 4 (Autumn 1970) pp. 370–1.
58. Ibid., pp. 371.
59. Ibid., pp. 370–1.
60. See Chapter 1, pp. 000.
61. F. Cooper, 'Long Range Defence Planning in the UK', *Long Range Planning* vol. 3 (December 1970) p. 18.
62. Donald R. Shell, 'Specialist Select Committees', *Parliamentary Affairs* vol. 23, no. 4 (Autumn 1980) pp. 399–400.

63. Partington, op. cit., pp. 370–1.
64. See Chapter 1, ch. 2, pp. 49–56.
65. Ann Robinson, *Parliament and Public Spending* (London: Heinemann, 1978) pp. 42–53.
66. Ibid., pp. 42–53.
67. Procedure Committee Report, *The Control of Public Expenditure and Administration* (London: HMSO, HC 410, 1968/69).
68. Peter Riddell, *Parliament and the Scrutiny of Public Finance* (London: The Economist Intelligence Unit, 1980) p. 55.
69. Robinson, op. cit., pp. 55–7 and 110–14.
70. Ibid., pp. 42–53.
71. David Owen, 'Parliamentary control of defence budgeting', *Brassey's Annual* (1973) p. 53.
72. Study of Parliament Group, *Specialist Committees in the British Parliament: the Experience of a Decade*, vol. XLII, no. 564 (1975).
73. *The Cumultive Effects of Cuts in Defence Expenditure* (London: HMSO, HC 254, 1976/77), and *Defence Policy after the Review* (London: HMSO, HC 431, 1976/76).
74. This information was provided by Brigadier Hunt in interview and is supported by Masood Hyder, 'Parliament and Defence Affairs: the Defence Sub-Committee of the Expenditure Committee', *Public Administration* vol. 55 (1977) pp. 62–3.
75. Interestingly, while there are Tribunites on the DEASC there was a tendency for all members to be anti-Soviet, in part because there was also a stong Jewish element within the committee.
76. Hyder, op. cit., pp. 77–8.
77. *Defence Policy After the Review*, op. cit.
78. *The Cumulative Effects of Cuts in Defence Expenditure*, op. cit.
79. *Gibraltar* (London: HMSO, HC 147, 1972/73); *Service Married Quarters in Gibraltar* (London: HMSO, HC 309, 1974); and, *Hong Kong and Cyprus* (London: HMSO, HC 270, 1975/76).
80. *Multi-Role Combat Aircraft* (London: HMSO, HC 99, 1973/74).
81. *The Defence Review Proposals* (London: HMSO, HC 259, 1974/75).
82. *Cyprus and Hong Kong*, op. cit.
83. *Logistical Support for the Front Line* (London: HMSO, HC 259, 1978/79).
84. *Reserves and Reinforcements* (London: HMSO, HC 393, 1976/77).
85. Ibid., pp. 42–88.
86. Nevil Johnson, *Parliament and the Administration: The Estimates Committee 1945–65* (London: Allen & Unwin, 1966).
87. The types of recommendations made included: moves to tri-service/unitary training under a single organisational head; the adoption of new, more stringent, contracting systems for procurement; a fundmental review of defence medical services; the provision for Parliament of MOD ten-year long term costings for future expenditure and costed option for all decisions; the standardisation of all documentations for all service personnel; the purchase of commercial stores and training skills; the acceptance of communality of helicopter purchase across all services; the use of laid-up trawlers rather than the purchase of new ships for off-shore patrol work; the scrapping of one of

the five naval dockyards; the independent review of all weapon system procurement; the creation of a new Minister of State responsible for equipment; and, the ability for MOD to carry over money not spent in any year to subsequent years instead of losing money allocated but underspent to the Treasury.

88. *Defence in the 1980's: Statement on the Defence Estimates 1980*, vols I & II, Cmnd 7826 (London: HMSO, April 1980).
89. *Central Management of the Services* (London: HMSO, HC 220, 1974/75).
90. Ibid., HC 220.
91. An indication of the delayed response of the MOD is provided in an article by an Assistant Under Secretary for Programmes and Budget, John Bourn, 'The Planning, Administration and Control of Defence Expenditure' (paper to the Centennial Conference, Department of External Studies, University of Oxford, March 1980) p. 17. Bourn argues that the MOD is currently studying and reviewing policy in areas, like Royal Naval Dockyards and research establishments, which the DEASC argued required review but which the MOD officially refused to countenance.
92. The impact of MOD prompting on DEASC was seen clearly in the evidence given to the committee by G. Ashcroft (MOD) over the problem associated with the inability of the MOD to carry over money unspent in any one year: *Defence Expenditure* (London: HMSO, HC 600-i, 1977/78).
93. 'Pym Takes Wraps Off New Nuclear Deterrent Project', *Guardian* (25 January 1980) p. 6.
94. Johnson, op. cit., pp. 158–66.
95. Robinson, op. cit., pp. 26–9.
96. On the nature of PAR's (Policy Analysis and Review) see Heclo and Wildavsky, op. cit., pp. 276–303. Under the Thatcher administration PARs have been abolished and replaced by internal reviews of efficiency and special studies undertaken by two special advisers to the government Sir Derek Rayner and Paul Channon. On the MOD internal studies see: Bourn, op. cit., pp. 15–18, and on the role of Rayner and Channon see: Richard Norton-Taylor, 'Official Paid Post Axed as Whitehall Gets Lesson in Thrift', *Guardian* (4 July 1980) p. 22.
97. An example of this being the provision of information on the Polaris replacement in the US rather than UK, See: Tony Geraghty, 'Thatcher To Put British Warhead in Trident', *Sunday Times* (6 July 1980) p. 1.
98. Robinson speaks of this problem, op. cit.: pp. 54–7 and it has been confirmed in interviews with Parliamentary Clerks and James Boyden, Chairman of SCOE between 1974 and 1979.
99. Interview with Clerks of the House of Commons (1982).
100. Peter Hennessy, 'Mr. Mulley angers specialists over successor to Polaris', *The Times* (30 April 1979).
101. Masood Hyder, 'Parliament and Defence Affairs: the defence sub-committee of the Expenditure Committee', *Public Administration*, vol. 55 (1977) pp. 59–78.
102. It was expressed in interview by senior clerks that Parliament could not and ought not to have a more extended role than that of scrutiny.

103. Hartley, op. cit., pp. 63–7.
104. 'Parliament redivivus?', *The Economist*, vol. 274 (9 February 1980) pp. 28–9.
105. First Report from the Defence Committee, *Sub-Committees* (HC 455, 1979/80).

Part III
Legislative Oversight and Defence Procurement

5 Reform and Procurement Oversight: Congress and the AV-8B

The weapons procurement process in the United States has long ceased to be the preserve of the armed services and the professional managers of the Pentagon. The process in America is more institutionally fragmented, and more politically visible and accessible than in other liberal democracies, especially the United Kingdom. It is fragmented in two important ways; the procurement process is effectively divided between the Pentagon and the Congress, and in both institutions the funding and development of a particular weapons programme is subject to the scrutiny and the influence of several, and often competing, committees or interests. It is politically visible in the sense that Congress is well informed about all stages of the procurement process from the definition of an operational requirement, through the stages of research, development and engineering to the eventual full scale production and entry into service of a piece of military equipment. It is also visible in the much more politically important sense that Congress is able to inform itself of any military, budgetary or political disagreement within the Pentagon management team about a particular programme. Unlike the public unity that the Ministry of Defence and the armed services maintain when the defence equipment issues are dealt with by the British Parliament, it is common for the political heads of Service departments and for military witnesses to give evidence to Congress that challenges the military assessment and the budgetary allocation made by the Secretary of Defense for a particular weapons system. Service Secretaries, professional servicemen and defence contractors are under little apparent pressure to prevent them giving an independent professional assessment to Congress and, for the Service

Secretaries, independence carries none of the implications of resignation that are enshrined in the British convention of collective responsibility.

The fragmentation and visibility of the procurement process make it very accessible to a variety of interested parties, including the members and staff of congressional committees, members of the Pentagon administration, defence contractors, and the armed services themselves. Given that the process is open, the supporters and the opponents of a weapons programme have many opportunities to promote their interests; what is denied in the Pentagon budget process can be restored by the Congress, and what Congress mandates or appropriates the Administration may veto or impound. To promote a particular weapons programme, its backers must build and maintain a coalition of support within the Pentagon and Congress or, if divided over a weapons programme the outcome is usually decided in favour of that institution which is least internally divided.

The operation of this highly political process is graphically demonstrated by the procurement history of the Marine Corps' AV-8B vertical and short take-off and landing (V/STOL) aircraft. From 1976, when the Marine Corps identified it as the light attack aircraft for the mid-1980s, until late 1981, when funds for the first 12 production models were voted by Congress, the future of the programme was in doubt. In 1978 the Department of Defense cut the research and development funds for the AV-8B by 50%, and in 1979 and 1980 it refused to include the aircraft in its budget request, recommending instead that the Marine Corps take the F/A-18 as its light attack aircraft. Nevertheless, Congress continued to fund the AV-8B programme at the level requested by the Marine Corps despite the advice and wishes of the Secretary of Defense. The history of the AV-8B shows that Congress has the ability both to make an independent assessment of military requirements and budgetary priorities in the weapons procurement field, and to make its assessment prevail against that of the administration.

The AV-8B issue demonstrates the potential of Congress to carry out a thorough going scrutiny of Administration procurement policy, and its ability to make its will prevail in respect of individual weapons systems. However, it also shows the minimal effect that the reform of the congressional budget system had on 'line item' issues of this kind. The reform was not intended to challenge the expertise and authority of the Armed Services Committees in assessing the most effective way to meet a military requirement nor their review of the cost and management efficiency of weapons programmes. Nor was it intended to challenge the Defence Sub-Committees of Appropriations in their scrutiny of the cost and budgetary implications of individual procurement decisions. Yet the Budget Committees did have the responsibility to encourage these committees to focus on 'priority setting' and on the broader implications for 'fiscal policy' of the decisions they made. Above all else, the reform was intended to make the work of committees more responsible, to lessen the influence of special interests and to make committees more conscious of national budgetary priorities and wider fiscal responsibilities, but there is no evidence that this happened. The AV-8B involved major budgetary issues such as the desirability of aircraft commonality to increase procurement efficiency, but there is no evidence that the Budget Committees or the Congressional Budget Office had any influence on the way the established committees considered these and other issues connected with the AV-8B. There is very little to distinguish the *method* that the reformed Congress used to consider the AV-8B from the method it had traditionally used for the procurement of aircraft.

THE POLITICAL BACKGROUND

The procurement of the AV-8B took place in a politically complex and an emotionally charged atmosphere in which it became a focus of attention in several politico/military disputes only one of which was directly related to the Marine Corps' request for it as a light attack aircraft. That issue revolved around the attempt by the Department of Defence to persuade the Marine Corps and Congress that the light attack role could be performed more efficiently by the McDonnell-Douglas/Northrop F/A-18, first on the grounds of its superior military performance and, after this had been challenged sucessfully by the Marines, later on the grounds of affordability. But this debate was always conducted against the background of wider issues. The first was the military viability of V/STOL technology compared to conventional take-off and landing (CTOL) aircraft. There existed within the Pentagon and Congress groups that regarded V/STOL as the military aviation technology of the future and one that should be developed despite the inability of current V/STOL aircraft to match the speed, range and payload performance of CTOL planes. Equally there were groups that saw V/STOL as a technology in search of a military mission, the pursuit of which would divert funds from programmes of much needed CTOL modernisation. For the first group the AV-8B was suppported as a way of ensuring that V/STOL technology had a future in the United States, for the second it was opposed on the grounds of current procurement efficiency.

The AV-8B was also a factor in the long-running dispute over the future of sea based aviation, especially the future of the large deck carrier. In the early 1970s there was a powerful group in Congress opposed to the building of additional nuclear powered supercarriers of the Nimitz class, each of which cost more than 2 billion in 1975 dollars. In 1977, under the influence of Admiral Zumwalt, the Navy outlined a plan to move to an all V/STOL carrier force that would be able to operate from a variety of small and inexpensive sea platforms rather than from supercarriers. Even though Congress upheld President Carter's veto of a Nimitz class carrier in 1978, there was considerable congressional opposition to the plan. This paralleled a progressive change, after Zumwalt's retirement, in the attitude of the navy itself and within a year of its publication the planned move to a force of small carriers was effectively shelved. The revival of Navy Department and congressional support for supercarriers was strengthened by the failure of American industry to establish a V/STOL programme which could produce an aircraft of sufficient performance within the time frame specified by the plan. This meant that large decked carriers, complete with catapaults and arrester gear capable of handling high performance CTOL aircraft would be required well beyond the 1990s. The only medium term threat to the large deck carrier was the AV-8B and its proposed naval derivative the AV-8B+.

The United States Navy, which presents the Marine Corps budget to Congress, wished to support the Marine request for the AV-8B but did not want a V/STOL develoment that might threaten the existence of traditional aircraft carriers. In truth the Navy was divided, with the surface fleet seeing the AV-8B development as a way of getting some organic air support aboard a variety of ships in the near future, whereas Navy aviators opposed it on the grounds that fleet air defence required planes with higher speeds and longer range. There is no doubt that many Navy pilots saw V/STOL aircraft and the possibility that they might proliferate throughout the fleet as a threat to their high status and their career prospects, and many Admirals were attracted to supercarriers more for their symbolic than their military value. As one congressional report notes, the AV-8B became a highly emotive issue in that it attracted not only the support of critics of the conventional aircraft carriers but also the opposition of proponents of a big-carrier Navy and CTOL naval aviation, despite the fact that the Marines requested the aircraft principally for the close air support of ground forces.[1]

The AV-8B was also a point of focus in the wider issue of lightweight fighter commonality. Congress, with the encouragement and active support of some members of the Department of Defense, had instructed the Navy in the Defense Appropriations Act of 1974 to participate with the USAF in the lightweight fighter flyoff between the General Dynamics single engined F-16 and the twin engined Northrop F-17. Intending to make the procurement of a new generation of lightweight fighters as efficient as possible, Congress further instructed the Air Force and the Navy to procure the same plane. However, the USAF selected the F-16 and the Navy chose the F-17 which was to be 'navalised' by McDonnell-Douglas, with Northrop as the major sub-contractor, and redesignated the F/A-18. The Navy argued that the twin engine reliability of the F/A-18 was essential for aircraft deployed at sea and, although they would have preferred more of the high performance F-14s, tentatively accepted the F/A-18 as the *fighter* for the Navy and Marine Corps F-4s. Congress reluctantly accepted this decision, but there were those in the Pentagon who wished to see as much commonality as possible, especially in the Navy which procured several kinds of aircraft each year but in numbers too small to be economic.[2] Therefore the Office of their Secretary of Defence (OSD) and the Programm Analysis and Evaluation (PA&E) department pushed the F/A-18 as the common replacement for *all* Navy and Marine aircraft, discounting the Marines' preference for the AV-8B as the attack replacement. These groups argued that an all F/A-18 buy would achieve great procurement efficiency and that a single aircraft in the fighter and attack roles would simplify the training, logistic and maintenance tasks of the Navy and the Marine Corps. This made the AV-8B an issue in the broader debate about the relative benefits of weapons commonality and procurement efficiency versus weapons specificity and operational performance. The problem of setting a priority on economic as opposed to military benefits in the weapons procurement process became a central one in the AV-18 debate.

Finally the AV-18 was an issue, or more accurately a symbol, in the broader debate about NATO's 'Two-way Street', which was the attempt to achieve greater equality in the trans-Atlantic arms trade by increasing American purchases of European military equipment. President Carter was concerned about the European view that America sold its arms aggressively in Europe but adopted a 'Buy America' policy at home which discriminated against European arms. He recognised the need to counter this view in order to maintain the unity and cohesion of the Alliance, and was aware of the political benefits that could be derived from a major European-American weapons agreement. The AV-8B went some way to fulfilling this requirement because it is a development of the British Hawker Siddeley Harrier and, even though produced in the United States, retains a substantial British technological imput in the form of the Rolls Royce Pegasus engine and part of the airframe built by British Aerospace. Undoubtedly, some of the support for the AV-8B came from factions in the Pentagon and in Congress which were as much impressed by the political benefit of having a major European-American programme on the 'Two-way Street' as they were by the operational and military arguments put up by the Marines.[3]

THE AV-8B PROGRAMME

The Marine Corps' interest in a V/STOL capability for the light attack and close air support (CAS) roles dates back to 1975,[4] and it has operated British built Harrier/AV-8As in these roles since 1971. The Marine Corps became interested in the Harrier after it had been demonstrated to German and American pilots in 1967 and it secured the Defense Secretary's agreement to acquire the aircraft in September 1968. The desire to deploy the aircraft as quickly as possible was demonstrated by the fact that the Navy budget for FY 1970 was amended in January 1969 to include $57 million for the procurement of 12 AV-8As and, in order to fit them in, the Marine Corps sacrificed 17 of the 51 F-4J fighters that it had originally requested.[5] 110 AV-8As were funded by Congress, the last of them delivered to the Marine Corps in march 1977 by which time they made up three of the Marines' twelve attack squadrons. The essence of the Marine case for the AV-8A was that its V/STOL capability gave it great basing flexibility, especially the capability of being deployed close to the forward edge of the battle area which would enable it to respond much more quickly to requests for ground support than the F-4.[6]

By 1973, the US Navy and Marine Corps and the British Navy and

Air Force were confident of the combat versatility of V/STOL aircraft, with the Marine Corps convinced that its future lay with an all V/STOL air arm.[7] A supersonic development of the AB-8A, the AV-16, was proposed which was to have not only greater speed but also improved range and payload capabilities. It was to be a joint UK/US project with manufacturing facilities in each country, and the major investment was to be in a new Pegasus 15 engine to be developed jointly by Rolls Royce and Pratt and Whitney. It was the cost of developing the Pegasus 15, an estimated $500 million, that led both to the cancellation of the project in 1974 and to the decision by the British Ministry of Defence in 1975 to develop the Sea Harrier using the existing Pegasus 11 engine. Marine interest in a Harrier development and the desire to establish a V/STOL production line in the United States led to a similar American programme. The Marine Corps submitted a 'needs statement' for a follow-on to the AV-8A in October 1975 and, although never officially approved by the Chiefs of Naval Operations, it remains the only statement of an operational requirement that was later to be developed as the AV-8B.[8] McDonnell Douglas, Hawker Siddeley's licensee, proposed a Harrier development which also used the Pegasus 11 engine but which improved range and payload capabilities by a combination of weight reduction and aerodynamic lift technology. The programme was officially approved in March 1976, with McDonnell Douglas as the prime contractor and Hawker Siddeley as the major sub-contractor.

The Navy had received funds for the development of the Harrier even before this decision. In its FY 1976 budget, debated in Congress in 1975, the Navy requested and was granted $4.3 million for development of the AV-8B as part of its V/STOL development programme. A year later, in the FY 1977 budget, the Navy informed Congress of the Marine Corps' specific requirement for the AV-8B The Corps planned to replace all its AV-8As and F-4s with 336 single seat AV-8Bs by the mid-1980s, which would provide a force structure of eight 20-plane squadrons, plus spares and aircraft for training and attrition losses. The Navy requested $33 million for the research and development of the AV-8B, with advanced development to begin in March 1976. Full scale development was planned to begin in 1979 and end in 1981. Full production of the aircraft was envisaged for FY 1982 with the Marines achieving their initial operating capacity (IOC) of thirty aircraft in 1984. The House and Senate Appropriations committees fully endorsed the Navy's V/STOL programme of which the AV-8B request was part.[9]

THE BATTLE FOR THE AV-8B

The FY 1978 Budget Cycle:

In 1977, however, the Navy radically altered the status of the AV-8B programme, and this was revealed in the Hearings on its FY 1978 budget request. Up until this date the aircraft had been an important part of the Navy's V/STOL development efforts and, in the AV-8B+ version, had been a candidate for Navy use even though definite plans for an Advanced Harrier deployment had been made only for the Marine Corps. The Navy decided, however, to consolidate its haphazard V/STOL research and development work into a structured plan for the production of two *types* of aircraft, a subsonic Type A and a supersonic Type B, but indicated that, although a variety of technologies would be considered for the programme, the AV-8B would not be amongst them. The Navy did request $60.3 million for the continued development of the AV-8B but exclusively for the Marine Corps, and it notified Congress that full production of the aircraft was to be delayed by one year to prevent too great an overlap with the development programme. There was considerable criticism in Congress about the failure of the Navy to define the Type A V/STOL programme objectives more precisely and only $14.1 million of the $28.2 million requested by the Navy was authorised. In contrast, Congress responded more positively to the clear programme objectives set for the AV-8B by the Marine Corps and both House and Senate authorised and appropriated the full $60.3 million request.[10]

The FY 1979 Budget Cycle

The AV-8B programme and the Navy's V/STOL plan were closely scrutinised by the Department of Defence throughout 1977. On 1 April, the Secretary of Defense, Harold Brown, informed the Navy that its plan was not specific enough about missions but that 'it unnecessarily restricts approaches to the solution to the problem',[11] by which he meant that he was unhappy that the Navy had specified V/STOL as the sole method of meeting the sea based air mission. He expressed a long standing concern about the military viability of V/STOL aircraft, a concern he had first outlined to Congress in 1964 when he was Director of Defense Research and Engineering.[12] He demanded the consideration of alternative programmes, especially CTOL aircraft, for the mission so that the most cost-effective solution could be found. The same demand was applied to the Marine's light attack and close air support missions, and this was the first indication of Brown's opposition to the AV-8B. Brown's misgivings about V/STOL aircraft were shared by Russell Murray, Assistant Secretary of Defense for Program Analysis and Evaluation, who emerged as the strongest opponent of the AV-8B within the OSD.[13] He advised Harold Brown in the summer of 1977 that the marine Corps *attack* mission could be carried out much more effectively by the F/A-18 which the Marines had already accepted as their *fighter* replacement. Any shortage in Marine attack aircraft that might occur while the F/A-18 was being developed could be filled by the procurement of an additional 72 A-4 planes. Although Murray claimed that his objections to the AV-8B rested on its military performance, press reports at the time suggested that the main reason for pressing the F/A-18 on the Marines was to increase its production run in order to reduce the unit cost of a fast inflating and politically unpopular programme.[14] In August 1977, after what Murray describes as 'some preliminary sparring' between the Marine Corps and the OSD, Brown ordered a cost-effectiveness study of the two aircraft.

Initially the study was to have been conducted by the Marine Corps, but Brown gave responsibility for it to the Secretary of the Navy's Office for Programs and Analysis. No official reason for the change was given but there were suspicions that Brown hoped that the Navy's analysts would simply endorse the view of their counterparts in the PA&E division. He also had reason to believe that tha Navy would be reluctant to support the Harrier development because 'the service is concerned that it may be forced into an AV-8B+ aircraft. The service generally is seeking to delay going to a smaller carrier for V/STOL operations'.[15] The report was submitted to Brown in October 1977 and, against expectations, it strongly endorsed the AV-8B and its superiority in the close air support role. It also indicated that the AV-8B would be less costly to procure and operate despite assumptions that favoured the F/A-18 in the cost analysis. Murray and his team of analysts in PA&E took issue with almost every point of the Navy/Marine study arguing that it had been constructed in a way that favoured the AV-8B over the F/A-18.

This view may have carried the day and led to the cancellation of the Harrier development had not the in-house debate on the future of naval aviation in general, and the AV-8B project in particular, created serious divisions within the Department of Defense that were exploited by the marine Corps and its supporters. As one well informed journal put it in October 1977, 'The directorate of defense research and engineering favors the AV-8B program, while the Program Analysis and Evaluation Office is against the AV-8B program and recommends termination.'[16] More importantly the Navy Secretary, W. Graham Claytor, Jr., emerged as a strong opponent of the PA&E's recommendations for naval aviation and as a strong supporter of the AV-8B. His awareness that the Navy chiefs wished to maintain traditional carriers led him to support the AV-8B only as a Marine close air support aircraft, and to support the Navy's demand for the high performance F-14s in preference to the F/A-18.

This fundamental disagreement about the future of Navy and marine aviation was taken to a new and official level on 10 December, 1977 when the Under Secretary of the Navy, R. James Woolsey, sent a memorandum to the Secretary of Defense to counter arguments made by Russell Murray in a memorandum that he had issued on the 9 December. The essence of the so-called 'Woolsey Memorandum' was that the Navy Department valued some of the capabilities of the F/A-18 but saw it not as a low cost compliment to the F-14, as the OSD described it, but as a lower capability substitute. Woolsey argued that in the light of fiscal constraints, 'it is far preferable to terminate [the F/A-18] than to suffer the disproportionate loss in other aviation and non-aviation programs which otherwise seem inevitable'. Those other programmes were identified as the F-14/Phoenix system which was, in Woolsey's view, the only one capable of dealing with the anti-ship threat posed by the Soviet Backfire bomber, and the AV-8B which he supported strongly as 'the right choice for the Marine light attack force'.[17] The dispute between the Navy and the OSD continued until the very eve of the presentation of the President's budget to Congrees and involved meetings at the highest levels in the Administration. A compromise was finally reached in late December 1977 that enabled the F/A-18, F-14 and AV-8B programmes to be continued but at reduced levels of funding. Although the Marine Corps had fought hard for the AV-8B in the budget formulation process, it was largely as a bargaining chip in the Navy's dispute with the OSD that it remained in the defence budget request for FY 1979.

It was in the congressional Hearings on the budget that the Marine Corps was able to reveal the substance of the AV-8B:F/A-18 cost effectiveness study and to defend publically its request for the AV-8B. It is worth noting that the marine Corps, although it took every opportunity to publicise its case, concentrated its effort on the Armed Services and Appropriations Committees. Indeed, there were few occasions when the Budget Committees had time to look specifically at tactical air programmes, and neither of them would trespass on Armed Services Committee business by looking at a single 'line item' weapons programme, whereas the traditional defence committees reviewed both annually. Nevertheless, the strategy of the Marine Corps reflected the reality of congressional power on defence procurement issues, and it did what it had always done; rallied its known supporters in the committees that had the authority to grant them what they wanted. Even on the issue of procurement efficiency, which should have been of major concern to the Budget Committees, the Marine Corps chose to argue its case before the Appropriations Committees. However, their case was considerably assisted by the failure of the DoD to present its case on the AV-8B effectively.

Harold Brown rather incautiously told the House Armed Services Committee that 'I feel that if forced to choose between the F-18 and the AV-8B, the Marine Corps would select the F-18 for both the fighter and the light attack force'.[18] This claim was intended to justify his decision to budget only $85.6 million of the $173.3 million requested by the Marine Corps for the AV-8B development programme. It was also intended to justify his choice of the F/A-18 as the Marine's light attack aircraft, and his direction to the Navy to request additional A-4s to meet any shortfall in Marine light attack forces. The testimony of the Marine Corps to Congress made it unequivocally clear that it did not prefer the F/A-18 to the AV-8B, and that it did not regard the A-4 as an adequate provision for any light attack shortfall that might occur. At no point did the Marine Corps compromise its opposition to the Defense Department's plans.

The marine Corps was given the best opportunity to promote its case by the Senate Armed Services Tactical Air sub-committee which held Hearings between 22 March and 12 April, 1978. The opportunity was particularly good because Senator Howard Cannon, the sub-committee chairman, and Charles Cromwell, the committee's staff expert, were established supporters of the Navy and Marine Corps. Cromwell's support was especially important because his training as an aeronautical engineer who had formally worked for the Naval Air Systems Command made him the formost tactical air expert on Capitol Hill. His opinion was respected and his recommendations were acted upon by the majority of committee members. He was also known to be a fierce opponent of interservice commonality projects like the F/A-18.[19] General Miller of the Marine Corps presented in outline, and in cautious terms, the results of the cost-effectiveness study that had been done the previous year. However, in response to what can only be described as a series of leading and obliging questions from Cromwell, the Marine Corps was able to rehearse its refutation of the OSD case against the AV-8B in detail and for the record.

Cromwell's opening questions allowed the Marine Corps to submit for the record the report of the Center for Naval Analysis which showed the AV-8B to be less expensive than the F/A-18. His second series of questions related to the responsiveness of both aircraft to requests for ground support. This allowed the Marines not only to confirm that the AV-8B could respond more quickly than the F/A-18, but also to emasculate the in-house criticisms made of their study by Russell Murray and the PA&E. Murray had criticised the marines for setting a response time of 30 minutes or less, and argued that if the time was doubled or halved then the AV-8Bs advantages would disappear. This, Murray argued, showed that the Marines had rigged the test to 'maximise their calculated advantage of the AV-8B over the F-18'.[20] The Marine response was caustic, pointing out that if response times were cut in half 'you are describing targets which must be attacked using other fire support means such as artillery', and that their combat experience in the Second World War, Korea and Vietnam showed 'that if we are not able to respond to the call for support from the ground forces within about 30 minutes, the effectiveness of air support is reduced considerably'. The point was forced home by the observation that 'The AV-8 concept was developed to match that tactical experience as a result of what we had learned from combat, not the other way round'.[21] Not for the first time a congressional committee accepted the lessons of Marine combat experience rather than the assessments of desk-bound analysts.

Further questions permitted the Marine Corps to extol the value of the ground loiter capability and high sortie rate of the AV-8B, to confirm their ability to supply and maintain it in austere forward bases, and to reassure Congress about its performance, safety and readiness record. Marine Corps witnesses also revealed that Brown had demanded improved reliability and greater combat effectiveness of the aircraft in 1976 and that those requirements had been met.[22]

Questions also allowed witnesses to describe the unique capacity of the AV-8B to fit into the Marine integrated air-ground team in a way that would assure the ground commander that air support would be available when needed. General Miller emphasised that if the Marines were to maintain their capability for amphibious operations and fighting flexibility then 'the Marine Corps cannot be dependent on air support from other services'.[23] The point had been made even more forcefully in one of the rare presentations to the Budget Committees a year earlier when General Miller said,

> We are proud of this closely integrated team. The Marine crossing the beach or assulting the hill can be confident of being supported by those with whom he has trained, and who understand and share his personal concern for reaching his assigned objective. Furthermore, this combined force of military effort is under a single commander.[24]

These were oblique but clearly understood references to the Marine Corps' experiences in Korea and Vietnam. In Korea the operational control of the First Marine Division and the First Marine Air Wing had been divided between the Army and the Air Force but, when the Division faced overwhelming odds at the Chosin Reservoir, the Marine Air Wing came to its rescue anyway ignoring the instructions of Air Force controllers. A similar splitting of the Marine air–ground team took place in Vietnam in March 1968 when the First Marine Air Wing was placed under the control of the Seventh Airforce. Airforce controllers diverted the majority of Marine aircraft from close air support of ground troops to deep interdiction missions. In both cases the division of operational control denied the Marines 'responsive and organic' air support at some considerable cost in ground force casualties. Clearly, one of the overriding qualities of the AV-8B for the Marine Corps was that it could be deployed so far forward and so close to the Marine ground commander that it would make little military sense to transfer its control to the Air Force.[25] It would, in other words, ensure that the Marine Corps retained control of its attack planes, and for this there was much support and sympathy in Congress.

For all these reasons the Marine Corps regarded the AV-8B as a priority programme and the Commandant, General Louis H. Wilson, indicated that he would rather delay the modernisation of the light attack force and wait for the AV-8B than accept any of the alternative plans offered by OSD.[26] OSD witnesses did offer some counter arguments to Congress, but they amounted to little more than that the F/A-18 had a better air-to-air capability than the AV-8B and that continuation of the programme would involve substantial research and development costs in the near-term.[27] The strength of these objections was diluted by the fact that Congress was fully aware that the OSD spoke for only one faction within the Department of Defense, and much was made of this by Marine's congressional supporters. Senator Hatch was one of eight senators who spoke up for the AV-8B as early as 20 October 1977, expressing his concern 'about recent news eminating from the DoD. It appears that Secretary of Defence Brown has attempted to stop the development of the Advanced Harrier program'. He noted that 'much has been made of the small differences between officials in the Navy and the Marine Corps over the development of the AV-8B. I find it reassuring to see the Navy Secretary, W. Graham Claytor Jr., has joined forces with Marine Corps Commandant, Louis H. Wilson, in support of the V/STOL programme'.[28]

In addition to this the full text of the 'secret' Woolsey Memorandum stating the Navy's support for the AV-8B and its opposition to the F/A-18 was published in the March edition of *Armed Forces Journal International*, just at the time when House and Senate Hearings on the two aircraft were taking place. The Armed Services and Appropriations committees of both Houses were unanimous in restoring the full funding of $173.3 millin to the AV-8B programme and in refusing the funds requested by the Administration for additional A-4s. The Reports of both Armed Services committees and that of the House Appropriations Committee indicated that full funding was intended to assist the efficient and orderly transition to an all AV-8B Marine light attack force by mid-1984.[29] In Congress at least the Marine Corps had won the FY 1979 budget battle hands down and had established a broad coalition of support, but its conflict with the OSD was far from over.

The FY 1980 Budget Cycle

In the early summer of 1978 Brown reconsidered the Marine Corps' cost-effectiveness study of the AV-8B and the F/A-18, the criticism of the study made by the PA&E analysts, and the Marine Corps' point-by-point rebuttal of the criticisms. He still felt that the cost-effectiveness of the AV-8B was in question and in July 1978 called for an operational test and evaluation of the two aircraft. The Marines nominated the fourth full scale development model of the prototype AV-8B for the flyoff which meant that it could not take place much before late 1981 and it was likely that some $1.2 billion in AV-8B development money would have been spent before the results of the test became available. In addition to this the General Accounting Office (GAO) learned that none of the Defense Department officials that it questioned about the flyoff felt that it would provide information that would resolve the cost-effectiveness issue, nor were they able to describe how the tests would be conducted. For these reasons a GAO report of January 1979 recommended against the flyoff and against the full scale development of the AV-8B unless 'a definite need has been established for this aircraft and there is an intention to deploy it operationally'. The report also noted that in early January 1979 the Under Secretary of Defense Research and Engineering, Dr William J. Perry, had refused to allow the Navy to obligate $108 million of the $123 million full-scale development funds that had been voted by Congress in the FY 1979 budget. The GAO were informed that no request for the programme would be made in the FY 1980 budget and that unless the action was reversed by Congress, 'the AV-8B program has effectively been terminated'.[30] Claytor immediately 'reclaimed' the project, that is to say he appealed officially to the Secretary of Defense against the decision to drop the AV-8B from the budget, but with no success. He and the Marines appealed unsuccessfully against the refusal to release existing AV-8B development funds in late January.

Once again the Marine's congressional allies came to the support of the project. Members of the House of Appropriations Committee wrote to Brown on 28 February 1979 to protest against the decision to exclude the AV-8B from the FY 1980 budget and against the deferral of the development funds. The GAO reported in March that the decision to withhold funds was an Executive impoundment and that the DoD had failed to notify Congress as required by the provisions of the Impoundment Control Act of 1974. On 4 April President Carter formally notified Congress of his decision to defer the funds. Yet, when William Perry appeared before the defense sub-committee of House Appropriations some days later he said 'The notification from the White House was an administrative error', and that 'All advanced development funds have always been available to the

Marines'.[31] It is difficult to avoid the judgement that this was more a change of mind than the rectification of an administrative error, since even an administration as accident prone as President Carter's would take care in responding to an official GAO enquiry about an impoundment and, as Perry was to make clear, later,[32] the decision to delay the programme was essentially an exercise in waiting for a judgement from Congress. By the time that Perry was called to give evidence, that judgement had been delivered unequivocally in the Marine's favour by a congressional coalition that was even broader and stronger than that of the previous year.[33]

Perry informed Congress that he had already released $40 million after the Marines had requested funds for a second time in February and that this would be sufficient to take the AV-8B development to its scheduled review by the Department's Defense Systems Aquisition Review Council in July 1979. The Navy and Marine Corps reported to the Review Council that all development goals had been met, that the programme was on schedule, and strongly recommended that AV-8B engineering development should begin. Despite the opposition of the Secretary of Defense and PA&E analysts to the AV-8B project, the Review Council, chaired by Perry, would not recommend either its constitution or termination.[34] The refusal to take action that would officially end the AV-8B programme was clearly influenced by the strength of congressional support throughout 1979, and confirmed the continuing battle within the Defense Department between the Secretary of Defense and Murray on the one hand and Claytor and Perry on the other.

The focus of interest of the House and Senate committees dealing with the Navy/Marine Corps budget changed slightly in the FY 1980 Hearings. The refusal to release $108 million of the money voted by Congress the previous year was, of course, a major issue, but Perry had largely reassured the committees that the money would be released and would be used to develop the AV-8B. Congress was much more interested in the reasons why the Department of Defense had not requested any funds for the continuation of the development programme. In reply to questions from members of the House Appropriations Committee, Perry explained that there was strong support in the DoD for the AV-8B but that,

> The price may be about a billion dollars for the luxury of having two different kinds of airplanes instead of one. The question is whether the virtues of the AV-8B, this exciting new V/STOL

technology with the operational advantage and flexibility it gives the Marines, are worth the price.

As a practiced observer of congressional opinions on defence issues he must have recognised that his was a rhetorical question, and it was intended perhaps to do no more than inform Congress of his support for the Marines and their 'exciting new V/STOL technology'. Perry's deputy for Tactical Warfare Programs, Robert Moore, was even more fulsome in his praise for the AV-8B prototype when he said, 'The performance, the handling qualities of the airplane are outstanding'.[35] Perry confirmed that performance was not a problem and that affordability, or the attempt to achieve 'production efficiency' for the F/A-18, was the major reason for excluding the AV-8B programme from the budget. He advised Congress that if other customers could be found for the aircraft, 'so that we have a larger production line, then those issues would diminish quite a bit'.[36] Perry was endorsing the AV-8B's technology, approving the Marine Corps' plans to deploy it for close air support, and indicating to Congress a way to surmount the problem of affordability.

Sympathetic questioning of the Navy and Marine Corps once again allowed them to challenge the position of the DoD. The first challenge was to the Department's estimate of affordability which claimed that an all F/A-18 buy would save \$1.38 billion. Appearing before the House Appropriations Committee, General Wilson was asked 'From the Marine Corps standpoint, what about this affordability problem?' and he chose to submit a formal answer for the record which read,

> The AV-8B is no less affordable than the proposed alternative USMC light attack aircraft, the F/A-18. It has been previously demonstrated that the life cycle costs of the AV-8B and the attack version of the F/A-18 are approximately equal. The real question, therefore, is not affordability, but which aircraft will fulfil the Marine Corps' mission best. The Marines are certain that the operational benefits and basing benefits offered by the AV-8B make it the best choice by far.[37]

Wilson's case rested on the fact that the DoD's comparison related only to research, development and procurement costs, but if operating expenditure were added, then the life cycle costs of an 'all F/A-18' programme and an 'F/A-18:AV-8B mix' programme were equal.[38] This direct challenge by the Commandant of the Marine Corps, both to the substance and the importance of the issue of affordability, focused attention on the priority that the Corps attached to the aircraft and on the treatment that it had received from the Secretary of Defense. Secretary William Claytor and General Wilson revealed that the AV-8B request had been submitted as part of the Navy's 'minimum' or highest priority budget, but that the OSD had insisted that it be moved to a lower level. Wilson reported that,

> It was then put in band 1, the next highest priority allowed under the rules. The Defense Department then moved it to band 3, and took some things that were initially of a lower priority within band 3, and put them ahead of it.[39]

In the House Armed Services Committee Hearings, Representative Bob Wilson allowed General Miller to make the same point more graphically. He asked if the AV-8B was the Marine's highest priority programme and was told that it was; he then asked 'You got slapped in the face and said no dice, we will cancel the whole program?', the General replied simply, 'Yes, sir.' Miller also indicated that he was not satisfied with the substitution of the F/A-18 because it could not fulfil 'the mission that we consider essential for the Marine Corps and for which the AV-8B was designed'.[40] The Armed Services and Appropriations committees once more unanimously showed their support for the Marine Corps by adding $203 million to the FY 1980 Navy budget to fund the AV-8Bs development; an increase that was accepted by the Budget Committees in the 2nd Concurrent Resolution without demur.

The FY 1981 Budget Cycle

The political events surrounding the FY 1981 budget were in many ways a replay of the previous year as congressional support continued to grow. Once again the Navy and Marine Corps placed the request for AV-8B development funds in their 'minimum' or highest priority budget, and once again the Office of the Secretary of Defense had relegated it to a level low enough to exclude it from the department's defence request which was sent to Congress in January 1980. Once again the Secretary of the Navy, and the Director of DR&E gave evidence to Congress that supported the Marine request, and once again the Armed Services and Appropriations Committees provided the Marine Corps with ample opportunity to make their case. Most of the Hearings were taken up with a repetition of the previous year's arguments about affordability and the suitability of the aircraft for the Marine mission.

One significant difference, however, was that the OSD's opposition to the AV-8B had considerably weakened, perhaps because the rapidly expanding defence budgets of the late 1970s meant that DoD could afford to do more, even for programmes, like the AV-8B, for which it did not have great enthusiasm. The first indication of this was that the OSD had relegated the AV-8B priority by only one level in the department's 1981 budget review compared to the three levels of the previous year. The second was indicated by Dr David Mann, an Assistant Secretary of the Navy, when he reported that although affordability was the only remaining objection made by the Department of Defense to the programme, it was now accepted that the life-cycle costs of the alternative programmes were equal.[41] He also reported that the United Kingdom had expreessed an interest in the American AV-8B but was concerned about Brown's apparent opposition to it. Congress knew that if Britain's interest were to be translated into a firm order for the aircraft, it would be the final nail in the coffin of the affordability argument. In its report on the DoD Appropriations Bill for FY 1981 the Senate committee encouraged the Secretary of Defense to accept the British offer without delay.

The third and most important indication that the Administration had moderated its opposition to the AV-8B, was that the Department of Defense had effectively abdicated responsibility for the programme's future to Congress. Mann reported that 'Future activity will be determined by Congressional action to the current program as no funds have been provided in the FY 1981 budget.' Perry conveyed the same message when he assured Congress that FY 1980 funds would be released to maintain the pace of the programme, and that 'we are not doing as we did in '79, actually stopping the program, delaying the program while we are waiting a judgement from Congress. We are keeping the program at its regular pace while we are waiting for Congress to decide'.[42] What Perry implied was that the DoD was maintaining the programme at a pace that assumed the continuation of funding. He also acknowledged that he had received the final report of the Defence Science Board on V/STOL aircraft in which the Director, Dr Eugene G. Fabini, identified the AV-8B as the only project in the United States that would yield an operational aircraft in the mid-1980s and recommended that 'we need to get V/STOL aircraft into an operational status in the Navy and the Air

Force, as well as the Marine Corps'.[43] Asked if he felt that this would lead the DoD to change its 'rather adamant stand against this aircraft', Perry replied 'Yes, I think this is a possibility.' He offered other reasons for such a change which were that the development programme for the AV-8B had gone exceptionally well, and that the Marines felt that V/STOL was extremely important for their operations and worth paying a premium price to get; both factors, said Perry, weigh heavily in our minds as a positive reason to go ahead'.[44]

Administration opposition to the AV-8B had collapsed under the combined weight of its own internal divisions and the unity of Congress. During the course of the formulation of the FY 1981 budget, Harold Brown and the OSD were faced not only with the opposition of the Secretary of the Navy and the Director of Defense Research and Engineering, but also by the Director of the Defense Science Board and by the Office of Management and Budget. It emerged that in 1980 the OMB had opposed Brown's willingness 'to bet everything on the common USN/USMC, common fighter/attack F/A-18 force'[45] recommending instead some equal-cost mix of F-14s, AV-8Bs and F/A-18s. In contrast all four congressional committees were unanimous in their treatment of the tactical air budget within which they provided $333 million for the AV-8B in FY 1981. The Senate Appropriations Committee Report directed the DoD to include adequate funding in its FY 1982 budget to ensure that the Marines had an initial operational capability for the AV-8B by 1984, and added that failure to fund the programme 'would constitute a direct contradiction of the explicit actions and consistent directions of the Congress for the past three years'.[46]

The FY Budget and After

The formulation of the Carter Administration's FY 1982 defence budget took place in the post-Afghanistan, post-Iran election year of 1980 and was dominated by the need to strengthen America's defence posture in order to meet the demand of the new right 'to make America strong again', especially since it had found in Ronald Reagan an enthusiastic and successful campaigner. It was the budget of a retiring administration that was presented to Congress in January 1981, and the fact that it contained a $230.7 million request for the full scale development of the AV-8B was a matter of small consequence and comment, even so there was no request for procurement funds. That omission was rectified by the incoming

Reagan administration which increased the FY 1982 budget extensively. It added no less than $13.7 billion for aircraft modernisation,[47] of which the $887.7 million for the development and procurement of 12 AV-8Bs in FY 1982, and long-lead funds for the procurement of 24 aircraft in FY 1983 was a small part. From this point onwards the programme was secure and it proceeded with the full support of the Reagan Administration. In February 1984 an important landmark was reached when the Marines received their first production AV-8B and the FY 1985 Five Year Defense Programme, presented to Congress in January 1984, provides for 233 more between fiscal years 1985 and 1989.

WHY THE AV-8B SURVIVED

One of the major reasons for the survival of the AV-8B programme was the longevity, consistency and tenacity of the Marine Corps' case for it. As early as 1957 the Commandant of the Marine Corps, General Randolph McC. Pate, had written to the Chief of Naval Operations to state that V/STOL capability was an 'ultimate requirement for all Marine aircraft in support of amphibious operations in the future. . . . Obtaining a STOL/VTOL capability is vital to Marine aviation'. Other studies conducted in 1963 and 1965 confirmed this interest, and led to the request for the purchase of the Harrier/AV-8A in 1967.[48] Very soon after acquiring and operating the first Harriers the Marine Corps defined the need for a follow-on version in 1973 leading to the approval of the McDonnell Douglas AV-8B programme in 1976. The Marine Corps also had a long established mission of close air support for which the AV-8s were particularly suitable, indeed they were regarded as the kind of aircraft that would allow the Corps to go back to first and cherished principles. Colonel Stanley P. Lewis wrote,

> The philosophy of close air support in the Marine Corps has not changed since the 1920s. Only the execution of this philosophy has varied as equipment has changed. Today's Harrier and tomorrow's AV-8B have brought the Corps full circle in the integration of aviation as a supporting arm.[49]

The Corps frequently emphasised that combat experience had defined the suitability of the Harrier for the air support role and not vice versa. When the Office of the Secretary of Defense opposed the procurement of the AV-8B in late 1977 it was challenging more than 50 years of Marine Corps combat experience in close air support, a 20 year old Marine requirement for a V/STOL capability and 10 year old procurement programme for AV-8s. Against this background Congress was very unlikely to conceed the Defense Department's case so long as the Marine Corps continued to regard the AV-8B as a high priority.

From the beginning the Corps regarded the AV-8B as its highest tactical air priority and, more importantly, did not waiver from this position even when its requirement was challenged. Of equal importance was the fact that the priority was assessed in terms of the capability of the aircraft to meet a well defined and specific mission in a way that CTOL aircraft could not. In FY 1973 the Senate Armed Services Committee recommended the deletion of funds for the AV-8A on the grounds that its range, payload and speed were too limited, but the Marine Corps' case that it enabled them to carry out the air support mission was the decisive factor in the House/Senate conference. The conference report supported the programme solely on the grounds that it 'fulfilled Marine Corps' requirements'.[50] When the OSD pressed the F/A-18 in the late 1970s the Corps was again consistent by defending the AV-8B on the grounds that it alone could meet the mission requirement. It was even willling to accept a modernisation gap to achieve that priority rather than take the Defense Department's recommendation. The Marine Corps witnesses who appeared before congressional committees were united in their unreserved support for the Harrier in the close air support role and, with one exception,[51] Marines who wrote about the aircraft did so to sing its praises. Against this kind of unity the divided Department of Defense made little headway especially since it measured the priority of the AV-8B mainly in terms of the procurement efficiency of *another aircraft* rather than in terms of its capacity to fulfil the close air support mission.

The fragmentation and the political accessibility of the procurement process within the Department of Defense are other major reasons for the survival of the AV-8B. There were two crucial divisions in departmental responsibility that the backers of the AV-8B were able to exploit. The first was that between Defense Research and Engineering, responsible for the technical validation of the programme, and the OSD, responsible for setting a budget priority on it. The second was that between the Department of the Navy, which saw its responsibility to lie mainly in ensuring that the Marine Corps and the Navy procured aircraft that fulfilled stated mission requirements, and the OSD and Program Analysis and Evaluation, which saw their joint responsibility to lie in achieving overall economic efficiency in the procurement of Navy and Marine aircraft. The success of the AV-8B development programme provided few grounds on which its technical validation could be challenged and goes some way to explaining the support given to it by Dr William Perry. His testimony that the AV-8B prototypes were meeting or exceeding their targets and his support for V/STOL technology won many legislative supporters for the programme. The willingness of William Claytor, the Navy Secretary, to endorse the aircraft as the Marine's highest priority programme and to reveal the manner in which that priority was treated in the Department's budget formulation process was also critical in winning congressional support for and in restoring full funding to the programme.

The unanimous support of congressional committees and of Congress itself, are yet other reasons that explain the survival of the AV-8B. Indeed, such unanimity in support of a weapons programme is rare and requires some explanation. The standing and reputation of the Marine Corps and the special affection that congressional committees have for it is an important factor in itself and committees consistently accepted the Marine's evidence at face value and without question.[52] The Budget Committees, which might have challenged the Marine's estimate of affordablity and at least should have claimed a legitimate interest in it, did not consider the issue at all. Instead the Defense Sub-Committees of the Appropriations Committees, each of which had a largely pro-defence and pro-Marine Corps membership, examined the affordability and procurement efficiency issue and found clearly in the favour of the Marines. The fact that the American procurement system allowed the Marine Corps to bring cost and performance data, produced for the DoD's internal budget formulation process, before these committees and to place their own interpretations upon it was of vital importance. Even so one cannot help but reach the conclusion that the overriding attitude of most members of the committees dealing with the AV-8B was that 'the Marines should have what they say they need'. The Corps lost no opportunity in expressing its thanks, and General Miller spoke no more than the truth when he said, 'You the Congess have consistently supported us over the years'.[53]

The unanimity of Congress is also explained by the fact that the competition between the two contenders for the Marine close air support role was not an equal one. The Marines were adamant that they required a V/STOL capability and, as Perry reported to the Defense Sub-Committee of House Appropriations in 1980, 'The AV-8B is the only game in town for the 1980s.'[54] Added to this, the development programme of the rival F/A-18 suffered miserably in comparison to that of the AV-8B. At the same time that the performance of the AV-8B prototypes were described as 'outstanding', and as 'meeting or exceeding' their development targets, the F/A-18 was described by the GAO as a 'high risk' weapons system which suffered from excess weight, high drag, low thrust and ineffective armaments. By February 1980 the cost of the F/A-18 had grown by $11.1 billion and the GAO estimated that poor contract and programme management ensured that costs would continue to grow throughout the development and production phases.[55] In a cruel irony of publishing, Russell Murray's defence of the F/A-18 over the AV-8B on grounds of cost and performance appeared side by side with an article which reported that the cost of the F/A-18 had 'soared' by $8 billion in just three months, and was once again the most expensive weapons system in the DoD's budget.[56] In contrast the overwhelming proportion of the $1 billion cost growth of the AV-8B resulted from political delays which the OSD, inspired by Murray, had inflicted on the development programme, rather than from any deficiencies in the management of the programme itself. The persistent congressional scepticism about the cost and performance of the F/A-18 stands in stark contrast to its wholehearted support for the AV-8B.

Weapons procurement normally generates conflicts of regional economic interest within Congress as Representatives and Senators are mobilised to protect investment, profit and jobs in their districts and States, but in this respect the AV-8B was an exception. This was a major contribution to the unanimity of congressional support for the programme and its explained in the main by the fact that McDonnell Douglas was the prime contractor for both the AV-8B and F/A-18. There were conflicting interests at sub-contractor level and between the manufacturers of the engines, but for a variety of reasons these were muted. Northrop had a major stake in the F/A-18 which was powered by the General Electric F404 engine produced in Lynn, Massachusetts, whereas British Aerospace was the sub-contractor for the AV-8B, which was powered by a Rolls Royce engine produced in conjunction with Pratt and Whitney. However, Northrop and

General Electric were well aware of the attempts of the Department of the Navy and of several Senators[57] to cancel the F/A-18 programme, and were therefore reluctant to press it as the Marine Corps' attack aircraft for fear of further underlining the fragile congressional support for the large number of F/A-18s that had already been funded for use as Navy and Marine fighters.[58] Nor could Northrop count on the support of McDonnell for the latter's interests were better served by the continuation of the AV-8B, which has made it the leading producer of V/STOL aircraft in the world, and a long running legal dispute over the foreign sales of the F/A-18 had soured the relationship between the two companies.[59] Without the support of McDonnell Douglas, Northrop could not win congressional approval for the purchase of more F/A-18s at the expense of the AV-8B.

Political events also conspired to increase support for the AV-8B and to erode the DoD's opposition to it. The Carter administration and Harold Brown had never been popular with the defence committees of Congress and there were major clashes over administration cuts of a Nimitz class super-carrier, the B-1 bomber and the MX missile. In the heat of defending its position on these major issues, the administration's opposition to the AV-8B lost some of its vigour, indeed Murray claims that 'the administration never really even tried to defend its position on the AV-8B, quietly acquiescing each year to the Congress' restoration of the AV-8B's funding.'[60] Carter was accused by powerful defence lobbies, such as the Committee on the Present Danger, and by the defence committees of neglecting American defence and of allowing the USSR to gain a dangerous military advantage in theatre and strategic nuclear weapons. It was also claimed that the USSR's 'expansionism' in the third world reflected a Soviet advantage in conventional 'power projection' forces over the USA. Against this background the Carter administration consistently increased defence spending and later, in the attempt to gain the Senate's ratification of the SALT II treaty, accommodated defence committee interests of which the AV-8B was certainly one.

Concern about the military consequences of the Soviet Union's alleged military advantages gave further support to the AV-8B. Carter's proposal for a Rapid Deployment Force, which could be deployed in areas of the world where the United States had no base facilities, provided the Marine Corps with the perfect opportunity to preach the virtues of an aircraft with a ferry range of 2500 miles and which could operate close to the forward edge of the battle area and independently of airfields. For the same reasons the United States Navy re-examined the potential of the AV-8B+ which could give a tactical air capability to no less than 87 ships in the fleet thus increasing its 'power projection' potential vastly.[61] The threat posed to NATO's airfields by the deployment of Soviet SS-20s revived United States Air Force interest in V/STOL aircraft, and this too renforced support for the AV-8B.[62] By 1980 the AV-8B could count on the support of the USMC, USN and USAF on military grounds, on DR&E and the Defence Science Board on technology grounds and on the OMB on budgetary grounds. In addition to this there were 'two-way streeters' in the DoD who also supported the AV-8B. All these interests were reflected in the congressional alliance that protected the programme.

Even when the AV-8B programme was secure in the vastness of Reagan's defence budgets there were factors that continued to reinforce it. In June 1981 John Nott, the British Secretary of State for Defence, announced an order for 60 McDonnell Douglas AV-8Bs in preference to the development of a British 'big-wing' Harrier, and this removed any lingering doubts about affordability. The Harrier was also gaining a considerable reputation as a fighter aircraft to add to its long established role as an attack and air support plane. In 1976 Marine AV-8As had outfought the supersonic F-14s in close aerial combat by six wins to three, with eleven engagements indecisive,[63] but the conclusive evidence of the Harrier's air combat capability was provided by the Falklands war in April and May 1982. Although there is still some dispute about the losses sustained by the two sides, the Harrier clearly equited itself very well. British sources claim that the Harrier force carried out 500 sorties per day with 32 confirmed kills, 65% of which were high performance Mirage 3s and 5s and Skyhawk A-4s. Against this there were eight Sea Harriers lost, 1 to a missile attack, three to ground fire and four in operational accidents.[64] There is no doubt that this performance surprised those in America still sceptical of the Aircraft's combat value and reinforced interest in the even more capable AV-8B and in V/STOL technology in general. Furthermore, there is every possibility that the AV-8B will not exhaust the potential of the Harrier line and a supersonic version is now technologically feasible. By November 1983 Rolls Royce were testing a 'Plenum Chamber Burning' version of the Pegasus engine that should produce sufficient thrust to produce supersonic speeds, and in February 1984 the UK and US held meetings to discuss a joint venture for the production of a supersonic V/STOL fighter for the year 2000.[65]

CONCLUSION

Defence procurement is an area where the effects of the reform of the budget process is likely to be minimal. It is here that the expertise and the interests of the traditional defence committees and sub-committees are at their greatest, and the integrity of authority over line items was the issue that the legislative committees wished to defend most when the powers of the Budget Committees and the CBO were established. Nevertheless the reformed budget process was intended to set line item issues within a broader context in which questions of national budget priorities and national fiscal policy were fully considered. One of the overriding concerns of the architects of the budget reform was that the traditional committees should be more responsive to national than to special interests, and that they should be able to exercise an independent judgement and review of contending arguments about procurement decisions. This seems to have happened in the case of AV-8B, but there is nothing to suggest that this was due to the work or the influence of the Budget Committees or the Congressional Budget Office.

The effectiveness of congressional review and the ability of Congress to overturn the Administration's unsound decision to exclude funding for the AV-8B from its defence budget request is explained more by a rare combination of political factors than it is by the effect of a reformed budget process. Of greatest importance was the unity of Congress and its committees behind the Marine Corps' request. That unity can be explained by the reputation of and the long established congressional support for the Marine Corps. This was reinforced on the AV-8B issue by the fact that the leading congressional staff expert on tactical aircraft, Charles Cromwell, happened to be an opponent of interservice commonality which was the basis of the DoD's case for an alternative to the AV-8B. The support of an acknowledged expert was vital in winning congressional support outside the defence committees since many Congressmen, unable to unwilling to spare time or energy to inform themselves fully about a single issue like this, simply follow the example of those that are reckoned to know. On line item issues the expertise is to be found outside the Budget Committees. The rare occurrence of a single aircraft manufacturer being the prime contractor for rival programmes also goes a long way to explain the unity of congressional committees since there were no regional economic interests that set one congressman against another.

The divisions within the DoD also assisted the Congress in making an effective scrutiny of this procurement decision, because the rival factions within the Department made available to Congress virtually all the information needed to make an informed and objective assessment of the military capability and the budgetary implications of the AV-8B and F/A-18 programmes. The underlying determination of Congress to give the Marine Corps what it wanted was assisted by the successful development and the efficiency of the management of the AV-8B compared to the F/A-18. In other words the established defence committees could afford to be rigorous in their assessment of the rival programmes because such rigour could not damage their case. For this reason there are several examples of the traditional committees using the work of the GAO and invoking the provisions of the Impoundment Control Act of 1974, but these are examples of the traditional committees using what ammunition was to hand rather than their response to the expectations of the new budget process.

Nevertheless, the AV-8B shows that in essence the established committees of Congress have the ability to conduct a rigorous and effective review of Administration procurement decisions; that they can require the Administration to account in detail for the decisions it makes and can force it to change decisions that are unsoundly based. But this case study also shows that this example rests on a rare combination of political events and in no way reflects the conversion of Armed Services and Appropriations Committees to the principles of the budget reform. It also shows that this successful attempt to hold the Administration accountable owed little or nothing to the work or the effect of the Budget Committees and the CBO. The underlying weakness, indeed the frustration, of the capacity of Congress to hold the Administration accountable on procurement is that the Budget Committees can do nothing to ensure that the defence committees act on other procurement issues as they did on the AV-8B.

NOTES

1. Bert H. Cooper, *The British Harrier V/STOL Aircraft* (Washington: Congressional Research Service [CRS], August 1981) p. 55.

2. See Russell Murray, 'Rising Vertically Through the Air, Invulnerable to Runway Cuts', *Armed Forces Journal International* (April 1981) *passim*. Murray was the head of the systems analysis department in the DoD and the main promotor of the F/A-18. See also Philip G. Hughes, 'Congressional Influence on Weapons Procurement: the Case of Lightweight Fighter Commonality', *Public Policy*, vol. 28, no. 4, (Autumn 1980) p. 417, and p. 23, for the influence of Deputy Secretary of Defense, David Packard, and the Deputy Director of Defense Research and Engineering, Charles Myers, on navy aircraft procurement and the attempt to make it more efficient by increasing aircraft commonality.
3. President Carter appointed William J. Komer to promote the idea of the 'Two-way Street' and it remained an important issue in NATO politics through his administration.
4. Cooper, op. cit., p. 76.
5. *Ibid.*, pp. 106–7.
6. US. Senate Appropriations Committee, *DoD Appropriations FY 1974*, Hearings, 93rd Congress, 1st Session, Part 3, p. 132.
7. Graham Warwick, 'AV-8B Advanced Harrier', *Flight International* (29 December, 1979) p. 2127.
8. See General Accounting Office [GAO], 'Is the AV-8B Advanced Harrier Aircraft Ready for Full-Scale Development?, (Washington: GAO, January 1979) p. 5.
9. See Bert H. Cooper, *V/STOL Developments: Background and Status of Navy/Marine Corps Vertical and Short Take-off and Landing Aircraft Programs*, (Washington: CRS, June 1979), Appendix IV, for a summary of congressional action on the AV-8B from FY 1970 to FY 1978.
10. See US House Appropriations Committee, *DoD Appropriations FY 1978*. House Report No. 95-451. 95th Congress, 1st Session, pp. 292, 306, for a comparison of Congress's treatment of the Navy's V/STOL programme and the AV-8B.
11. Quoted in GAO, 'Status of the Navy's Vertical Short Takeoff and Landing Aircraft', (Washington: GAO, February 1978) p. 19.
12. Brown gave evidence to the House Armed Services sub-committee on Research and Development which held special Hearings on V/STOL aircraft on May 13th, 1964. See also Cooper, *V/STOL Developments*, op. cit., Appendix I, 'Early V/STOL Programs'.
13. See Murray, op. cit., *passim*, for the substance of the PA&E's opposition to the AV-8B.
14. See Drew Middleton, 'Navy's Sea Control at Stake in Plane Dispute, Planners Say', *New York Times*, 14 October 1977, p. 12. and David Anable, 'Thousands of Jobs Ride on Fighter Contract', *Christian Science Monitor*, 18 August 1977, p. 5.
15. The dispute within the DoD is well reported in Clarence A. Robinson, Jr., 'AV-8B Pivotol in Navy Aviation Flight', *Aviation Week and Space Technology*, 31 October 1977, pp. 18–20.
16. *Ibid.*, p. 19.
17. Woolsey's views were reported in the press in February, but the full text of the memorandum was published, with an introduction by Benjamin

F. Schemmer, in *Armed Forces Journal International* (March 1978) pp. 41–4.
18. US House Armed Services Committee, *Military Posture FY 1979*, Hearings, 95th Congress, 2nd Session. Part 1, p. 493.
19. See Hughes, op. cit., p. 40.
20. Murray, op. cit., p. 52.
21. US Senate Armed Services Committee, *DoD Authorisations for Appropriations for FY 1979*, Hearings, 95th Congress, 2nd Session, Part 7, p. 5091.
22. Ibid., p. 5099.
23. Ibid., p. 5066.
24. US House Budget Committee, *Tactical Air Warfare*, Hearings, 95th Congress, 1st Session, p. 54.
25. The point is implied by Col. Stanley P. Lewis, USMC., in 'V/STOL Close Air Support in the US Marine Corps', *US Naval Institute Proceedings*, vol. 29 (October 1976) pp. 113–16. See p. 113 for guarded references to Korea and Vietnam. Murray, op. cit., makes the point much more clearly on p. 58, and regards the Marine Corps' determination to retain control of their aircraft as the 'unspoken issue' in the AV-8B debate.
26. *DoD Authorisations for Appropriations for FY 1979*, op. cit., p. 5102.
27. See Cooper, *V/STOL Developments*, op. cit., p. 166 for a summary of the OSD's objections. Interestingly enough the OSD made no reference to the F/A-18's substantially greater R&D costs of $900 million.
28. *Congressional Record* (daily edition), vol. 123, 20 October 1977: S.17629. See S.17622 for the comments of Senators Bartlet, Hart, Williams, Leahy, Garn, Danforth and Hayakawa.
29. See the House Appropriations Committee Report, p. 273, Seanate Armed Services Committee Report, p. 83, and the House Armed Services Committee Report, p. 90.
30. GAO, 'Is the AV-8B . . .' op. cit., p. 12.
31. US House Appropriations Committee, *DoD Appropriations For 1980*, Hearings, 96th Congress, 1st Session, Part 6, pp. 511–12.
32. US House Appropriations Committee, *DoD Appropriations For 1981*, Hearings, 96th Congress, 2nd Session, Part 3, p. 397
33. For a brief description of this coalition, see CRS Issue Brief No. IB78020, 'V/STOL Aircraft Development' (Washington: CRS, August 1981) p. 8.
34. See GAO, 'A Decision by the Secretary of Defense is Needed on the AV-8B Aircraft Program', (Washington: GAO, February 1980) p. 8.
35. US House Appropriations Committee, *DoD Appropriations For 1980*, Hearings, 96th Congress, 1st Session, Part 7, p. 459.
36. Ibid., Part 6, pp. 513–15.
37. Ibid., Ppart 2, p. 149.
38. Ibid., Part 7, p. 500.
39. Ibid., Part 2, p. 144.
40. US House Armed Services Committee, *Military Posture FY 1980*, Hearings, 96th Congress, 1st Session, Part 2, pp. 601 and 605.
41. *DoD Appropriations For 1981*, Hearings, Part 3, op. cit., p. 884.

42. Ibid., p. 397.
43. Final Report of the Defense Science Board Task Force on V/STOL Aircraft (US Department of Defense, Office of the Under Secretary of Defense Research and Engineering) p. iii.
44. *DoD Appropriations For 1981*, Hearings, Part 3, op. cit., p. 396.
45. Deborah B. Meyer, 'F/A-18 at Another Critical Juncture', *Armed Forces Journal International* (April 1981) p. 60.
46. See Senate Appropriations Committee Report (H.Rept. 96–1020) p. 15.
47. For a survey of the changes that Reagan made to the FY 1982 defense budget see CRS Issue Brief No. IB8 1002, 'Defense Budget – FY 1982', (Washington: CRS, September 1981) *passim*.
48. See Col. R. A. Gustafson, USMC., 'The Marine Corps View', *Armed Forces Journal International* (April 1981) p. 58.
49. Lewis op. cit., p. 116.
50. US House Armed Services Committee, *DoD Authorisations for Appropriations FY 1973*, Conference Report (92-1388), 92nd Congress, 2nd Session, p. 12.
51. See Lt. Col. J. L. Cunningham, USMC., 'Can the Marine Corps Really Use V/STOL Aircraft?', *Marine Corps Gazette*, vol. 61 (January 1977) pp. 18–24. The article was refuted almost immediately by Lt. Col J. W. Orr and Lt. Col R. E. O'Dare, 'V/STOL Will do the Job from Carriers, Sea Platforms, Airfields – or Parts of All. Even Roads, Pads or Whatever', *Marine Corps Gazette*, vol. 61 (May 1977) pp. 39–46. As the title suggests the refutation was comprehensive.
52. This point was confirmed by interviews with members and staff members of all four committees in March and April 1981. Murray (op. cit., p. 53) also refers to the Marine's 'powerful congressional connections.'
53. The Marine Corps was punctillious in giving its thanks to all the committees that supported its request for the AV-8B, this quotation comes from *Tactical Air Warfare*, op. cit., p. 55.
54. *DoD Appropriations For 1981*, Hearings, Part 3, op. cit., p. 397.
55. See GAO 'An Unclassified Version of a Classified Report Entitled 'Need to Demonstrate F-18 Naval Strike Fighter Weapon System Effectiveness Before Large-Scale Production', (Washington: GAO, February 1979) *passim*, and GAO, 'F/A-18 Naval Strike Fighter: Its Effectiveness is Uncertain', (Washington: GAO, February 1980) *passim*, but especially p. 17.
56. Meyer, op. cit., p. 59.
57. Senator Gary Hart made several attempts to cancel the F/A-18 programme, but the congressional support that McDonnell Douglas and Northrop could muster was sufficient to prevent this, although this alliance was not powerful enough to promote the F/A-18 at the expense of the AV-8B.
58. Art Harris and George C. Wilson in, 'Fighter Plane Contracts Stir Dogfight', *Washington Post*, 5 December 1977, p. A1, note the conflicting regional interests, and the weakness in the F/A-18 coalition. they also note that McDonnell Douglas had little incentive in seeing the F/A-18 push the AV-8B out of the budget.

59. Some of the effects of the McDonnell Douglas/Northrop legal battle are noted in CRS Issue Brief no. IB78087, 'Fighter Aircraft Program: F/A-18' (Washington: CRS, January 1981) p. 3.
60. Murray, op. cit., p. 53.
61. The figure of 87 ships was given in a study produced by the McDonnell Douglas Corporation; it also claimed that there was the potential to use the AV-8B on 174 other ships including about 100 merchant Marine container ships. See Congressional Record (daily edition), 12 March 1979, S2555.
62. See John W. Fozard, 'Sea Harrier – First of a New Wave', *Aeronautical Journal*, vol. 81 (January 1977) p. 34; Peter J. Taylor, RAF, 'The Impact of V/STOL on Tactical Air Warfare' *Air University Review*, vol. 29 (November/December 1977) *passim*. and Cooper, *V/STOL Developments*, op. cit., pp. 72–3.
63. See Taylor, ibid., p. 72. Cooper, op. cit., p. 19 notes that the AV-8A won 14 of 19 close engagements with the F-14 in 1977. Fozard, op. cit., p. 23, notes that the AV-8s have a very high thrust to weight ratio and enjoy all the rapid acceleration and climb characteristics of a supersonic fighter. In addition to this the Harrier has the unique capacity to vector in forward flight (VIFF) which allows it to outmanoeuvre supersonic CTOL aircraft, and it is also more fuel efficient and can outlast CTOL aircraft in combat. Fozard notes that it is usually the first to turn for home that loses in a modern dogfight.
64. See William H. Gregory, 'New Lessons for Combat', *Aviation Week and Space Technology*, 19 July 1982, p. 13 for an assessment of the effect that the Harrier's Falklands performance had in the US Javier E. Palencia and two other Argentinians claim in 'Argentina Looks at the Falklands', *Aviation Week and Space Technology*, 23 August 1982, that the UK lost at least 20 Harriers, but does not make it clear if these were in combat, accidents or on ships that were sunk. The figures given here come from, 'Post-Falklands Briefings Spurring British Missile System Interest', ibid., pp. 22–3.
65. See 'US, British Discuss Supersonic Joint V/STOL', *Aviation Week and Space Technology*, 19 December 1983, p. 19.

6 Reform and Procurement Oversight: Parliament and the Case of the MRCA-Tornado

The creation of SCOE and DEASC in Britain did not lead to a more effective or significant role for Parliament in setting defence priorities than had been the case before. Unfortunately, as we shall see in this chapter and later in Chapter 8, the desire to extend Parliamentary scrutiny and influence over intra-defence resource allocation decisions was also to founder. The relative failure of the 1971–79 reform to influence resource allocations *within* the defence budget is indicated by study of DEASC's attempt to influence MOD procurement policy – in this case the decision to develop and produce two variants of the Anglo–German–Italian Multi-Role Combat Aircraft (MRCA), later named the Tornado. Before looking at DEASC's role in relation to the MRCA-Tornado in some detail it is first of all necessary to indicate how Parliament fits into the system of military procurement in Britain and, if we are to assess the impact of reform, indicate how successful Parliament had been in its oversight of procurement policy before the creation of SCOE and DEASC.

THE SYSTEM OF MILITARY PROCUREMENT IN BRITAIN AND THE ROLE OF PARLIAMENT TO 1971

Until 1971 the British military procurement process was characterised by Service autonomy and a relative lack of civilian control or co-ordination. By the 1960s it gradually became clear that this independence was dysfunctional as the number of major weapons projects that had to be cancelled due to time and cost over-runs and obsolescence increased. The 1960s witnessed a number of organisational and procedural reforms in the procurement field, but these were only to be the precursors to a more fundamental change which saw in August 1971 the creation of a single agency for the purchase of military equipment. The Procurement Executive, an independent agency within the Ministry of Defence, finally ended the procurement autonomy of the separate Services in Britain.

From 1945 up until the 1960s at least it could be argued that decisions about major weapons developments in Britain were left to the individual Services' Boards and their respective Service Ministries. Thus the Royal Navy and Admiralty, with strong civil and military ties, purchased their equipment (although not missiles) from private suppliers and the Royal Naval Dockyards through the War Office. The Army with the War Office was less fortunate in that it had to purchase its supplies through a 'middleman' up until 1959. The Ministry of Supply had been created in 1939 to co-ordinate the supply of Army equipment and until 1959 most Army procurement came through this Ministry and from the Royal Ordnance Factories and from private manufacturers.[1] After 1959 the War Office purchased its own equipment independently and directly from producers. Finally, the RAF and Air Ministry, while determining their own operational requirements independently, were also forced to purchase their aircraft through a 'middleman'. In 1940 Beaverbrook's Ministry of Aircraft Production was created and was superceded after the war by the Ministry of Supply, which until 1959 procured equipment for both the Army and the RAF. After 1959, while the Army found new autonomy, the RAF and Air Ministry found themselves involved in a 'middleman' relationship through a number of agencies – the Ministry of Aviation (1959–67), the Ministry of Technology (1967–70) and the Ministry of Aviation Supply (1970–71).[2]

Despite these continually changing relationships it was the case that the ultimate decision on Service operational requirements rested squarely with the Service Boards and the Service Ministries. The creation of a Ministry of Defence in 1946, which was supposed to introduce a greater measure of civilian control and co-ordination into the process, did not really detract from this independence since this fledgling organisation was poorly staffed and the military experts were located within the Service Ministries and Boards. This meant, effectively, that the Minister of Defence had to rely on the co-operation of the Services with civilian Ministries and producers to ensure that weapons systems were adequate and operationally sound and necessary.[3] Light on this procurement process is shed if we consider for a moment the way in which a new aircraft would proceed through the research–development–production process in Britain in the 1950s and early 1960s. Responsibility for specifying operational requirements for military aircraft rested squarely with the Air Staff – in particular with the Deputy Chief of Air Staff and the Assistant Chief of Staff (Operational Requirements). It was the job of these two men to convince the Air Council, the MOD (Defence Research Policy Committee), Treasury and Ministry of Aviation (Research and Development Board) of the need for, and desirability of, particular aircraft to meet specific 'threats' and tasks. Once approval was given the Ministry of Aviation had delegated powers from the Treasury to then place contracts for engines, airframes and avionics and also chaired (with MOD, Air Ministry and Treasury participation) any subsequent modification committees which might be necessary in the light of changing technological or operational requirements.[4] In this respect it was clear that the system of aircraft procurement was one which was dominated by the Service (subject to Treasury financial controls) and was also wholly divorced from other Service procurement decisions. The only semblance of co-ordination was haltingly provided by the MOD in its Defence Research Policy Committee, which was responsible for general military research, but this was hardly the central co-ordinator of procurement for all the Services.

It was hardly surprising therefore that, in an age of rapidly escalating inflation, rising worker militancy, massive advances in technological sophistication and declining economic resources in Britain, that this antiquated, leisurely and Service dominated system should come into serious question in the 1950s. It was not just that costs for military equipment were increasing – this might have been accounted for by inflation and the need for ever more complex and sophisticated weapons systems – it was that the whole defence budget was coming under serious financial pressure. Since 1945 the Services had not really been confronted with serious choices on commitments and equipment. There were two reasons for this: a ten year rule had been adopted by the Labour government after 1945, which stated that there should be no fundamental re-equipment of the forces until future requirements could be foreseen (this was not problematic at the time given the need to run down the war machine); and, there was a massive rearmament in the early 1950s after Korea which allowed all of the three Services to obtain new equipment without conflict and on the basis of 'equal shares'. This system could not be maintained and throughout the period after 1955 there were attempts by first Macmillan and then by Sandys at the MOD to reduce the defence budget. This approach had been foreshadowed in the 1952 Global Strategy Paper on the future primacy of nuclear weapons and was to find its most effective expression in Sandy's Defence White Paper of 1957. This document clearly stated the government's intention of relying on massive nuclear retaliation in order to downgrade conventional forces.[5] The implication of this document was clear: there were harsh choices to be faced in the defence budget as Britain's economic performance failed to meet expectations and there was a growing feeling that difficult resource allocation decisions *vis-à-vis* the Services could not be taken when these Services were independently responsible for their own procurement.

Unfortunately, it was not just that there were going to be difficult choices as Service rivalry intensified over defence cuts, but it became painfully apparent in the late 1950s and into the 1960s that the procurement system as a whole was totally inefficient. It wasn't just that costs rose or that delays held up delivery of systems – all other countries trying to maintain defence forces at the peak of technologial expertise were facing similar problems – it was that Britain seemed to be unable to research, develop and produce *any* effective weapons systems on time or within costs. One estimate indicated that only one military aircraft (the Buccaneer) which was started in the 1950s was ever completed by the 1960s.[6] It was further clear that, compared to the United States, Britain was unable to produce aircraft within anything like the same timescale. One estimate averaged military aircraft gestation in America in this period at 6 years and 3 months, compared with Britain's 8 years and 4 months.[7] Furthermore, Howard has estimated that up to 1967 32 major equipment projects were cancelled costing a total of £500 million.[8] Of these cancellations missiles and aircraft were by far the most numerous casualties: it was not simply manned aircraft (like the supersonic bomber) which were scrapped after 1957 but the missiles which were to replace them (the Blue Streak, Skybolt and Blue Water). Further aircraft cancellations followed in the 1960s with the decisions not to proceed with P-1154 (Mach-2, V/STOL), HS-681 (Transport), AFVG (Variable-Geometry fighter) and, most acrimoniously of all, with the TSR-2 (Strike/Reconnaissance and Strategic Bomber).[9] The result of this being a need to buy from

America and a complete demoralisation of the British aerospace industry.

It became apparent in the 1960s in a series of studies and government reports that there were serious weaknesses in the British procurement system. The Gibbs/Zuckerman report into the management and control of research and development for defence which was published in 1961 pinpointed many of the problems of the procurement system.[10] There were delays in decisions due to government recalcitrance and bureaucratic 'in-fighting' and due in part to the desire of the Services to try to obtain the best rather than what was practicable. As a result there was far too much modification of specifications and operational requirements throughout the research and development stage and evidence of the Services being unable to agree on what they wanted. Perhaps the classic case of this was the inability of the RAF to decide what type of strategic bomber it required and therefore opting for three different 'V' bombers.[11] Further difficulties experienced with the system were the inability by the government to specify what its commitments were; the production of aircraft at such a sophisticated level that there was no chance of a market for them;[12] a lack of close collaboration with industry;[13] the duplication of effort by the production of identical systems (it was discovered that the Services were each producing relatively identical surface to air missiles in the 1950s – the RAF Bloodhound, the Army Thunderbird and the RN Seaslug);[14] and, a tendency either to start projects when they would be obsolete before becoming operational or to insist on aircraft that required completely new development from scratch in airframe, engine and avionics (the TSR-2 being a classic example).[15]

These problems were apparent in the 1950s and 1960s to those involved in military procurement and it gradually became the case that the inefficiencies of the process were becoming known to a wider audience. The Public Accounts Committee in Parliament began, in the 1950s, to unearth serious deficiencies in the government contacting system. First of all it was discovered that there had been serious cost under-estimations in the Swift aircraft (1955/56), then came the revelations in the 1963/64 on the excessive profits made by Ferranti in its production of the Bloodhound SAM missile. This was followed to the end of the decade with similar contracting problems being unearthed with Bristol-Siddeley engines and with Rolls-Royce; whose Spey engines for the US Phantom aircraft almost doubled the price that the planes would have cost 'off the shelf'.[16] It was apparent to PAC and to the government, therefore, that contracting was far from perfect; that the government relied on guesswork; and that there was a lack of competition in tendering for contracts; too much information was controlled by the manufacturers; and there was insufficient trained and qualified staff in the defence procurement process. It was also apparent that Britain, if it retained global pretensions, would have to end wasteful contracting and cancellations and try to ensure that it could meet its commitments at less cost.

The Gibbs/Zuckerman reforms, therefore, called for the development of a functional approach to defence procurement with more use of check-points and reviews built into a 'step-wise' approach to research and development. These goals were supported by numerous PAC reports in this period and by the Lang Reports of 1965/66 which studied the problems of Ferranti and Hawker-Siddeley contracting.[17] Both reports called for more incentive in contracting and more technically trained and professionally qualified cost officers in the defence field. These studies were mirrored by the 1965 Plowden Report which studied the state of the aircraft industry and argued for a fundamental reorganisation and avoidance of costly projects, and a willingness to buy sophisticated systems from the USA or to indulge in international collaboration.[18] Similar demands for organizational reform were enunciated by the 1968 Fulton Committee Report into the Civil Service (the use of guesstimates and the lack of forward planning, the lack of management by objectives and lack of economist and accountants in the defence field came in for serious criticism);[19] by the Downey Report on development cost estimating in the Ministry of Technology in 1969;[20] and, by the 1969 Elstub Report into productivity in the aircraft industry (which attacked the lack of partnership between users, industry and the defence Ministries).[21]

Interestingly enough, the move to reform here was parallel with a demand for reform of central control over the defence field as a whole. This had resulted, in 1963/64, in the creation of a single Ministry of Defence and the downgrading, within MOD as Service departments, of the previously autonomous Services Ministries. Similar moves to greater central control were adopted in a piecemeal fashion throughout the 1960s. A Defence Operational Analysis Establishment was created to provide an independent study of operational requirements and two new committees were introduced into the newly expanded MOD. These two committees were the Weapons Development Committee and the Operational

Requirements Committee. These two committees (on which all the three Services, plus scientific and civilian staff sat) were given procurement co-ordination roles for the review of development programmes and the harmonisation of long-term operational requirements respectively.[22] A similar innovation aimed at great efficiency in procurement was the creation of a Contracts Review Board in 1968, which renegotiated contracts subject to excessive profits or loss,[23] and the 1969 introduction of a National Defence Industry Council to encourage better industry-user partnership.[24]

Despite these changes, and the further attempt at functional control in 1967,[25] the procurement system was still characterised by diversity and a degree of Service autonomy. It was not, however, until the election of the Conservative government in 1971, with its Rayner Report into defence procurement, that Britain witnessed the end of Service independence and the culmination of this gradual move towards the unification of defence procurement in one agency. The basic tenet of the Rayner Report, which led to the creation of the Procurement Executive as an independent agency within the MOD in August 1971,[26] was that there should be a civilian head of all procurement. This old system of 'decision by committee' was to be replaced by 'accountable management' in which project teams would be responsible, under their project managers, for weapons systems from conception to production and for all of the financial, technical and time issues involved.[27]

Since 1971 there have of course been a number of changes in this new administrative process – in particular a reduction in the number of major weapons Systems Controllerates which were created in the Procurement Executive in 1971 and, after the Management Review of the MOD in 1976, a reduction in the number of officers accountable to Parliament – but in essence the procurement system in 1981 is similar in most respects to the Rayner conception. The new system can be divided into two – the organisation itself and the process for the gestation of procurement. Taking the organisational structure first, the administrative support staffs in the Procurement Executive are divorced from project management. Under the civilian, Chief of Defence Procurement are the three major Controllerates for the procurement of Sea, Land and Air Systems, which are headed by civilian Controllers, who are the accountable officers for these systems to the MOD and to Cabinet and Parliament and who sit on their relevant Service Boards. Similar accountable Controllers exist for Research and Development Establishments (which had been fundamentally reorganised from 25 to 12) and there are two Controllers on the administrative side for Policy and Management and Sales. The rationale for this system is to divide administrative back-up from specific project management so that, while there is an administrative input into specific projects, the lines of responsibility and management are always clearly apparent. Thus under the Controllers for Air, Land and Sea Systems are teams of financial and technical staffs under project managers who are collectively responsible for individual projects as they move from feasibility to production and these tasks are completey separate from normal administrative duties.[28]

Turning finally to the process itself, it can be characterised as an approach to procurement which emphasises 'step-wise' functional project gestation, with limited approval for discrete stages and subject to continuous review. The overall aim of the process being of course to monitor time and cost delays and to weed out potentially disastrous projects before they are too well developed to cancel without massive cost and embarrassment. Built into this system are attempts to co-ordinate the requirements of the three Services. The process follows the following stages (aircraft related examples are used but the process is not dissimilar for other Service procurement):

Operational Requirement Definition – Air Staff military requirements start as a *Staff Target* (which specifies function and desired performance) and derive from work carried out in the Service Board, RAF Scientific and Intelligence Staffs and the Air Force Board Standing Committee (AFBSC) which looks at aircraft concepts. This Staff Target is also sent to producers for tentative comment. The Target is also discussed with the Procurement Executive and is sent to MOD Operational Requirement Committee (MOD/ORC) and MOD Defence Equipment Policy Committee (MOD/DEPC).[29] It is in these committees, assisted by the Defence Operational Analysis Establishment that co-ordination of single Service requirements and the other Services, with financial constraints, takes place. Alternative equipment solutions within a single Service or by another Service are considered (i.e. manned aircraft versus missiles), as well as the scope for international national collaboration or purchase 'off the shelf'. The Cabinet is not normally heavily involved at this stage though the Treasury will be. Once approval is given by the two commitees, and therefore by the Secretary of State for Defence, the relevant

Controller (in this case for Air Systems) will commence the embryonic research and development stages.

Research – The Controller (Air Systems) in the Procurement Executive then forms a project team which conducts a *feasibility study* on the most cost-effective way of proceeding. This stage ends with tentative time and cost scales being provided for the project which has been chosen by the likely contractor. If the project is costly a review stage occurs here. The feasibility study leads to the definition of a *General Staff Requirement*, now to be built into the Long-Term Costings in the Defence Budget, before this occurs the project and the study will be sent back to AFBSC, MOD/ORC and MOD/DEPC for re-approval. Once again, in so far as this is not likely to prejudice the Defence Budget, the Cabinet is not likely to be involved. The Treasury will be appraised of course.

Development – From this research stage the approved *GSR* passes to the *project definition stage*, which is one of the crucial and most important stages in the process. It is here that contractors look at the technical problems in the *GSR* and draw up detailed comprehensive development plans, often assisted by the government research establishments. A firm commitment to time and cost scales is developed and tentative unit production costs are presented. At this stage the idea begins to take physical form and it is estimated that over 15% of the research and development budget is spent here in a stage which may last over twelve months. The intention is to solve as many problems before detailed development commences. Before full development a review is undertaken by the project team and, depending on the likely time and cost consequences, full cabinet discussion of the project may be necessary – especially if there are serious implications for government expenditure. *Full Development* is the second stage under which the Project team supervises the technical testing of the project. This stage may itself be sub-divided into stages for prototype and pre-production models of the aircraft in which airframe, engine and avionics quality control and performance specifications in flight are tested and approved. Built into this stage is the proviso that if costs rise above 20% or delays threaten to add one year to the gestation of the project it must be sent back to MOD/ORC and MOD/DEPC. This may also necessitate Cabinet approval.

Production – This is the final stage in the process prior to RAF acceptance in service. It is normally preceded, even if there have been no major cost or time problems, by Cabinet approval of the number to be produced. Procurement Executive project teams continue to monitor production quality at all times.

Having outlined the system of military procurement that has evolved in Britain since the Second World War it is clear that Parliament's role in this process has been relatively slight. Indeed it can be seen that Parliament's role in the gestation process, in formal terms, is nil. Although it has been argued however that prior to the creation of the Procurement Executive the PAC did create a dysfunctional role for Parliament in procurement. The Elstub Committee for one argued that through its insistence on 'value for money' and the trepidation that its revelations imposed on civil servants involved in contracting, then there was an in-built tendency to delay and caution which militated against commercial criteria in project management.[30]

Despite this negative impact, the positive role of Parliament in procurement has been negligible. Notwithstanding the theory that the government is unable to enter into expenditure commitments without Parliamentary approval, in practice the process of government procurement contracting has always been able to circumvent the annual approval of expenditure by Parliament. As we saw (and this is no different now with the creation of the Procurement Executive) the government may enter into military contracts which, while involving only derisory sums of money in the initial years, actually commit the government to expenditure in the future on a massive scale. A clear example of this failure of Parliamentary control over project development was seen at the beginning of the examination of the MRCA project by DEASC in 1971. David Owen asked the MOD why it was that there was no mention of the MRCA in its initial submission to DEASC when he in fact knew it was to be the single most expensive piece of defence equipment throughout the 1970s. The MOD blandly replied that the programme had not yet come fully into operation and the expenditure so far allocated to MRCA was located in the figures in the Defence White Paper on research and development![31] In this sense contracts entered into are, or can be, a form of uncontrollable expenditure and clearly indicate the problem facing Parliamentary scrutiny of defence projects.

It would not however be fair to Parliament to argue that it failed to create any role for itself in project management or scrutiny between 1945 and 1971. Parliament did create a limited role for itself and was successful in its audit of past expenditure. In this respect

Parliamentary oversight of defence procurement between 1945 and 1971 mirrored the general experience of the legislature in the defence field. Policy influence was limited to indirect references to the mismatch between military commitments and resources in Estimates Committee reports.[32] This Select Committee however maintained its continuous scrutiny of the inefficiency of Service organisation and research and development agencies and procedures after 1945. The Admiralty, the War Office, the Royal Naval Dockyards, the Research and Development Establishments and the Ministry of Supply coming in for particular criticism as the Estimates Committee pursued its *managerial* role of efficiency.[33] In this sense then we can argue that the Estimates Committee at least contributed to the critical environment which surrounded the procurement field in the 1950s and 1960s and probably assisted, thereby, in preparing the ground for the centralising reforms that were to come. Similarly the work of the Select Committee on Science and Technology, which undertook a comprehensive study of defence research and development in 1968, and highlighted for the public many of the inefficiencies and problems which were by then common knowledge in government circles, also extended Parliament's scrutiny role in the procurement field. This committee, in particular, illuminated the poor relationship between the MOD and industrial contractors. The committee paid particular attention to the failure of MOD to notify the industry of the avionics it required in the MRCA before proceeding to research and development, and was also instrumental in the creation of the National Defence Industries Council, which was to reforge government–industry relationships in the defence field after 1969.[34]

The main impact of Parliament came however not in these areas but through the work of the Estimates and Public Accounts Committees in tightening government contracting procedure. Colin Turpin has argued that the Estimates Committee spent considerable time highlighting contracting inefficiencies in fields like naval research, contracts for army buildings, aircraft and store supplies. Undoubtedly this complemented the continuous review of contracting by the PAC, which had led it in turn to reveal glaring anomolies in contracting for the Swift aircraft (1955/56), Ferranti (1963/64), Bristol Siddeley (1965/66) and Rolls Royce Spey Engines (1967/68).[35] Overall, then, Parliament's role prior to 1971 relied heavily on the audit of past decisions and procurement contracts by the PAC and, though it was not without its successes in changing procedures, the role was limited. Indeed it was felt by the beginning of the 1970s that with the creation of the Procurement Executive, the MOD and Industry were creating a 'new partnership' which would further erode Parliamentary scrutiny of procurement decisions. As a result there was hope that the creation of SCOE and DEASC would extend Parliament's ability to make procurement accountable by setting in motion a continuous and comprehensive review of the whole procurement process.[36] Unfortunately, and this is a fundamental criticism of the work of DEASC in general, no comprehensive review of procurement was instituted between 1971 and 1979, even if there was more detailed scrutiny of individual procurement projects under DEASC. DEASC instituted detailed studies of major equipment projects like the MRCA, the Chieftain tank, guided weapons and the Cruiser programme. Nevertheless the question that remains to be answered is whether (notwithstanding the new desire to get at the policy behind the procurement projects and provide alternative) these DESC studies were anymore effective in influencing procurement policies than the more limited work of earlier Select Committees?

THE BACKGROUND TO THE PROCUREMENT OF THE MRCA-TORNADO

Before we assess the impact of DEASC on the procurement of the MRCA-Tornado and its variant, the MRCA-ADV interceptor, it is as well to provide a brief outline of the overall gestation of this aircraft which was the single most expensive piece of equipment in the defence budget in the period 1975–85.

The Multi-Role Combat Aircraft (MRCA) developed out of the twin desires to resolve time and cost over-runs, plus the crippling financial burden of developing advanced aircraft, by the use of international collaboration. It was argued that such collaboration reduced the national costs of research, development and production by increasing the number of planes to be built.[37] There were of course other reasons for aircraft collaboration. There had been continual talk of a move to standardisation of equipment in NATO and also fears that, if European countries did not collaborate, the United States would take over Western civil and military aircraft production by default.[38] There may also have been a desire to show 'good Europeaness' in this decision as Britain attempted to enter the EEC throughout this period.[39]

There can be little doubt, however, that Britain's RAF required a new aircraft (or indeed several aircraft depending on one's tactical and strategic perception of operational requirements) at the end of the 1960s. As we saw, few new aircraft had entered service in the 1960s due to time and cost over-runs and declining economic performance. Only the Buccaneer and Harrier had entered service in the 1960s as wholly British built frontline aircraft.

The RAF also needed a replacement for its ageing Lightnings and US Phantoms which had been purchased to protect the UK Air Defence Region (UKADR) from Soviet low and high flying aircraft and missiles. On top of this, there was also a desire by the RAF to ensure, after the TSR-2 debacle, that it was equipped with the most modern up to date aircraft to fulfil its roles in NATO and home defence. It was clear, therefore, that, given advances in air defence missiles, Britain's perceived operational roles of long range interdiction and strike (IDS) and Air Defence (ADV) would not be met by existing aircraft. The RAF felt that a new low flying, terrain following aircraft capable of Mach-2, as well as low speed loitering, with all weather operational capabilities like the US F1-11, would be necessary. The RAF obviously regretted the loss of the multi-role TSR-2 and the F1-11 (which was originally to be bought after the TSR-2 was scrapped) and was determined to ensure that a new advanced aircraft would be procured for the 1970s and 1980s.[40]

Fortuitously for the RAF at the end of the 1960s there were a number of NATO airforces which were also involved in trying to replace their ageing planes – notably Canada, Holland, Belgium, West Germany and Italy. These countries had all purchased the US F104 Starfighter because they did not have the capacity to develop their own aircraft. It was out of this that international collaboration was developed. Although Canada, Holland and Belgium withdrew and decided to buy from America a Memorandum of Understanding to produce an MRCA was signed in July 1968 by Britain, West Germany and Italy. The intention was to produce a plane that would operate from 1975 to 1985 to meet the six operational requirements specified by these three countries. Britain had a requirement for long-range, deep interdiction and strike (IDS) reconnaissance, air defence (ADV) and support of naval operations. West Germany had two requirements – close air support on the battlefield for the Luftwaffe and air support for the German Navy. The Italian's wanted an aircraft for air superiority and close support.[41] To meet these requirements two variants of the MRCA were to be built. For the interdiction, strike, reconnaissance, naval and battlefield support and air superiority roles there was to be a common variant (the IDS type) and for the British requirement for air defence there was to be a second type, which would be based on the IDS, but which would have different characteristics in avionics, weapons and airframe, all of which would be met by the British alone. This ADV-type was expected to have 80% commonality with the IDS version.[42] It was due to this myriad of role requirements that the aircraft was particularly complex technically. For the IDS role the plane required high speed (Mach-2) and low-level, all-weather fighting capabilities plus short take off and landing ability (STOL); but for the ADV role it required the ability to loiter in the air and then have dash capabilities at instant high speeds to intercept bombers and missiles. This placed immense technical difficulties on the airframe and the RB 199 turbo-engine, because the plane had to have both height and low speed performance characteristics and required variable-geometry wings which could be swept backwards and forwards depending on the performance required.[43]

It was decided that the project would be administered through a joint organisation based in Munich called the NATO MRCA Management Agency (NAMMA), on which representatives from all three countries would sit, and that it would give the contract to a consortium drawn from the three major firms involved in the construction of the airframe. This consortium was called PANAVIA and consisted of BAC (responsible for the front fuselage and cockpit), Messerchmitt-Bolkow-Blohm (responsible for design leadership, the central fuselage and wing pivots) and Aeritalia (responsible for the wings). PANAVIA was the prime contractor for the project and sub-contracts were then placed for the engine, avionics and other equipment. A consortium was created for engine construction, known as TURBO-UNION, under Rolls-Royce design leadership, with participation by Fiat and Motoren-Turbinen-Union (MTU). The avionics caused some difficulty because it was eventually decided to buy a system from the US firm, Texas Instruments, for the IDS, while for the ADV Britain opted for a Marconi/Ferranti system.[44]

Design leadership and work sharing was decided on the basis of the number of aircraft that each country intended to buy at the end of the project. Thus, because in July 1968 West Germany envisaged purchasing 600 IDS types she was given 40% of the work on engine construction and 56% of the work and design leadership on the airframe. Britain was given design leadership and 40% of the engine work and 24% of the airframe, because of her combined commitment to around 350 IDS and ADV types. The Italians were given 20% of the engine work and 20% of the airframe on the basis of their commitment to 200 IDS variants. Subsequently, as the project developed and the likely costs and time scales began to stretch beyond the original £1.7 million per plane estimates West Germany and Italy reduced their commitments. In April 1970, at the pre-development stage, West Germany reduced its order to 400 and in March 1973 it cut back to 324 due to budgetary constraints. Italy reduced its requirement to 100 in April 1970. This resulted in work sharing percentages being altered. In April 1970 West Germany and Britain received 42½% each of the airframe; Italy received 15%.[45] During the life of the project Britain did not cut its requirement of 385 (220 IDS and 165 ADV); although due to declining economic growth the Labour government twice had to 'stretch' the production programme to delay aircraft coming into service to cut defence spending. In both 1975 and 1977 the 'in-service' production of MRCAs was reduced by up to a third.[46]

The gestation of the MRCA was subject to major time and cost difficulties, which were compounded by the problems of having to operate a complex international collaborative organisational structure. On time alone the aircraft was and is seriously behind schedule. It was intended that the operational life of the MRCA-IDS would be 1975–85, with the MRCA-ADV following in 1979–89. But, while the IDS variant started life on time, with the feasibility stage completed three months early in March 1970, major delays occurred as serious difficulties were experienced in engine, avionics and airframe construction.[47] The development stage experienced such slippage that the first official flight of the IDS did not take place until 1974 and production did not begin until July 1976.[48] The ADV also experienced horrendous technical difficulties with the project definition stage alone lasting two years and full development only beginning in March 1976.[49] The result of these difficulties was that instead of 1975 the 'in-service' dates for the MRCA-IDS were respectively 1980 (with full complement by 1986) for West Germany; 1981 (with full complement by 1985) for Britain; and, 1981 (with full complement by 1986) for Italy. The British MRCA/ADV was eventually expected to be coming into service by 1984 rather than 1979.[50] Added to this the cost of the project escalated from the original 1968 estimate of production costs per aircraft at £1.7 million rising to £7.9 million by 1977 prices for the IDS and from over £2 million to £9.4 million (1977 prices) for the ADV (it was estimated that the inclusive 1981 cost for the IDS was now £11 million per plane).[51] At September 1977 prices this, according to PAC estimates, meant a four and one half increase in production and development costs on 1970 estimates.[52]

Obviously much of this increase can be accounted for by the effects of inflation and, because this was an international collaborative scheme, by the deleterious effects of variations in exchange rates which, with the pound falling against the D-mark, ensured higher costs for Britain.[53] But there were also 'real' problems with the programme which were of immense importance in raising the cost and delaying the in-service date of the plane. In particular, the MRCA copied the problems of the TSR-2. By trying to build from scratch an aircraft requiring a new engine, airframe and avionics there were serious difficulties in all these fields. The airframe experienced fewest problems due to the fact that BAC had already a well developed design team used to variable-geometry airframe construction. Nevertheless, there have been claims that the plane is too heavy, that it lacks manoeuvrability and that its angle of attack load limits are below the maximum airframe values possible.[54] There have also been major problems with the airframe for the ADV, which had to be stretched by three feet to reduce drag and reshaped to build in the new radar system and to enhance the dash speed of the plane.

Indeed it has been argued that despite the hopes that the ADV would be fairly common with the IDS, it is in fact, due to these design changes and its completely separate air to air radar and weapons, a completely different aircraft.[55] The IDS also experienced major difficulties in engine and avionics construction. In particular there has been a need to revamp the specifications on electronic counter measures (ECMs) completely to avoid the advances in strike capability experienced in surface-to-air missiles (SAMs) during the 1973 Yom Kippur War. Only the US Air Force was originally fitted with active rather than passive ECMs and there has had to be a crash development in this field for the MRCA to ensure that it can get to its intended targets. This has off-set the gains made in buying the terrain-following radar 'off the shelf' from Texas Instruments.[56] Finally, there were serious difficulties experienced with the thrust to weight ratio of the RB-199 engine which manifested themselves in the disintegration of the turbine blades, problems with high and low temperature characteristics and difficulty in obtaining the speed performances required.[57] Although this is only an educated guess it would appear that the engine performance has not met the original design specifications set nor the operational requirement desired by the RAF.[58]

These basic design problems were compounded by additional problems related to the international nature of this project. Not only was there difficulty over the increased costs to Britain through its own high inflation rates in the 1970s and due to exchange rate variations, but the West German decision to reduce numbers in 1973 seriously distorted the work sharing arrangements. The decision meant, in effect, that Britain had less of the work than she was entitled to and therefore was paying more proportionately than the other countries for each MRCA. On top of this it gradually became clear that the assumed savings from collaboration were being eroded by the delay it took to make decisions for a plane with six different operational requirements, managed by countries using different languages and procedures and requiring ratification of all important decisions by three national governments and procurement systems.[59] The result of this was a slowness in decision-making, an increase in development costs over time and conflict and a lack of total communality in even the IDS variant. It was decided, for example, that the countries would each go their own way on the type of 'crash recorder', the radio, internal radar computer management system and external fuel tanks, and there was serious conflict over whether the RAF should have its way and have a two man plane rather than the one man that the Italians and West Germans had originally proposed.[60]

Despite the blandishments of the British defence establishment the MRCA project as a whole appears to confirm the view of *The Economist*[61] that 'the three countries have spent millions of pounds discovering the wheel; there is nothing wholly new in the MRCA', and of one critic who has called it the:[62] 'egg laying, woolgathering, milk producing sow'. There are a number of reasons for this conclusion. According to some estimates the MRCA-IDS does not have the range nor the weapon load of the F1-11, though it does have all-weather capability and a STOL ability, which the F1-11 does not. It does not, for those who wish to use it for close air support, the fighter capacity of the F1-11 or the F-14, F1-15 and F-16 (any one of which West Germany or Italy could have purchased off the shelf in the 1970s at a similar or cheaper price). The IDS is an up to date long range strike aircraft but, as we shall see later, the F1-11 could have been bought earlier to meet the 1975–85 operational timespan and there are now doubts about whether this IDS role is possible today.[63] Turning to the ADV, this aircraft is only slightly better in performance than than Phantom's which are already in use for air defence, although the MRCA does have low-flying and STOL ability and all-weather capabilities that the Phantom does not. The ADV does not however have a particularly effective dog-fighter capability when compared with the F-15 and F-16[64] and, according to one estimate, the F-15 could have been purchased 'off-the-shelf' in 1975 for £1 million less than MRCA was then costing.[65] Overall then, while it is true that the MRCA is an advanced aircraft and that it is what the RAF wanted and that by modern standards it is not a particularly costly plane, it is unfortunate that because of the time and cost delays it is not now, as it comes into service, a very modern aircraft. Nor is it clear that there are not other more effective and cheaper ways of fulfilling the operational requirements for which the IDS and ADV are destined.

THE IMPACT OF REFORM ON PROCUREMENT: DEASC AND THE MRCA-TORNADO

What then did DEASC, as a reformed and more active policy scrutiniser, make of the MRCA programme? The first thing to say is that compared with the old Estimates Committee, DEASC was much more diligent, conscientious and detailed in its perusal of the MRCA project. DEASC studied the general issue of the MRCA in 1970/71, 1971/72, 1974/75, 1976/77 and, in detail, in 1973/74 and 1975/76 when substantive policy recommendations were made.[66] This work was assisted also by three studies of the project by the PAC in 1974, 1975 and 1977/78.[67] This meant that, unlike the old Estimates Committee approach, DEASC was able to study part of the policy for the MRCA as it was being made. This was particularly true for the ADV type because the important decisions to proceed were not made until 1975/76. It was, however, less true of the IDS type because the crucial decisions on full development had been made in the summer of 1971, well before DEASC had been able to study the project.[68]

It was the case, however, that DEASC was studying the project when crucial decisions had to be made by the government on the number of planes to be produced in both variants in 1975/76. Unfortunately, when it came to policy impact DEASC had very little impact on government behaviour, and when it tried to extend its 'value for money' role it resulted in a confusion and conflict of roles *vis-à-vis* the PAC.

If DEASC had wanted to adopt a *strategic* role it would have had to question the whole basis of policy behind the decision to procure both variants of the MRCA. This would have meant that the committee ought to have asked whether Britain could afford it, why the RAF and NATO saw an operational need for this plane, and whether a multi as opposed to several single role aircraft ought to have been purchased.[69] Furthermore, one would have expected DEASC to ask whether there were other ways of fulfilling the requirement that were cheaper or perhaps permissible through other systems. In particular one might have expected DEASC to get at the range of issues in the defence literature which argue that the RAF's IDS role is no longer possible due to the strike capability of SAM missiles, which makes this long range role undesirable for manned aircraft.[70] Similarly, one would have expected DEASC to look at whether or not it would be cheaper and more effective to replace expensive air defence aircraft with SAM missiles (like the British Rapier). This option would then have left the RAF to buy more sophisticated fighters for single purpose air superiority in its air defence and NATO roles.[71] Finally, one would have expected DEASC to be assessing the future of multi versus single role aircraft; as well as the future of international collaboration and a European defence industry,[72] in relation to national production or purchase from the Americans.[73]

Following on from this one might have expected DEASC to study the efficiency of the management structure; whether or not there was sufficient national control of the project; and, whether or not the MOD and Procurement Executive were doing their job in the best interests of the nation. Such issues as the viability of overseas sales, the balance of work sharing and the equal distribution of the cost burden and defence of national design and technical skills might well be expected to have arisen in the role of Parliamentary scrutiny of executive efficiency.[74] Finally, one might have expected DEASC to leave it to the PAC to raise issues relating to the efficiency of contract and work sharing arrangements and whether or not there were avoidable time and cost over-runs through different contracting and management arrangements.

Turning to what was actually achieved we can argue that DEASC was able to make a number of recommendations about policy alternatives, and it did get at the policy issues behind the MRCA decision. Furthermore, it did extend Parliamentary scrutiny of defence decision-making and ensure there was far more information available to Parliament and the public than had been the case before. But, having studied the policy behind the procurement decision in the end DEASC recommendations were totally rejected by the government and, in a number of respects, DEASC failed to raise fully many of the important policy questions that we might have expected it to.

DEASC did raise fundamental questions about the need for the MRCA and discovered from the RAF the strategic and tactical thinking, as well as 'threat' perceptions, which lay behind this operational requirement for both the IDS and ADV variants. In particular, some members of DEASC were concerned that the RAF had a long range interdiction and strike requirement that was shared only by the US Air Force, and not by the allies who were collaborating in the scheme. The interesting line of questioning that developed in committee on this mismatch, and on whether or not the RAF actualy needed the IDS role, was, however, curtailed by the chairman's interventions and it was not subsequently pursued in detail.[75] This intervention by a Conservative, pro-defence orientated chairman to protect MOD and RAF witnesses from difficult questioning was one of the major problems facing DEASC in its scrutiny of this, and other issues. Indeed when the Committee returned to this question in 1974/75 they took evidence from David Greenwood, a defence specialist at Aberdeen University, in which he raised the very issues of whether or not Britain needed the IDS role and perhaps ought to concentrate on close air support due to the likely attrition rate that the MRCA-IDS would face.[76] Surprisingly, DEASC made nothing of this evidence or argument in its subequent questioning of the MOD and RAF and, in completely ignoring this issue, it failed to discharge its policy role effectively. The tenor of its approach was that while:[77]

> We think it right to draw the attention of the House to the substantial increases, and potential increases, in expenditure borne by the British Government and to the fact that some slippage has occurred in the development programme. Neither this nor our request that the British air defence requirement should be stringently reviewed should be construed as an attack of the project. During their visits to Strike Command Headquarters and to RAF Wattisham the Sub-Committee were impressed by the RAF's need for modern aircraft such as the MRCA, and it must be

expected that these cannot be provided on the cheap or without accepting the risk that the programme may have to be varied.

Thus while there was some discussion of the need for single role combat aircraft and the problems of the increased efficiency of SAM missiles this was never effectively brought to bear on the discussions over the IDS variant but was, rather, raised in relation to the RAF's ADV requirement. Interestingly enough, while DEASC chose to take issue with the decision to buy the ADV because our partners did not see a need for this plane and because of its rising costs, it would appear that there was a stronger case for the ADV than for the long-range IDS role. Britain has a massive sea area to police in the UKADR and there is a threat to Britain from low-flying aircraft which attempt to get under radar cover. This provides a clear rationale for an aircraft able to loiter in the air and then dash to intercept bombers.[78] Clearly, the Phantom and the Lightning do not possess sufficiently advanced air to air radar or loiter capability since they were designed to intercept high altitude intruders and the MRCA looks a useful aircraft when compared with these two. This cannot be said for the IDS variant which cannot match the fighter capability of the F-14, F-15 or F-16 and which is being built for a role that its arguably cannot fulfil. Unfortunatley, DEASC ignored this and chose to recommend that the ADV variant should be dropped – or as they euphemistically put it . . . 'stringently reviewed'.[79] The government chose to ignore this recommendation for a number of reasons which DEASC was able usefully to elicit. First of all the government accepted the RAF need for the IDS variant and the committee did not attack this role. Secondly, while there might have been a case for cutting the MRCA programme in total the RAF was already the recipient of the most swingeing cuts of the three Services in the 1974/75 Defence Review conducted by Labour.[80] Thirdly, the government had always seen the project as having industrial benefits at home. To cancel MRCA-ADV and perhaps buy US F-15s (as DEASC was recommending) would have meant a loss of jobs and exchange problems with the dollar.[81] Fourthly, and perhaps crucially, the government had already decided on its final production commitment and to have cut the ADV would have meant higher unit costs for all the planes that were purchased; the possibility of severe penalties; and the possible total withdrawal from the project by West Germany and Italy. The ADV then went ahead even though William Rodgers (the Minister of State at MOD) admitted that the government had in part accepted that SAM missiles might make a better job of air defence and that, due to the need to reduce specifications to keep the plane in cost, the government had considered reducing the number or buying fighters from the Americans.[82] In the end, however, the Labour government was locked into an international agreement which would have had as many costs as benefits to renage on. Shades indeed of the Concorde fiasco!

In the end then, if DEASC did nothing else it provided a wealth of information on why policy decisions had been taken, even if it did not influence policy directly itself. Surprisingly, however, having deliberated for so long on the project it was strange that the committee did not make any recommendations on an MRCA replacement; on whether operational requirements should stay the same for the future in the light of SAM technology; or on the difficult choices the government would have to face in the future between Service roles (Navy versus RAF according to Greenwoods evidence);[83] nor on whether international collaboration or multi-role concepts were useful experiments to continue with in the future of procurement. The only halting suggestions as to the future that were made related to the need to speed up SAM emplacements and airfield hardening against attack and the need for the RAF to reduce its sophistication in specifications to ensure that it obtained aircraft more quickly (did this imply no more multi-role types?).[84]

In the end then DEASC failed to achieve all it might on the policy side. The major reasons for this have been touched on in some detail in Chapter 4 and were clearly apparent in the scrutiny of the MRCA. DEASC lacked the staff, expertise, time, information and inclination to operate as an effective policy scrutiniser. In particular there was a tremendous problem of sidelining of information by the MOD – amongst other things it refused at first to give either the percentage or actual breakdown of cost increases attributable to various causes.[85] DEASC also had to operate with a chairman who intervened to deflect difficult questions. Furthermore many of the crucial papers which were necessary for informed lay discussion – on threat perceptions, on development cost problems, on the feasibility studies and on MOD work on ECMs – were only provided for DEASC confidentially. Obvious there are problems with security issues here, but the unwillingness by the MOD to provide information on the actual design and technical problems experienced with the engine and avionics smacked of bureaucratic convenience in hiding problems and mistakes than the defence of the national interest. This point DEASC made itself and it was implied in David Greenwood's strictures on the paucity of information provided to Parliament on defence when compared with the United States and West Germany.[86]

If DEASC failed therefore to discharge its policy role fully a similar criticism cannot be made of its activities elsewhere. Although the committee suffered from a lack of staff and a poor style of questioning it did spend considerable time assessing the 'value for money' and efficiency of the MRCA project. The criticism that can be made there however is that it could have been more effective and that it all too often duplicated the work of the PAC. This wasted effort could more usefully have been spent in pursuing policy issues.

DEASC and PAC were, nevertheless, both extremely effective in discovering problems associated with the decision to operate on an international collaborative basis.[87] The committees felt that this approach led to a failure to agree on operational requirements; led to an increase in 'real' costs; and fostered delay due to a lack of true standardisation of equipment.[88] It was also argued that there were serious unforeseen exchange rate problems and difficulties in work sharing that could not be resolved satisfactorily;[89] and, that there was a definite loss of design and technical skill to Italy and West Germany (the latter was clearly using British aerospace expertise to develop its own aerospace industry).[90] Furthermore, there was evidence that the MOD and Procurement Executive had not protected British design leadership and that the United States was benefiting from off-set agreements with West Germany.[91] Finally, it was argued that there had never been any true assessment of the costs and benefits of collaboration other than 'guesstimates';[92] that there was little potential for any overseas sales;[93] and, that the RAF had been forced to reduce their own optimal specifications to obtain any overseas participation in the scheme.[94] Surprisingly enough, despite these findings DEASC was of the view that international collaboration was a beneficial approach and that the problems were reasonable and to be expected. Only the PAC was slightly more sceptical and, in its 1974 Report, warned the government to be more cautious in entering into these arrangements and to consider buying from the USA in future.[95]

In this respect it is possible to argue that the more circumspect approach of the PAC was more realistic given the evidence unearthed as to the deleterious consequences of international collaboration. Indeed that fact that multi-role aircraft are no longer being considered by the Americans after the F1-11, and the British replacement (AST-403) for the Jaguar fighter experienced difficulties in finding an international collaborator, indicates that the anodine conclusions of DEASC when compared with those of PAC are an indication of its failure to discharge it scrutiny role as conscientiously as it might.[96] PAC questioning and recommendations, when compared with the questioning style and somewhat uncritical conclusions of DEASC, appear at once more intelligent and expert. In this sense DEASC duplicated the PACs 'value for money' role without contributing anything novel to the process – there was similar evidence of this unsatisfactory duplication in the audit role.

The PAC, in scrutinising the MRCA contracts and the problem of time and cost delays, made a number of important recommendations for the future. It recommended that no work sharing arrangements should be left until well into the project but that contracts should specify at an early date what development costs and work burdens should be.[97] Furthermore, and in an implied barb against the unfair use by West Germany of contracts to obtain design leadership on the airframe, it was argued that there should be penalties in the future for partners who reduced their planned purchase number before production began.[98] The PAC was also extremely critical of the lack of residential government technical officers with contractors in West Germany and Italy.[99] Most of this work, involving detailed scrutiny of why costs had risen, was extensively duplicated rather than extended by DEASC.[100]

CONCLUSIONS

We saw how changes in the organisation of defence procurement in the 1960s and 1970s led to fears that the old system of Parliamentary scrutiny would be eroded and that legislative oversight of procurement would become more difficult. It was also an expectation that legislative oversight of defence procurement would be greatly aided by the creation of SCOE and DEASC. One basic criticism of SCOE and DEASC was that they failed to institute the fundamental 'root and branch' review of research and development (defence and civilian) that Turpin for one had argued was necessary. Despite this it would not be fair to argue that SCOE and DEASC totally failed to extend legislative oversight of defence procurement. Taking the detailed study of the MRCA project, plus the similar detailed studies of guided weapons, the Cruiser programme, nuclear weapons and the main battle tank into account there can be no doubt that legislative scrutiny of both the 'efficiency' of procurement policy-making and the workings of the process itself was extended. If the PAC still tended to undertake these scrutiny and audit functions more effectively than DEASC then this is only to be expected given the experience and staff resources that the PAC has historically commanded. But DEASC contributed in one way that PAC could not and that was in gleaning information from the MOD and government about the policy behind procurement decisions.

This study of the MRCA procurement experience indicates both the strengths and the weaknesses of the SCOE and DEASC experiment. On the one hand Parliament and the interested public outside are now much better informed about how the procurement process works and why certain decisions were taken. But, while this is a definite plus, DEASC's experience with the rejection of its recommendations clearly shows the limits to the reform movement of the 1970s in Britain. DEASC could not always obtain the information that it required; it did not have the time and staff to discharge its investigatory role effectively (in particular DEASC failed to notice inconsistencies in MOD and RAF submissions which might have led it to strengthen its case against both the IDS and ADV variants):[101] its reports and recommendations did not cause an uproar in either Parliament or the press; and, (perhaps most worrying of all) because of its need to present a bipartisan approach the most difficult questions were either not asked or deflected and the most damning conclusions – on the perceived inadequacy of international collaboration as an approach to procurement – were not drawn. Hamstrung by party politics and unable to overcome executive pre-eminence DEASC could not hope to change the governments priorities over MRCA even when it was in a position to develop a viable case. Nor could this be otherwise when the effective decisions on procurement are taken up to ten years before the full financial impact ever appears in Parliamentary estimates. In so far as DEASC broke into this procurement process before decisions had been taken to give an alternative view we can applaud the Parliamentary experience of the 1970s. But in terms of policy impact it is doubtful that DEASC went any further than the old Estimates Committee was able to. Nevertheless DEASC did illuminate the procurement process in a way that the Estimates Committee could not and, while this did not overturn executive dominance of procurement decision-making, DEASC contributed to extending the accountability of the process.

NOTES

1. Clive Ponting, 'The Reorganisation of Defence Procurement' (paper to Centennial Conference of the Extra-Mural Department, University of Oxford, 1980) pp. 2–4; and, Colin Turpin, *Government Contracts* (Harmondsworth, Middlesex: Penguin, 1972), pp. 112–15.
2. Richard Worcester, *Roots of British Air Policy* (London: Hodder & Stoughton, 1966) pp. 38–9; and, Angus Rae, *The Organisation of Defence Procurement and Production in the United Kingdom* (Aberdeen University, Centre for Defence Studies, ASIDES no. 13, 1979) p. 13.
3. Michael Howard, *The Central Organisation of Defence* (London: RUSI, 1970) p. 5–33.
4. Worcester, op. cit., pp. 38–9.
5. Arthur Reed, *Britain's Aircraft Industry, What Went Right? What Went Wrong?* (London: Dent, 1973) pp. 71–3.
6. For a useful introduction to the problems of the industry and its cost and time over-run problems see: Reed, ibid., *passim*; Derek Wood, *Project Cancelled* (London: MacDonald & James, 1976); and I. Cheeseman, M. Edmonds and J. Simpson, 'The Procurement of Military Aircraft 1945–1970', E. J. Feutchtwanger (ed), *Perspectives upon British Defence Policy* (University of Southampton, 1978).
7. Keith Harley, 'Development Timescales for British and American Aircraft', *Scottish Journal of Political Economy*, vol. 19 (1972) p. 115.
8. Ponting, op. cit., p. 5.
9. G. Williams, *Crisis in Procurement: a Case Study of the TSR-2* (London: RUSI, 1969); and, Wood, op. cit., ch. 9.
10. *Report of the (Gibbs/Zuckerman) Committee on the Management and Control of Research and Development* (London: HMSO, 1961).
11. Reed, op. cit., pp. 28–9.
12. Ibid., p. 61; and, Worcester, op. cit., pp. 39–40.
13. Martin Edmonds, 'Government Contracting and Renegotiation: a Comparative Analysis', *Public Administration*, vol. 39 (Spring 1972) p. 50.
14. F. R. U. Crocker, 'Quality or Quantity?', *RUSI Journal*, vol. 116 (March 1971) p. 50.
15. Ponting, op. cit., p. 7.
16. Turpin, op. cit., pp. 169–70; and, Worcester, op. cit., pp. 39–40.
17. *Cmnd* 2428 (1965/6); and, *Cmnd* 2581 (1965/6).
18. *Report of the Plowden Committee on the Aircraft Industry (Cmnd 2853)* (London: HMSO, 1965).
19. *The Fulton Report (Cmnd 3638)* (London: HMSO, 1968).
20. *Report of the Steering Group on Development Cost Estimating (Downey)* (London: Ministry of Technology, 1969).
21. Reed, op. cit., pp. 82–4.
22. Turpin, op. cit., p. 122.
23. Edmonds, op. cit., pp. 54–5; and, Keith Hartley, 'Evaluating Military Aircraft Outlays, The British Experience', *Economic Journal*, vol. 79 (December 1969) p. 880.

24. Turpin, op. cit., p. 262; and, R. Verdon-Smith (Sir), 'The Need for Closer Relations Between Defence and Industry', *RUSI Journal*, vol. 116 (March 1971) pp. 11–12.
25. Turpin, ibid., p. 122.
26. *(The Rayner Report) Government Organisation for Defence Procurement* (Cmnd 4641) (London: HSMO, 1971).
27. Rae, op. cit., pp. 1–6; and, Turpin, op. cit., pp. 115–16.
28. Further details can be gleaned from Ponting; Rae and Turpin, op. cit., *passim*; and, M. Cary (Sir), 'Military Procurement', *RUSI Journal*, vol. 119 (March 1974), pp. 18–24; G. H. Green, 'British Policy for Defence Procurement', *RUSI Journal*, vol. 121 (September 1976) pp. 20–7.
29. The MOD/WRC is normally constituted of the three Services, MOD civilian staffs, Procurement Executive civilian staffs, Scientific Advisers, Treasury and the Secretary of State. It is normally concerned with alterations and specifications for operational requirements. MOD/DEPC is chaired by the Chief Scientific Adviser and normally has civilian staffs involved (MOD/Procurement Executive). It considers long-term weapons and equipment issues and their Service harmonisation within the overall constraints of the defence budget.
30. Turpin, op. cit., p. 262; and, Verdon-Smith, op. cit., pp. 11–13.
31. *HC 629* (1970/71), pp. 82–3.
32. *Military Expenditure Overseas, HC 302* (1963/64).
33. This is discussed at length in Chapter 3, pp. 140–55.
34. Turpin, op. cit., pp. 222–3.
35. Ibid., pp. 79, 38–9 and 42–5.
36. Edmonds, op. cit., and, Turpin, ibid., pp. 263–5.
37. On the need for international collaboration in weapons acquisition see: M. Edmonds, 'International Collaboration', in *International Affairs* (April 1967) pp. 320–37; W. Schutze, *European Defence Co-operation and NATO* (London: Atlantic Papers 1969) C. Layton, *Advanced European Technology* (London: Allen & Unwin, 1969); *Military Aircraft Procurement and Its Effect on the British Aerospace Industry* (London: RUSI, 1968); John Calmann, *European Co-operation in Defence Technology: The Political Aspect* (London: ISS, 1967); and, *Weapons Procurement, Defence Management and International Collaboration* (London: RUSI, 1972).
38. For recent developments see: Clifford Cornford (Sir), 'European Equipment Co-operation', *RUSI Journal*, vol. 124 (March 1979) pp. 46–9; and, Stephen Kirby, 'The Independent European Programme Group: the Failure of Low-Profile High Politics', *Journal of Common Market Studies* (December 1979) pp. 175–96.
39. G. Lea & J. Meacham, 'Today's Few: a Survey of the RAF', *The Economist*, vol. 265 (17 December 1977) pp. 8–9.
40. Ibid., pp. 3–4; and, *HC 155* (1975/76) paras 57–60.
41. A. H. C. Greenwood, 'MRCA – The Future System of Military Procurement', *RUSI Journal*, vol. 117 (September 1972) p. 8; Mark Hewish, 'Tornado for the Future', *New Scientist* (6 May 1976), p. 302; and, Angus Rae, *Collaborative Weapons Acquisition: the MRCA*

(TORNADO) – PANAVIA Project (Aberdeen University, Asides No. 12, October, 1979) pp. 6–9.
42. Hewish, ibid., p. 304; and, Rae, ibid., pp. 31–2.
43. Rae, ibid., pp. 13–14.
44. A. H. C. Greenwood, op. cit., p. 11; and, *HC 141* (1971/72) para. 38.
45. Rae, op. cit., p. 8; and, *HC 169* (1973/74) p. 35.
46. *HC 259* (1974/75) para. 26; and, *HC 254* (1976/77), para. 8.
47. Hewish, op. cit., p. 303; and, *The Economist*, vol. 2552 (21 September 1974) p. 44.
48. 'Pink Elephant', *The Economist*, vol. 259 (12 June 1976) p. 56.
49. *Defence Expenditure, Cmnd 6489* (London: HMSO, May 1976) paras 54–5.
50. Rae, op. cit., p. 8: and, Lea and Meacham, op. cit., p. 32.
51. *HC 298* (1977/78), p. 41.
52. Ibid., para. 34; and, *The Times* (25 February 1981) p. 16.
53. *HC 303* (1974) p. 136.
54. *HC 298*, (1977/78) p. 33; and M. Hirst, 'Flying in the Tornado', *Flight International* (28 October 1978) p. 1585.
55. *HC 298*, (1977/78) pp. 25–8, 33; *HC 169* (1973/74) pp. 33–5; and, Rae, op. cit., pp. 12–14.
56. *HC 303* (1974) pp. 144–5; and, Lea and Meacham, op. cit., p. 15.
57. *HC 169* (1973/74) pp. 25–7.
58. This conclusion is based on the authors' reading between the lines of published sources and is of course belied by official government and defence establishment arguments that the aircraft is exactly what is required and that the RAF is very happy with its performance. However, see also the somewhat more sceptical views of: *Interavia*, no. 11 (1977) pp. 1111–75; David Fairhall, 'Take off for the 1980's', *Guardian* (16 September 1974) pp. 15–17; *The Economist*, vol. 250 (16 March 1974) p. 40 and vol. 258 (13 March 1976) pp. 55–6; and, Robin Cook, 'Into the Tornado', *New Statesman* (23 July 1976) pp. 100–1.
59. Rae, op. cit., p. 17; Hewish, op. cit., p. 304; and, A. H. C. Greenwood, op. cit., pp. 9–13.
60. *HC 169* (1973/74) pp. 34–5.
61. *The Economist*, vol. 258, op. cit., p. 5.
62. Cook, op. cit., p. 101.
63. Lea & Meacham, op. cit., p. 31; and, in particular see David Greenwood, 'Some Economic Constraints on Force Structure', in Feuchtwanger, E. J. and Mason, R. A. (ed), *Air Power in the Next Generation* (London: Macmillan 1979) pp. 12–37; and, *The UK Current Defence Programme and Budget* (Aberdeen University, ASIDES Spring 1980).
64. Lea & Meacham, ibid., pp. 31–3.
65. *The Economist*, vol. 258, op. cit., p. 55.
66. The DEASC Reports included: *HC 628* (1970/71); *HC 141* (1971/72); *HC 169* (1973/74); *HC 99* (1973/74); *HC 259* (1974/75); *HC 155* (1975/76); and, *HC 254* (1976/77).
67. Although PAC looked at MRCA on three occasions, only *HC 303* (1974) and *HC 298* (1977/78) looked at the project in detail.

68. *HC 99* (1973/74) p. 164.
69. On the issue of multi versus single roles see: W. T. Gunston, 'Communality in Aircraft design', *Brasseys Annual* (1966) pp. 246–57; and, 'Multi-role or Single Purpose? a Problem in Procurement', *RUSI Journal*, vol. 117 (March 1972) pp. 33–7.
70. For an extended discussion of this issue see Greenwood (1979) op. cit., pp. 25–40 and (1980) pp. 36–7. Greenwood's views on this have also received support from: Allan W. Hall, 'Tornado: Will the Multi-Role Capability Work?', *Aviation News* (15–30 September 1978) p. 7; Lea & Meacham, op. cit., p. 12–16; F. R. U. Crocker, op. cit., and, Noel Falconer, 'Too Few of the New – or More as Before?', *RUSI Journal*, vol. 120 (September 1975) pp. 34–8.
71. Lea & Measham, ibid., p. 15.
72. The case for such an industry is developed in Layton, op. cit., Cornford, op. cit.; Per-Eric Jansson, 'Defence Procurement – a European View', *RUSI Journal*, vol. 124 (December 1979) pp. 19–22; and, Gunston, op. cit. The case for a purely national approach to procurement can be found in: Oliver Stewart, 'The Future of Britain's Aerospace Industry', *Brassey's Annual* (1966) pp. 227–36.
73. On the possibility of buying from the USA see: Keith Harley, *A Market for Aircraft* (London: IEA Hobart Paperno. 57, 1974); and, Ian Bellany, 'Defence Procurement – a Heretical View', *RUSI Journal*, vol. 117 (March 1972) pp. 37–9.
74. These issues have been raised variously in Bellany, ibid., pp. 38–9; Cook, op. cit., Reed, op. cit., p. 6; Verdon-Smith, op. cit., p. 15; Cornford, op. cit., p. 46; Gunston, op. cit., p. 256; A. H. C. Greenwood, op. cit., p. 11; and, Ponting, op. cit., p. 7. It is worth pointing out however that while these studies have tended to be critical of international collaboration within MRCA, there are studies which generally see the system as worthwhile and worth repeating. Rae, op. cit.; Interavia, op. cit.; and, Jansson, op. cit.
75. *See HC 141* (1971/72) pp. 256 & 257 in particular; and also, *HC 169* (1973/74) para. 25.
76. *HC 259* (1974/75) pp. 1–20.
77. *HC 169* (1973/74) para. 25.
78. *HC 155* (1975/76) paras. 25 and 57–9; and, *Defence Review: an Appreciation of the Problems of Air Defence Affecting the UK* (D 103) – Memorandum by the Ministry of Defence (SCOE 77/1) pp. 111–17.
79. *HC 141* (1971/72) p. 250; *HC 169* (1973/74), paras 1–15 and p. 31; *HC 155* (1975/76) para. 80 and p. 135; and, *HC 259* (1974/75) para. 28.
80. *HC 155* (1975/76) para. 64: Lea & Meacham, op. cit., pp. 4–9; and David W. Wragg, 'Defence – the Politics of Staying at Home', *The Spectator* (14 December 1974) pp. 758–9 provide details of the cuts affecting the RAF. The RAF lost 17 000 men, around 50% of its transport aircraft, the closure of 12 Home Bases, a squadron from Singapore, a 25% cut in its helicopter force and a reduced maritime-reconnaissance role amongst other things. The RAF with MRCA after 1975 clearly had all their equipment eggs in 'one basket'.
81. *HC 155* (1975/76), paras 76–80 and pp. 228–32.

82. Ibid., paras 76–80 and pp. 228–32.
83. *HC 259* (1974/75) pp. 5–6.
84. *HC 155* (1975/76) p. 232; and, *HC 259* (1974/75) para. 28.
85. *HC 141* (1971/72) pp. 71–2 and, pp. 260–6; and, pp. iv–vii.
86. Ibid.; and, HC 259 (1974/75) p. 7 and p. 14–15.
87. *HC 628* (1970/71) pp. 81–2; *HC 141* (1972/72) para. 38; *HC 99* (2973/74) pp. 157–9; *HC 155* (1975/76) para. 75; and, *HC 303* (1974) paras. 184–6, 191–4 and 203.
88. *HC 141* (1971/72) pp. 257–8; *HC 628* (1970/71) pp. 81–2; *HC 169* (1973/74) p. 35; and, *HC 303* (1974) paras 184–6.
89. *HC 303* (1974) para. 192; and, *HC 298* (1977/78) paras 22–25.
90. *HC 141* (1971/72) para. 42 and p. 259; and, *HC 303* (1974) p. 134, 142 and 150.
91. *HC 141*, ibid.; and, *HC 303,* ibid.; and, pp. 1423–50.
92. *HC 259* (1974/75) p. 61; *HC 303* (1974) pp. 139 and 150–1; and, *HC 298* (1977/78) pp. 29–30.
93. *HC 141* (1971/72) p. 252; *HC 169* (1973/74) p. 36; and, *HC 259* (1974/75) para. 26.
94. *HC 303* (1974) para. 18.
95. Ibid., paras 191–4 and 203.
96. Greenwood (1980), op. cit., p. 38 and *The Economist*, vol. 70, (24 February 1979) p. 65; vol. 261 (2nd June 1979) pp. 16–17; and vol. 273 (24 November 1979) p. 95. See also Public Accounts Committee, *International Collaborative Projects on Defence Equipment, Monitoring and Control of Procurement Expenditure* (HC 84, HMSO, 1985)
97. *HC 303* (1974), para. 193–194; and, *HC 298* (1977/78), para. 26.
98. *HC 303* (1974) para. 142.
99. Ibid., p. 132.
100. Vilma Flegman, 'The PAC: a Successful Select Committee', *Parliamentary Affairs*, vol. 33 (Spring 1980) pp. 166–72.
101. In particular it was apparent that while the RAF was arguing that Britain needed the MRCA-ADV to ensure air defence and that SAM missiles were simply not flexible enough against low-flying aircraft, the MOD was arguing to the Americans and the DEASC that the Rapier SAM missile was so flexible that it could be moved quickly and easily into new locations and that new developments would ensure that it could operate against low-flying intruders. Unfortunately, DEASC neither had the time nor the expertise to notice these glaring inconsistencies. See, in particular, *Defence Review: an Appreciation of the Problems of Air Defence Affecting the UK* (D 103) for the RAF view (*HC 55* (1975/76) pp. 111–17) and compare this with the submission from the Ministry of Defence, *Surface to Air Missiles: Air Aspects of the Defence Review: Possible Sale of Rapier to the USA* (D 104) (*HC 155* (1975/76)) p. 118.

Part IV
Legislative Oversight and Defence Policy Issues

7 Congressional Reform and Defence Policy: the Manpower Issue

The creation of the congressional Budget Committees and the Congressional Budget Office (CBO) was not intended to interfere with the powers of the Armed Srvices and Appropriations Committees for the oversight of defence policy and programmes, including their responsibility for setting the level of US manpower in NATO. *Managerial* and *Audit* questions relating to the NATO commitment, such as recruitment and retention of personnel for the All-Volunteer Force, levels of pay and service conditions, the provision of weapons for the general purpose forces, and the structure and deployment of those forces were considered to be, and remained, strictly the province of these established committees. The Budget Committees did not concern themselves in any detailed way in 'line-item' issue of this kind. They and the CBO were expected, however, to assist the Armed Services and Appropriations committees to examine the *strategic* or policy implications of manpower decisions more fully than before, and in this respect the Budget Committees and, to a more marked degree, the CBO had some limited success in the mid-1970s.

Yet it became clear within a very short time that this success was more a reflection of the established committees' willingness to consider the full implications of manpower decisions than it was the Budget Committees' ability to force such a consideration onto the congessional agenda. And in any event the 'policy context' of manpower deployments was more properly the province of the House Foreign Affairs and the Senate Foreign Relations committees and they remained more likely to influence congressional opinion on these issues than the Budget Committees. Indeed, in the immediate aftermath of the Soviet invasion of Afghanistan when Congress responded, or more precisely over-responded, to public and pressure-group demands for increased defence spending, the Senate Budget Committee had little success in getting the Congress to consider either the need for or the policy implications of increased defence spending,[1] and the CBO tended to reflect rather than to question the populist demand for a stronger defence posture including an increased military role in Western Europe.

THE IMPORTANCE OF THE NATO MANPOWER ISSUE

It is difficult to overestimate the importance of the US committment to NATO in either executive or congressional politics; it has played a vital role in shaping post-war defence and foreign policy and has had a major impact not only on the defence budget, but also on the balance of the entire federal budget. Ever since the committment of American troops to NATO in 1951, the defence of Western Europe has been the basis of military planning for America's general purpose forces. As the CBO commented in 1979, 'The defence of Europe holds a dominant position in establishing US defense policies and in fashioning the capabilities of US conventional forces'.[2] Even in 1983, when the Reagan Administration was emphasising the Rapid Deployment Force and the need to project military power beyond the NATO area, the CBO observed

> . . . under current planning, all active army divisions but one are committed to NATO (the one in Korea would remain there). Moreover, virtually all of the active Air Force fighter squadrons, supplemented with reserve fighter squadrons, are committed to NATO.

The report also pointed out that substantial contingents of the United States Navy were on patrol in the NATO waters of the Atlantic Ocean and the Mediterranean Sea.[3] In effect virtually all America's conventional land forces and equipment, its tactical air forces and a substantial part of its navy are devoted to, and must be justified by, the requirements of the defence of Western Europe. Only the strategic nuclear forces and that part of the navy devoted to 'power projection' do not fall clearly within this category. Even then the demands of the NATO commitment often determine the scope for the development of these forces. Manpower costs alone account for over 50% of defence spending[4] and, together with equipment costs, the conventional general purpose forces account for the greater part of defence spending. Decisions about their size, location, equipment and level of readiness determine the shape of the defence budget and all these decisions are taken in the light of the perceived state of the NATO/Warsaw Pact military balance. It is in this sense that NATO is the very foundation of America's military planning.

The commitment to NATO has also been the most enduring and most important feature of American post-war foreign policy. Successive administrations have emphasised both the importance of the European allies as trading partners and the volume of direct US investment in Western Europe. The importance of the alliance itself as the front line for the defence of US strategic interests has also been frequently stressed. In the early 1970s, when there was considerable congressional pressure to reduce the number of US troops in Europe, Senator John Tower, then the ranking Republican on the Senate Armed Services Committee, expressed just this sentiment when he said,

> We do not remain in Western Europe solely because we wish to help our European allies and contribute to their defense. We are there because we have pursued a foreign policy and a defense policy that holds that it is far more desirable for us to maintain our defense perimeter as far from our shores as possible and as close to any potential enemy's shores, as possible.[5]

Clearly the Atlantic Alliance, which embraces political, strategic and economic links, has been the most important relationship that the US has maintained with any group of nations in the post-war world. In a Congressional Research Service (CRS) study of American interests in NATO it was noted that the interdependence of the nations of Western Europe and North America was so well developed that only rarely could one member of the Atlantic Alliance act in the political, military or economic spheres without taking into account and affecting the interests of other members of the alliance. Even during the Carter Administration, when the general principles of American foreign and defence policy enjoyed very little bi-partisan support, there was 'a reasonably broad measure of consensus in the American foreign policy community on US policy toward NATO', the general objectives of which were the preservation of collaborative political, economic and military ties with the countries of Western Europe, the minimisation of Soviet influence upon them and the lessening of East–West tensions.[6]

There is a much more direct link between the NATO defence commitment and America's foreign policy links with the states of Western Europe. The Atlantic Alliance is a collective defence arrangement and Congress is very much concerned that America's European allies should match, and should be seen to match, the efforts of the United States for the defence of Europe. In practice this has meant that any increase in the defence budget provision for the maintainance and modernisation of conventional forces, the overwhelming majority of which is deemed to be for the defence of Europe, has to be part of a collective NATO defence effort. This in turn means that the European allies are under considerable pressure to increase their defence effort one way or another whenever Washington decides to increase its defence budget. This requirement produces few problems when there is a genuine alliance-wide consensus that defence spending should be increased, as there was immediately after the Soviet invasion of Czechoslovakia, but it is a major irritant in trans-Atlantic relationships when America increases its defence spending beyond a level acceptable to or thought necessary by the Europeans, as has been the case throughout much of the Reagan Administration.

There is little doubt that trans-Atlantic relationships have been strained whenever the European allies have felt that they are being pressed to increase their defence spending more to justify the growth of the American defence budget, which is still determined largely by domestic political and economic factors, than to deal with a perceived Soviet threat. There is, of course, a reverse side to this coin and there has been much resentment in America that the Europeans are enthusiastic to maintain close cooperation for a collective defence but follow essentially nationalistic and protectionist economic policies and, on many issues, aspire to a diplomacy independent of the USA.

The NATO commitment has been no less important in determining the size of the defence budget and has also been the major determinant of the balance of the federal budget. With some 60% of the defence effort devoted to the security of Western Europe it is not surprising that it dominates the defence budget. In 1980 it was estimated that pay for the 300 000 plus American troops stationed in Europe amounted to more than $6 billion annually, and that the total cost of supporting the NATO commitment was in excess of $50 billion for FY 1979.[7] It has been regularly estimated that America spends substantially in excess of half its defence budget on the direct support of NATO and even in recent years, when the costs associated with the extra-European Rapid Deployment Force have increased, the General Accounting Office has estimated that this is still the case. In FY 1982 for example, 56% of the defence budget, which amounted to \$122.3 billion or 4% of America's GNP, was allocated to NATO defence.[8]

In a major review of defence commitments made at the beginning of the Carter Administration Alice Rivlin, the Director of the CBO, noted that 'How the United States plans to fulfil its defense commitments to . . . NATO is the major determinant of the defence budget', and commented further that this same concern would 'provide much of the backdrop as the Congress decides on budgetary targets for the First Concurrent Resolution on the Budget'.[9] In other words the sheer size of the defence budget has become a major determinant of the volume of welfare expenditure as well as of taxation policy. In addition to this, defence spending has other important economic consequences. Overseas defence spending, especially in Europe, is recognised as having an important effect on America's balance of payments account, and defence spending for equipment has a particularly marked effect on the size of the federal deficit and the rate of inflation.[10]

CONGRESS AND THE NATO MANPOWER ISSUE BEFORE 1974

The central importance of the NATO commitment in US foreign and defence policy, and its effect on the defence budget in particular and the federal policy, and its effect on the defence budget in particular and the federal budget in general has meant that Congress has periodically accorded it great significance. On two occasions before the budget reforms there has been a 'great debate' not only on the size and nature of the US contribution to the defence of Europe but also on its wider defence and foreign policy implications and on the burden that it imposes on the American economy. The first was occasioned by President Truman's decision of September 1950 to assign an additional four US divisions to Europe and his authorisation of General Eisenhower to serve as the Supreme Allied Commander Europe (SACEUR). These decisions were a reaction to the North Korean invasion of South Korea in June 1950 which was widely interpreted as a clear indication of the readiness of Communist states to use force to gain political ends. The Truman administration gave serious consideration to the possibility of a Soviet attack against the state of Western Europe and decided upon the troop deployment as part of a forward defensive strategy for NATO. These decisions and the strategy upon which they rested were examined by the Senate committtees on Foreign Relations and Armed Services in joint hearings held in February 1951.[11]

The hearings took place at a time when the United States was heavily engaged in the Korean war against the forces of 'monolitiic communism' and the majority of witnesses were overwhelmingly in favour of the troop deployments to Europe and the creation of an integrated command structure for NATO. In April 1951 Resolution 99 was passed expressing the 'sense of the Senate' and endorsed the President's decisions but there were certain conditions and reservations. These reflected the misgivings of Republican Senators like Robert Taft and Kenneth Wherry about the economic effects of the deployment and about the strategy on which the Resolution was based. Both men were fiscal conservatives and fears that overseas defence spending on this scale would fuel inflation which in turn might require extensive federal intervention in the economy, and it was the latter prospect to which they objected most. They also feared that the Resolution committed the United States to fight communism on the Eurasian landmass where it would be at the greatest disadvantage in a war with the Soviet Union, and were equally concerned that the Europeans would become excessively dependent on the United States for their security. In order to prevent this, Taft and his supporters were successful wording the Resolution to require the European allies to make 'the major contribution to the [NATO] ground forces'.[12]

The second 'great debate' was sponsored by the Democatic majority leader in the Senate, Mike Mansfield, and engaged the attention of Congress, mainly the Senate, on and off from 1966 to 1975. The background to this debate was more complex than that of the 1950s and was sparked off by growing congressional concern that the Europeans had become poor allies. This assessment reflected congressional resentment of the failure of the majority of the Western European allies to give wholehearted support to the United States in Vietnam and concern that the Europeans took the defence of Europe less seriously than did the United States. The decision of General de Gaulle, announced in March 1966, to withdraw French troops from

NATO's integrated military command was the event that did most to forge this congressional attitude, but other European states had also allowed their military contributions to NATO to run down and this reinforced the view that the Europeans had become complaisant about the Soviet threat. The depth of congressional concern and resentment was increased by the extent of Western Europe's post-war economic recovery which, in the view of Mansfield and others, enabled the European allies to take on a greater part of the NATO defence burden than they had so far been willing to accept.

The progress of the Mansfield 'great debate' can be divided into two main periods,[13] the first of which ran from mid-1966 to the end of 1970, during which time Mansfield introduced several 'sense of the Senate' resolutions none of which was taken to a vote.[14] The first resolution was introduced in August 1966 and noted the increased capacity of the United States to wage war and to move military forces rapidly so that US troop reductions in NATO would not reduce either its resolve or its ability to defend Europe. The resolutions called simply for 'a substantial reduction of United States forces permanently stationed in Europe' and was co-sponsored by the 13 members of the Democratic Policy Committee, and within a month had attracted an additional 18 co-sponsors.

An identical resolution was introduced in January 1967 with the support of 41 co-sponsors, and it was agreed that it should be referred to a Joint Subcommittee of the Committees of Armed Services and Foreign Relations to be chaired by Mansfield. The subcommittee hearings held during April 1967 allowed the fullest airing of the arguments for and against US troop reductions in Europe, but once again Mansfield decided not to push the issue to a vote, and he announced at the end of the hearings that no resolution would be reported out of the subcommittee. During 1968 it was Senator Symington rather than Mansfield who pushed for a reduction in the US NATO commitment, but his initiative was dropped in the face of congressional reaction to the Soviet invasion of Czechoslovakia in August. It was not until December 1969 that Mansfield again introduced his resolution, and by February 1970 it had the support of a slim majority of the Senate. However, the administration was adamant that the current level of US troops in Europe should be maintained and in November 1970 the Defence Secretary Melvin Laird, having had earlier plans for a 30 000 troop reduction vetoed by President Nixon, announced that the number of US troops in Europe would remain unchanged for at least the next 18 months. It was this decision which changed Mansfield's strategy and in December 1970 he announced that he would no longer introduce 'sense of the Senate' resolutions, but would seek to enforce US troop reductions by legislation or by an amendment to a military authorisation or appropriation bill.

Mansfield's objectives in this first period were essentially to place indirect pressure on the Administration to reconsider the scale of the US contribution to NATO which he felt reflected policy inertia rather than a realistic assessment of the security threat to Western Europe. However, he was largely unsuccessful in changing the Administration's policies. He was informed in the April 1967 hearings that US troops had already been withdrawn from France and that 35 000 would be withdrawn from Germany in the first six months of 1968, but the re-deployments from Germany were described as simply part of the routine rotation of US troops stationed there.[15] His second objective was to encourage the European allies to carry more of the NATO defence burden, and here he met with more success. The West German government accepted in May 1967, June 1968 and July 1969 a variety of off-set agreements to reduce the foreign exchange costs to America of stationing troops in the Federal Republic. The Europeans also set up the Eurogroup within NATO in 1968 which had two primary objectives. The first was to publicise the considerable part of the defence burden that they already carried, and the second was to decide collectively what measures they could take to increase their share of the burden in order to assuage congressional demands.[16] In December 1970 the Eurogroup members of NATO accepted a 5 year programme estimated to cost in excess of $1 billion for the improvement of specified forces and NATO's infrastructure.

These responses from the European allies did little to alleviate the pressure from Mansfield, although it is fair to say that from 1971 onwards he was as much, if not more, concerned about national spending priorities and the inroads of Nixon's 'Imperial Presidency' on the constitutional powers of Congress as he was to achieve some redistribution of NATO's, defence burden. From 1971 and 1975 Mansfield and his supporters changed strategy and introduced a number of amendments designed to legislate US troops withdrawals from Europe. In May 1971 an amendment to the draft extension bill would have limited America's NATO commitment to 150 000 troops by the end of the year but it was defeated by 61 to 36, and a Senate Appropriations Committee amendment to the FY 1972 Defense

Appropriations Bill[17] to fund no more than 250 000 troops in Europe was defeated in November by a similar margin.

Although no amendment was offered in 1972, the cost and the number of US troops in Europe were discussed by the Senate Appropriations and Armed Services Committees, and the latter issued a report in July calling upon the 'newly affluent' Europeans to reinburse the US with the incremental costs associated with stationing troops in Europe rather than at home.[18] Mansfield came closest to success on 26 September 1973 when his substitute amendment to the Defence Procurement Bill to reduce US land forces stationed overseas by 40% by June 1976 was passed by a narrow majority of 49 votes to 46. For procedural reasons the original amendment had to be voted upon before the Mansfield substitute could be deemed to be adopted, and this vote did not take place for several hours. This provided the Nixon Administration with the opportunity to lobby vigorously key Senators in an attempt to reverse the majority. In the event this was done comfortably and the original amendment was modified by Mansfield was rejected 51 votes to 44. Mansfield offered his resolution again in June 1974 but could muster no more than 35 votes for it, and a year later he announced that the collapse of South Vietnam and threats to Western interests elsewhere made it the wrong time to seek US troop reductions overseas.

In the second period from 1971 the 'great debate' continued to look at the substance of US foreign and defence policy in respect of NATO. Fundamental questions such as the nature of the Soviet threat, the alternative strategies available to meet the threat, the relationship between conventional and nuclear forces and their effect upon deterrence and defence, and the importance of an American presence in Europe were all examined in depth. Mansfield's amendments allowed and encouraged the major committees of Congress to examine these *strategic* questions repeatedly during the late 1960s and early 1970s, and it also required the Administration to offer a much fuller account of its foreign and defence policies to Congress than was usually the case before 1975. But the Mansfield resolutions and amendments were more important still for they addressed directly the question of political and budget priorities and raised fundamental questions about the constitutional control of foreign and defence policy.

A consistent theme of Mansfield's criticisms of the foreign and defence policies of successive Administrations during the Vietnam War was that the United States could not pay for the war in Southeast

Asia and maintain substantial numbers of troops elsewhere in the world and still afford to fund all the domestic programmes that he and the leadership of the Democratic Party felt were necessary.[19] In order to protect these domestic programmes, or in other words to alter federal spending priorities in their favour, he wanted the Administration to reassess the extent to which its foreign policy could profitably be supported by armed force. This was done in the expectation that many alliance obligations, especially NATO, no longer required the levels of US forces that past conditions and inertia had assigned them. He also wanted political and economic realities of America's alliance relationships to be reflected in US defence policy and in this respect he continued to press that the European allies should carry a proportion of the NATO burden commensurate with their newfound economic strength.

In the pre-reform Congress Mansfield and his opponents had to work through the traditional committees which dealt with foreign and defence policy and the funding associated with them, but this enabled him only to challenge the defence priority rather than to examine that priority within the context of the federal budget as a whole. In the 1966–70 period he relied upon the Democratic Policy Committee, his membership of the Senate Committee on Foreign Relations and his standing as the Majority Leader to promote and win support for his 'sense of the Senate' resolutions. The fact that he never succeeded in winning majority support from Senate Armed Services, the committee most directly responsible for overseeing the Administration's policy on US troop levels in Europe, explains a great deal about his failure to win more widespread support. Indeed, it is interesting that the most bitter criticism of the first resolution was concerned with its sponsorship by a Party committee which had trespassed on the responsibilities of the established legislative committees. Members of the Senate Armed Services Committee acted as the main suppporters of Administration policy on NATO and effectively organised the opposition to Mansfield. In this respect John Stennis, the chairman of Armed Services and a member of the Appropriations Committee, together with John Tower, the ranking Republican on the Armed Services Committe and the chairman of the Republican Policy Committee, were the most effective actors, although Senator Sam Nunn was to emerge as a respected specialist on military issues during the course of the debate.

These Senators sponsored counter-resolutions such as that calling for 'substantial and effective combat forces in Europe' co-sponsored by Tower in February 1967, and amendments more moderate than, and designed to undermine support for, those offered by Mansfield. It was in this area that Nunn was to emerge as a considerable Senate tactician. On 25 September 1973 he and Senator Jackson offered an amendment to the Defense Procurement Bill which required the European allies to off-set the balance of payment costs of US troops in Germany. This few some support from Mansfield's more radical amendment of the 26 September to cut by 40% US forces stationed overseas. By early 1974 the German government had agreed to off-set payments in line with the Jackson–Nunn amendment and this reduced support for Mansfield even further. Nunn, in some senses, assumed the mantle of a critic of NATO but with the very limited purpose of attempting to stimulate a European commitment sufficiently strong to enable him and other Administration supporters to defend existing US troop levels in NATO. His report to the Senate Armed Services Committee of April 1974 was critical of the structure of US forces in NATO and called for a cut of 60 000 support personnel, but he emphasised the need to maintain the combat effectiveness of US troops, to reduce the cost of stationing them in Germany and the need for the European allies to do more.[20] In 1974 this was no more than a reiteration of Administration policy.

The Mansfield 'great debate' on US troops in Europe served to illustate both the weakness of the congressional procedures for examining the extended *strategic* implications of military decisions, and the inability of Congress to examine the relative priority of major spending programmes. It also showed the ability of the established legislative committees to fend-off challenges to policies that fell within their jurisdiction. The fact that Mansfield had to work through the established and fragmented committee system meant that he could not tackle the defence/welfare priority issue directly or effectively. The fact that he had to pursue his campaign after 1971 by attempting to amend the Bills of powerful legislative committees that jealously guarded their jurisdiction meant that support for his proposals could never be considered in isolation from the emotive question of 'committee turf'. Clearly many Senators supported the counter-resolutions and amendments of Stennis, Tower and Nunn as much to support the priorities of the committee system as to defend the Executive's NATO policy.

The more lasting contribution of Mansfield's campaign is not to be found in America's relationship with the European allies in NATO, but rather in the part that it played in the congressional challenge to

Nixon's Imperial Presidency and in the attempt to restore to Congress the power to defend its priorities for public spending. Mansfield believed that US military spending overseas had come to distort Presidential spending priorities to the detriment of domestic programmes, and in this he spoke for most Democrats and many northern Republicans in Congress. He had been critical of the President during his first term for his lack of responsiveness to these sentiments, but was even more concerned after Nixon's re-election that the President was flouting the constitutional powers of Congress and ignoring the political mandate of the Democratic majorities in both Houses.[21]

At the beginning of 1973 Nixon seemed determined to provoke conflict by announcing impoundments[22] of over $11 billion on the funds voted by Congress for welfare programmes in FY 1973, and by announcing his intention to place a limit on the FY 1974 federal budget largely by holding down welfare spending. This overturned a clearly expressed congressional priority for welfare and ensured that the Mansfield resolution became a central part of the political battle over national priorities and an important agency in mobilising support behind the move to reform the congressional budget system. Because Mansfield's 1973 resolution was part of this more general process it was drafted with the assistance of the Democratic Policy Committee and was considered by the Senate Democratic caucus, and Mansfield was also involved in discussions with the chairman of the Senate Appropriations Committee and prominent members of the Senate Committees on Armed Services and Foreign Relations as well as the Director of the Office of Management and Budget and the Speaker of the House of Representatives.[23] Despite all this, the combined opposition of the Administration and the Senate Armed Services Committee was sufficient to defeat him.

Mansfield's campaign was overshadowed in late 1973 and early 1974 by the revelations of the Watergate affair, and by 1974 the new Budget process was in place and offered the prospect of examining the President's budget more comprehensively than in the past, and of setting congressional spending priorities in a more direct way than that attempted by Mansfield. It is perhaps ironic that at just the time that the new budget system offered Congress the opportunity to examine the defence priority more fully than in the past, public and congressional pressure began to shift in favour of an expanded defence role. The pressure for increased defence spending was later to become so strong that few Congressmen were prepared to undertake more than a cursory examination of the need for it. Senator Muskie, the Chairman of the Senate Budget Commitee, noted how in the three months after the invasion of Afghanistan there were proposals to add $440 billion to the $805 billion five year defence programme approved by Congress only two months before the invasion. In reply to a defence witness in the same hearing who said 'Senator, I might just say that I may be one of the few testifying before you who have offered you savings', Muskie replied 'But you see, you are not a Senator responding to constituents.'[24]

CONGRESS AND THE MANPOWER ISSUE IN THE REFORMED CONGRESS

The very limited powers of the Budget Committees and the deference that their chairmen paid to the interests of the established committees[25] meant that the consideration of NATO manpower and funding levels would remain in the hands of the Armed Services and Appropriates Committees repectively, whilst the House Foreign Affairs and the Senate Foreign Relations committees would continue to take the major responsibility for examining America's foreign policy in respect of Europe. However, the Budget Committees were expected '. . . to perform new fiscal policy and priority-setting functions which, properly executed, will enable other committees to perform their tasks with greater focus and effect'.[26]

The Senate Budget Committee attempted to encourage the traditional committees to give greater focus to priority-setting in the oversight of manpower issues and to examine the *strategic* implications of manpower decisions, but the attempt was both indirect and didactic. The House Committee was rather less ambitious and tended to conduct *managerial studies*, such as that on *Defense Manpower and the ALL-Volunteer Force*,[27] which complemented rather than examined the work of the authorisations and appropriated committees. In this sense the House Budget Committee tended to act as a congressional publicist for defence problems that might have budgetary consequence, but it rarely aspired to 'educate' the established committees about the strategic implication of their work as did its Senate counterpart with the assistance of the CBO.

Indeed the first attempt to set manpower in a broader policy context than was usual was taken on the initiative of the CBO itself. In January 1977 at the beginning of the Carter Presidency it published the first of a series of six Budget Issue Papers on the general purpose forces which set out to identify the

> most significant assumptions underlying current planning of the general purpose forces, to discuss the match between those assumptions and the current or projected forces, and to suggest what might change in defence programmes if somewhat different planning assumptions were adopted.[28]

The timing was intended to assist Congress in its consideration of Carter's FY 1978 budget, the defence section of which placed a strong emphasis on reinforcing the general purpose forces and America's NATO commitment. The CBO examined the DoD's 'one and a half war' scenario for general purpose forces but noted that it was difficult to see in the current US military posture any reflection of a coherent view of foreign policy objectives and threats to those objectives.[29] However, it identified from the Annual Defense Department Report for FY 1977 the planning assumptions for the one war. That report states,

> Since the centerpiece of our strategic concept is to have the ability, in conjunction with our allies, to manage one major contingency, we believe that the most prudent way to arrive at the specific requirement for general purpose forces is to consider what we would need to establish and maintain a forward defence in Central Europe.[30]

However, there appeared to be a serious mismatch between the DoD's estimation of the requirements of forward defence on the central front and the structure and deployment of the general purpose forces and the plans for their modernisation.

The combination of the intention to defend NATO's central front as far east as possible and the assessment that Warsaw Pact doctrine and structure was designed for rapid offence using 'blitzkrieg' tactics, made the initial stage of any conventional war in Europe particularly critical. In order to minimise the loss of NATO territory against the Warsaw Pact it would be necessary to maintain high levels of ready forces in Germany with substantial stocks of military consumables. Yet, despite the facts that the primary role of the Army is to fight a land war in Europe and that nearly all army forces are justified by the DoD's NATO scenario, only five of America's 16 divisions were stationed in Germany and only two more divisions could be airlifted to Europe before the fighting began, provided that the DoD assumption of several weeks 'political warning' time of a Warsaw Pact attack held good. Even then pre-positioned stocks for them would not be at required levels until the end of FY 1979. The CBO also noted that,

> Although recent DoD reports have pointed out the importance of the initial battle in Europe, much of the present Department of Defense force expansion and modernisation program is aimed at improving US military forces' capability to fight the longer war. Expansion of the Army from 13 to 16 active divisions might not improve its contribution to early NATO defence, and might even reduce it.[31]

Much the same conclusion could be drawn about the planned conversion of two army infantry divisions to armoured or mechanised divisions because their equipment would have to be moved to Europe by sea and would not arrive in time to affect the early stages of the war. Planned naval and tactical air force improvements also contributed more to a sustained European war than to its initial stages. Only the DoD's planned modernisation of strategic mobility capability and the decision to make good shortfalls in US military stocks pre-positioned in Europe – collectively a small part of the general purpose forces modernisation programme – reflected its concern with the initial phases of a war in central Europe.

The six Issue Papers also examined current theatre nuclear deterrence doctrine which, it contended, had been rendered questionable by the growth of Soviet theatre nuclear forces. It was not at all certain that a fire break between conventional and nuclear war could be maintained in such circumstances, and in any event the US use of nuclear weapons to counter massive Soviet conventional forces could spark a nuclear response so massive that 'it might lead to a situation considerably less favourable to US interests than loss of the battle on the European mainland'.[32] The very likelihood of a Warsaw Pact attack on NATO was questioned given the current level of US troops in Europe and the probability of escalation to nuclear war. Indeed, as the CBO pointed out, the Europeans had never taken the idea of a conventional response for NATO seriously and had acquired neither the active forces nor the war reserves to support it, and there was nothing that the US could do alone in its sectors of the central front to make a NATO conventional response credible. In such circumstances it was prudent for Congress to look at competing needs for national resources that were more pressing than the need for a substantial increase in US military capability for Europe.[33]

There is no evidence that the Armed Services Committees or the Foreign Affairs and Foreign Relations Committees took this council of prudence into account; certainly there are no references to the Issue Papers in the hearings of these committees, and the FY 1978 defence budget approved by Congress founded virtually all the general purpose forces modernisation programme despite the fact that it could not contribute in any substantial way to the DoD's NATO scenario which was supposed to be the basis of military planning. If nothing else the CBO studies served to highlight both the irrelevance and vacuity of the policy accounting rendered by the DoD to congressional committees, and the willingness of those committees and Congress to accept it uncritically. It is difficult to avoid the conclusion that at best the DoD planning assumptions were rationalisations for force structures and weapons programmes that reflected the remorseless inevitability of the weapons procurement process and the effect of Armed Service and special interest lobbying more than they did a realistic assessment of the contribution that the US could best make to NATO defence.

From December 1977, the CBO published another series of Issue papers to analyse the *strategic* policy implications of the US military role in NATO, but this time at the request of the Senate Budget Committee. This reflected the very strong NATO orientation of President Carter's FY 1979 defence budget[34] and the fact that the NATO commitment determined most of the defence budget which in turn determined the scope for growth or the necessity of contraction in the non-defence programmes of the federal budget as a whole; issues that would be vital in the Senate Budget Committee's work for the First Concurrent Resolution in FY 1979.[35] The Issue Papers took up the task of educating Congress and its committees rather more directly than before by examining in detail the assumptions and perceptions that underpin the DoD's requests for funds. It observed that,

> For more than two decades, perceptions of the military balance between NATO and the Warsaw Pact have been a major determinant of US force requirements and have affected Congressional debate and action on the defense budget. The

Congress is presented an official assessment of the military balance each year by the Secretary of Defense, intended in part to justify the department's funding requests.[36]

However, perceptions of that balance can vary considerably because they are based less upon actual information than on a number of political and military assumptions and judgement many of which are implicit. This gives the DoD great scope in the estimation of the state of the balance and, therefore, equal scope both in the presentation to Congress of the threat to NATO interests and in the requests for specific forces to meet the threat.

The CBO noted that the assumptions and judgements made by DoD have changed over time so that the official view of the NATO/Warsaw Pact balance 'shifted from pessimism in the 1950s to optimism in the 1960s. In the 1970s it seems to have slipped back toward pessimism'.[37] The pessimism of the 1970s was in part due to the tendency of the DoD to present Congress with 'static bean counts'; that is comparisons of things like crude troops numbers, units and weapons. However, if assessments become more dynamic and move away from gross numbers of troops and weapons and take into account interactions, constraints and capabilities the more they become optimistic for NATO. This was a veiled invitation for Congress and its committees to be less credulous in its treatment of the DoD's assessment of the NATO/Warsaw Pact balance and to look more closely at the assumptions and political judgements that informed it. The advisability of discounting French troops and of assuming Warsaw Pact unity in a central front war were elements of the DoD balance assessment that Congress was encouraged to look at most closely.

A more fundamental reservation about DoD planning assumptions was that they were based almost exclusively on the central front balance of force which meant that planning was focused on the Warsaw Pact rather than on NATO. However, the report pointed out that it is equally important to make an assessment of European allied forces for they comprise the greater part of NATO ground forces and have responsibility for the most vulnerable parts of the central front. It is the Europeans' military capability that determines not only the strength of NATO, but also the conditions under which US forces would fight and the effectiveness of further improvement in American forces. Yet the known strengths and weaknesses of the European allies had 'been given much more limited consideration in structuring US forces than have the less certain attributes of a Warsaw Pact attack',[38] nor had official defence planning addressed the question of what role the US forces could be play in an alliance in which the allied armies differ in overall military capability and have responsibility for the defence of different sectors of the central front. The CBO study observed that 'For NATO as a whole, the most important improvements would be those that would bring Western European forces to equivalent capabilities with US forces'.[39]

Nevertheless, the Administration was continuing with its modernisation programme which included equipment for the three new army divisions and the replacement of current weapons inventories. In all the Administration's FY 1979 procurement programme for major items of equipment required a 16% real increase over expenditures for FY 1979, including provision for pre-positioning in Europe the equipment for three additional US divisions.[40] The forces provided could contribute to NATO defence in at least three ways; the defence of the US sector of the central front, the provisions of mobile assets in the US sector that could be used to assist allies in other sectors, and forces stationed in the United States for the reinforcement of NATO. Congress was encouraged to be more discriminating that the DoD in funding the modernisation programme by considering which of these roles could most profitably be developed to take account of NATO's structure and the difference between US and Western European military capabilities. In particular it emphasised the importance of pre-positioned equipment in Europe as one of the few ways in which the US could unilaterally improve NATO's military capability.

Once again there is very little in the proceedings of the authorisations and the appropriations committees for FY 1979 to suggest that the CBO Issue Papers had had much effect. The Armed Services Committees in particular continued to be uncritical of the DoD's emphasis on the NATO/Warsaw Pact balance and of the fact that it was a pessimistic 'static bean count' which contained many questionable assumptions. The Administration's rather indiscriminate programme of NATO modernisation was dealt with in essence as a line by line authorisation of separate weapons systems and manpower levels.[41] However, the Papers did assist in the promotion of a growing congressional awareness of the importance of the military capability of the Western European allies and to an understanding that US force improvements would be of little value unless accompanied by corresponding improvements in their European capability. If the United States attempted to improve

NATO's military capability alone it would be militarily futile and politically dangerous because the Europeans would do even less.

The work of the CBO, and the publicity that the Senate Budget Committee gave to its work, did much to ensure congressional support for the Administration's initiation of the NATO 'Long Term Defence Programme' which committed all members to increase their NATO related defence expenditure by three percent annually. This policy made considerable sense in FY 1979 by seeking balanced and complementary improvements in all NATO forces and, in a period when increases in the US defence budget were still moderate, placed only minor strains on trans-Atlantic relationships and allied budgets. However, improvements in Western European military capability was seen by Congress, and indeed the Administration, as no longer just a question of equity, as in Mansfield's day, but also of the effectiveness and security of US forces in Europe. NATO was America's front line of defence against the Soviet threat and it depended virtually on the contribution of the European allies. Thereafter, any US perception of an increased Soviet threat was to be accompanied by even more insistent Congressional and Administration demands that the Europeans match the defence spending of the United States. In this respect the work of the CBO did much to enable Congress to recognise the links between US foreign and defence policy which the fragmentation of the congressional committee system had disguised.

In FY 1980, the Senate Budget Committee again sponsored CBO studies of NATO manpower issues,[42] but there was a marked change in their character. The issues that the studies addressed were concerned with reinforcing a conventional war in Europe and emphasised pre-positioned (POMCUS) material and strategic airlift which had been identified by the DoD as the key elements of the FY 1980 defence posture. However, the studies did not in any sense attempt to question the need for additional POMCUS supplies or an expansion of the strategic airlift capability, nor did they examine the DoD's estimate of the NATO/Warsaw Pact military balance even though it was a clear example of the kind of 'static bean count' that the CBO has warned the Congress to treat with scepticism in earlier studies. The POMCUS study simply accepted the DoD's contention that the balance required more NATO forces, or quicker US reinforcements, or both[43] and simply examined the budgetary implications of two alternatives to the DoD's method of provision. It also accepted as the justification for improved reinforcement capability the contention that 'the alliance cannot be confident of its ability to conduct a conventional defense of Europe',[44] but did not see fit to repeat its scepticism[45] about the DoD's NATO war scenario assumption that a war in central Europe could be kept at the conventional level. Had this assumption not been accepted by Congress, as it was not accepted by many European legislatures, the need for DoD's entire POMCUS and strategic airlift programmes would have been questionable.

These Issue Papers simply laid before Congress and its committees slightly more and slightly less expensive alternatives to the DoD's programme, but the Armed Services Committees spent their time examining only the Administration's request which they accepted almost without reservation, and the Senate Budget Committee endorsed it as part of the defence request forwarded to it by the Armed Services Committee. There was no attempt to encourage Congress to examine the assumptions and judgements that support the request, and this probably reflected the sensitivity of the Senate Budget Committee and the CBO to the growing 'hawkishness' of the Senate as it struggled with the ratification of the SALT II Treaty. These studies were a reflection of the fact that the Senate was in no mood to question the need for an increase in the defence budget, and if the defence budget were to be expanded it was almost inevitable, given the size and importance of the NATO element of the budget, that some of those resources should be allocated to European oriented forces.[46]

The almost total failure of the Budget Committees and the CBO to get the authorisations and appropriations committees to exercise the priority setting function and to examine the strategic implications of defence decisions in the post-Afghanistan FY 1981 budget cycle has been dealt with in Chapter 3, and a similar failure has been evident in each of the budget cycles of the first Reagan Administration. For example, a CBO report to assist Congress in its consideration of an army modernisation programme priced at $37.6 billion over the five year period 1983–87[47] accepted without reservation DoD assumptions about defensive/offensive force ratios on the central front, and its assessment of the effects of modernisation on those ratios. It endorsed the contention that Warsaw Pact modernisation meant that the $37.6 billion programme could be expected only to maintain the current adverse central front balance, but repeated none of its early scepticism about DoD assumptions – that it might be impossible to keep a central European war conventional, that static force comparisons of the central front are likely to be unduely pessimistic, that the Warsaw Pact might not maintain its political unity in the opening phases of a war – that characterised the reports of the CBO in its more didactic phase. It even failed to encourage Congress to ponder the problems of transporting to Europe the equipment that the modernisation programme provided. The 5096 M1 tanks, 3897 M2 Fighting Vehicles, 221 Multiple Launch Rocket Systems, 435 Apache helicopters and 568 DIVAD guns in the programme far exceeded the current and anticipated US life capability and, indeed, the European 'reception' capacity.[48] They also seemed to exceed the training needs of the army. This uncritical review of the budgetary implication of the army modernisation programme was typical of the period and again reflected the CBO's recognition that the Reagan Administration and the public placed a high priority on defence and that Congress was unlikely to make major cuts in the defence budget. The report had been commissioned by the defence subcommittee of the House Appropriations Committee and this too was likely to make the CBO less critical of the Administration's defence request than in the past.

CONCLUSIONS

The reform of the budget system made only indirect changes to the process by which Congress considered issues like manpower levels in Europe. The Armed Services Committees retained the major responsibility for the review and oversight of manpower policy and funding, and the Budget Committees were able to review the work of these committees only in general terms. The attempt to encourage Congress to examine the Administration's manpower policies in a broader *strategic* context was made by the CBO, often at the invitation of the Senate Budget Committee. In the mid-1970s the CBO reports on this issue provided Congress with a number of insights into DoD force planning scenarios which demonstrated that current force structures and modernisations did not fit the scenarios, or that the force structures and levels suggested and justified by the scenarios were questionable. As the momentum of public and congressional opinion gathered in favour of increased defence spending so the work of the CBO became more reflective of DoD policies. At precisely the time that congressional committees *should* have been subjecting the NATO manpower policies to closer scrutiny the work of the CBO not only failed to assist such a scrutiny but also became more supportive of those policies.

Irrespective of the work of the Budget Committees and the CBO, the consideration of NATO manpower levels continued to be carried out by the same committees and in the same manner as before the reform. The Budget Committees were able to provide Congress with the opportunity to examine the defence priority against other public spending programmes only in the most superficial way, and it was completely unable to influence directly the assessment of manpower policy in the established committees. The more critical and didactic the report the less likely it was to hae been requested and used by these committees. Only when the work of the CBO became supportive of the Administration's defence programmes did any of the established committees request its assistance. As in Mansfield's day the opportunity for Congress to conduct a 'grand debate' on NATO manpower issues is not provided by any of the committees or by the CBO, but by individual Senators using the same methods and tactics as Mansfield. Indeed there has been a revival of the demand to reduce the level of US troops in Europe, this time led by Senator Sam Nunn who, as recently as June 1984, introduced legislation to cut US troops levels in NATO by 90 000 unless the Europeans honoured their commitment to increase defence spending by 3% per annum.[49] In essence the consideration of manpower issues today remains every bit as much the preserve of the traditional committees as it did in the pre-reform Congress.

NOTES

1. See Chapter 4, pp. 26–40 for Budget Committee action on the FY 1981 defence budget request.
2. *Strengthening NATO: POMCUS and other Approaches* (Washington: CBO, February 1979) p. 1.
3. *Rapid Deployment Forces: Policy and Budgetary Implications* (Washington: CBO, February 1973) p. 20.
4. US House Budget Committee, *Defense Manpower and the All-Volunteer Force*, Hearings, 95th Cong., 1st Session, July 1977 (Washington: US Govt Printing Office, 1977) p. 1.
5. Senator Tower, *Congressional Record*, 23 November 1971, p. S19494.
6. Stanley R. Sloan, *European Security, American Interests, and Alternatives to NATO*, (Congressional Research Service Report JX 4005 C, Washington, January 1978), see pp. 60–6 for an examination of US interests in NATO.

7. Center for Defence Information, *US Military Force – 1980: An Evaluation* (Washington: CDI, 1980) pp. 40 and 45.
8. General Accounting Office report noted in the *Royal United Services Institute for Defence Studies*, New Sheet No. 43, August 1984, p. 1.
9. *Assessing the NATO/Warsaw Pact Military Balance* (Washington: CBO, December 1977) p. iii.
10. See *Defence Spending and the Economy* (Washington: CBO, February 1983), *passim.*
11. See *Assignment of Ground Forces of the United States to Duty in the European Area*, Hearings, 82nd Cong., 1st Session, February 1951, (Washington: US Govt. Printing Office, 1951), and also Edward T. Lampson, *The United States and NATO: Commitments, Problems, and Prospects*, Washington: Congressional Research Service, July 1972) pp. 19–32.
12. Ibid., p. 21.
13. Phil Williams, in various works which have been of great value in the preparation of this part of the chapter, has divided the Mansfield debate into more detailed sections than this. However, the simple division used here effectively highlights the different congressional tactics that were employed by Mansfield and his supporters.
14. See Lampson, op. cit., Appendix F which lists all the Senate resolutions and amendments relation to US troops in Europe from 1966–71.
15. See the Hearings of the Joint Subcommittee of the Committees on Foreign Relations and Armed Services, 90th Cong., 1st Session, April 1967 (Washington: US Govt. Printing Office, 1967) *passim.*
16. See William C. Cromwell, *The Eurogroup and NATO*, (Foreign Policy Research Institute, Philadelphia, Pennsylvania), and also *The Eurogroup* (Brussels: NATO Information Service) various editions.
17. HR. 1173, 18 November 1971.
18. This point is dealt with by Phil Williams in 'The Senate and US Troops in Europe: the 1973 Debate', (paper delivered to the Political Studies Association, April 1981).
19. See Lampson op. cit., and Mike Mansfield, *International Responsibilities: Reappraisal and Reapportionment* (University of Akansas, March 1968) *passim*.
20. Senator Nunn's report *Policy, Troops and the NATO Alliance* was designed to support the Administration's NATO policies and at the same time to indicate to the European allies that there was a price to pay for continued congressional support for existing troop levels in Europe.
21. See Williams op. cit., pp. 14–15.
22. See Chapter 4, pp. 14–15 and Allen Schick, *The Impoundment Control Act of 1974: Legislative History and Implimentation* (Washington: Congressional Research Service, 1976), especially pp. 3–4.
23. These meetings are documented in the *Mansfield Collection*, (held at the University of Montana) and are assessed in Williams, op. cit., pp. 18–19.
24. US Senate, Committee on the Budget, *First Concurrent Resolution on the Budget – Fiscal Year 1981*, Hearings, 96th Congress, 2nd Session, March 1980 (Washington: US Govt. Printing Office, 1980) pp. 352 and 355.

25. See the authors' 'Congressional Reform of Budgetary Decisions', *The Parliamentarian*, vol. LXIV, no. 2, April 1983.
26. George Gross, 'The Congressional Budget and Impoundment Control Act of 1974: a General Explanation', (House Budget Committee, Washington, 1975) p. 6.
27. For full reference see note 4 above.
28. *Planning US General Purpose Forces: Overview* (Washington: CBO, January 1977) p. iii.
29. Ibid., p. 2.
30. Donald H. Rumsfeld, *Report to the Congress on the Fiscal Year 1977 Budget and its Implications for the Fiscal Year 1978 Authorisations Request and the Fiscal Year 1977–81 Defence Programs*, 27 January 1976) p. 116.
31. *Planning US General Purpose Forces*, op. cit., p. 39, and also *US Army Forces Design: Alternatives for Fiscal Years 1977–1981*, (CBO Staff Working Paper, July 16, 1976) *passim*.
32. *Planning US General Purpose Forces*, op. cit., p. xiv, and see also *The Theater Nuclear Forces*, (Washington, CBO, 1977) *passim*.
33. Ibid., pp. 46–7.
34. The Carter Administration's defence policy *statements* gave great emphasis to NATO, but this was not reflected in his defence *spending* despite the 'NATO budget' tag that was attached to his first three military budgets. In fact the big increases in spending were for nuclear weapons the funding of which rose 42% between FY 1979 and FY 1981.
35. *Assessing the NATO/Warsaw Pact Military Balance*, op. cit., p. iii.
36. Ibid., p. 1.
37. Ibid., p. xv.
38. *US Air and Ground Conventional Forces for NATO: Overview* (Washington: CBO, January 1978) p. 3.
39. Ibid., p. 1.
40. see *Strengthening NATO*, op. cit.
41. US Senate, Committee on Armed Services, *Department of Defense Authorisation for Appropriations for Fiscal Year 1979*, Hearings, 95th Congress, 2nd Session, March/April 1978 (Washington: US Govt. Printing Office, 1978), US House, Committee on Armed Services, *Department of Defence Authorization for Appropriations for Fiscal Year 1979*, Hearings, 96th Congress, 1st Session, January 1979 (Washington: US Govt. Printing Office, 1979).
42. See *US Airlift Forces: Enhansement Alternatives for NATO and Non-NATO Contingencies*, (Washington: CBO, April 1979) and *Strengthening NATO*, op. cit.
43. Ibid., p. xviii.
44. Ibid., p. 47.
45. See in particular Chapter III, 'How to Make the Balance Look Good/Bad', *Assessing the NATO/Warsaw Pact Balance*, op. cit., and also Stanley R. Slone, *Some Perspectives on the NATO/Warsaw Pact Balance*, (Washington: Congressional Research Service, April 1976). These and other reports make the point that the assumptions used by the DoD are very pessimistic and are likely to generate a demand for very

high levels of troops, but there is no evidence that any member of either Armed Services Committee attempted to examine or call into question these assumptions.

46. Interview with John Tilson of the Senate Budget Committee Staff, April 1982.
47. *Army Ground Combat Modernisation for the 1980s: Potential Cost and Effects for NATO* (Washington: CBO, November 1982) *passim*.
48. The reception capacity is determined by the number of ports and airports that are likely to remain operational during the course of a conventional war and also upon the capacity of the European road and rail infrastructure.
49. See Phil Williams, *US Troops in Europe* (London: Routledge & Kegan Paul, 1984) p. 2.

8 Parliamentary Reform and Defence Policy: BAOR and the Manpower Issue

Despite the hopes built into the 1970s reforms DEASC did not come to grips with the fundamentals of defence. This was revealed in the procurement issue, but it was also indicated over manpower as well. Instead of taking issue with government policy over force levels and their balance with conventional and nuclear weapons DEASC concentrated, instead, on value for money/efficiency and audit concerns. Despite this DEASC did have more impact than the old Estimates Committee which it replaced. In particular, it did have a fairly influential role on the issue of the restructuring of BAOR and the organisation of the reserves and reinforcements. Overall, however, DEASC did not achieve all that it might have due to its willingness to eschew consideration of crucial policy questions. To understand this we must first understand the issues which DEASC might have aired over British manpower and force levels.

THE ROLE OF BAOR AND BRITISH PROBLEMS WITH MANPOWER SINCE 1945

It has generally been the case in Britain, given its historic antipathy to conscript armies, that one major problem facing the armed forces has been the search for an adequate number of recruits willing to volunteer for the Services. But since 1945, due to Britain's declining world and economic roles, this perennial problem of a *shortfall* in recruitment has been linked with a difficulty in *financing the cost* of manpower as living standards have risen in society generally. Indeed in recent years the two problems have been seen as inter-dependent:

low wages and poor service conditions are seen as an effective barrier to the recruitment of sufficient troops to meet even the reduced manpower targets of the 1960s, 1970s and 1980s.[1] These two problems have not, however, had equal importance in the decades which followed 1945. Until the 1960s *cost* rather than *shortfall* was the major issue; it is only since the 1960s that there has been a fusion of these two problems.

Britain did not return to an all-volunteer army until 1962/63 and this meant that recruitment to the armed forces was not a major difficulty in the period between 1945 and 1960. Indeed, while it was true that there were difficulties in finding adequate recruits after 1948, the problem in this immediate post-war period was not recruitment but demobilisation as the Labour government attempted to shift something like 4½ million people out of the armed services into civilian life.[2] The major problem after this was obviously financing both the cost of demobilisation and the cost of the retention of a conscript army. An army which was substantially increased after 1950 during the period of Korean rearmament, when the numbers in the Services were targeted to rise from around 690 000 to 875 000 (of which 50% were to be conscripts).[3] Obviously the problem for the armed forces, of which the army bore the largest burden, was the need to retain a large training establishment and continually recruit manpower which was not always enthusiastic about service and which, once trained, tended to leave. The armed forces obviously felt this created problems of inefficiency and a weakness in esprit and fighting morale, but they clearly needed the manpower given the numerous commitments into which Britain had entered in this period of rapid decolonisation. British armed forces experienced active service in Malaysia, Palestine, Singapore, Hong Kong, Kenya, Cyprus, Aden, Jordan, Lebanon and Western Europe, to mention just a few of the locations where post-war difficulties were experienced.

If manpower in quantitative rather than in qualitative terms was not an issue in the 1950s then financing this defence establishment was. It soon became apparent with the 1952 Global Strategy White Paper that the Conservative governments under Churchill, Eden and Macmillan (notwithstanding the temporary aberration of Suez) had to look for ways in which to reduce the defence burden on the national economy.[4] The solution which was agreed upon, and which was finally laid out in the 1957 Defence White Paper, was to rely on nuclear weapons to maintain as many existing foreign and defence policy commitments, while allowing for a reduction in conventional force structures and defence costs on the economy. There were obviously a number of broad strands which contributed to this policy decision: the perception that conscription was politically unpopular and economically wasteful in keeping men out of export and high technology industries; the antipathy within the services to conscription due to its erosion of morale and the need to maintain a costly and wastefully large training establishment; and, the perception that Britain would no longer require a large conventional force to garrison its colonies because it had decided upon a gradual retreat from Empire. As a consequence conscription was set to end by 1960 and an all volunteer army was to be created. In effect this White Paper was the beginning of the process of global retrenchment which was to see Britain committed mainly to a NATO role in the 1970s and 1980s.

By the early 1960s, then, British armed forces were being drastically reduced in manpower – falling from the 875 000 of Korea to approximately 350 000 by the early 1970s.[5] But as these measures were introduced they also shifted the problems facing manpower from cost alone to those of shortfall in recruitment and service pay and conditions. These twin problems were to become the themes of manpower concerns in the 1960s and 1970s. Indeed it was not cost but the shortfall in manpower recruitment which was to emerge in the 1960s as an important constraint on defence planning.[6] It became apparent to the Conservatives that it would be politically damaging to return to conscription to solve the shortfall problem in the early 1960s. Labour concurred with this view even though it became apparent that there was an over-reliance on recruitment from only a few regional areas with high unemployment (like Lancashire and Central Scotland) and a worrying tendency for officers to come from a relatively narrow socio-economic background.[7]

These problems helped to explain why there was, for instance, an actual shortfall of 10 000 men in 1968.[8] The government was, however, unwilling to countenance radical reforms and concentrated instead on two fronts. Firstly, the government followed the logic of the 1958 Grigg Committee which had studied the problems of recruitment, pay and conditions in the Services.[9] Grigg recognised that there was a problem of shortfall and argued that the Services would have to buy recruits, although it was agreed the soldier should not be overpaid because this might lead to the wrong type of recruit who was more concerned with mercenary pay than service. This recruitment policy was accepted by the governments of the day and three broad lines of approach were adopted. First of all, many former dirty and boring Service occupations were civilianised (driving and cleaning) to encourage the notion of a professional fighting role. Secondly, attempts were made (with some success as one third of recruits were taken in from this method) to catch potential recruits at early age by introducing a Junior Leader entry scheme for 15 to 17 year olds. Finally, better and more flexible conditions of service were adopted. The measures introduced under this heading included the biennial reviews of pay recommended by Grigg (later given an annual basis by the National Board for Prices and Incomes in 1967); the adoption of short-servce commissions and basis enlistments (3 to 5 years as well as more traditional 9 to 22 year contracts); recruitment of graduates and University secondments to stimulate the technically proficient entrant which the armed forces required to run and operate a modern army; and, major improvements in social welfare and accommodation for servicemen and their families.[10] It is however doubtful if these changes had a profound effect on recruitment because, as the table below indicates, there was still a shortfall in recruitment well into the 1970s:

TABLE 8.1 *Tri-Service recruiting results*

FY	*Required male* entrants	*Numbers* obtained	*Percentage* achieved
1963/64	45 000	35 694[a]	79.3
1964/65	47 000	42 990[b]	91.4
1965/66	45 500	37 200	81.7
1966/67	40 700	39 500	97.0
1967/68	43 000	31 900	74.1
1968/69	38 000	28 100	73.9
1969/70	46 100	34 300	74.4
1970/71	49 100	38 900	79.2
1971/72	46 300	46 493	100
1972/73	43 000[c]	39 120	90.7
1973/74	43 000[c]	25 800	60.0
1974/75	43 000[c]	34 960	81.3

a represents CY 1963.
b represents CY 1964.
c represents a minimum annual requirement, which does not includes shortfalls from previous years; *Statements on the Defence Estimates 1971*, Febuary 1971 (Cmnd 4592), p. 31.

SOURCE T. A. Fabyanic, 'Manpower Trends in the British All-Volunteer Army', *Armed Forces and Society*, vol. 2 (August 1976) pp. 555.

The second major reorientation over manpower questions by the governments of the 1960s, and later in the 1970s, was seen in the changed attitude to reserve forces now that there was a reduced number of men in the armed forces and a continuing problem of shortfall in recruitment. During the period of the conscript army the reserves had consisted largely of the Territorial Army, organised on a county basis and responsible for home defence. But in line with cutbacks in the defence establishment in the 1960s these formations were also restructured and slimmed down, and in the 1966/67 period were replaced by a new organisational structure called the Territorial Army and Volunteer Reserve (TAVR).[11] This restructuring was based on a number of new assumptions formulated in line with the shortfall problem and the new strategic doctrines of both massive retaliation and flexible response. Firstly, it was argued that the old home defence role of the TA could be left on a 'care and maintenance' basis and that the new TAVR would be given a much more effective operational war role. Given the assumption that the thin line of regular NATO troops in the front line could be reinforced quickly enough in a period of political conflict before war broke out, it was intended that the new British TAVR would be trained and equipped not for home defence but to be rushed in the NATO Central Front to reinforce the full-time regulars of BAOR. These troops were to make up one-quarter of the British front line fighting strength and would be trained for a front-line war role to supplement existing front-line regular formations. This meant of course a reduction in the number of reserves, the disbanding of the old county territorial units, the assigning of TAVR units to specific regular units and an emphasis on better equipment and training to bring them into line with existing front-line troops. It was an attempt, in other words, to allow Britain to maintain a small force in BAOR, with low recruitment potential, and still ensure the possibility of an adequate fighting force of 130 000 men if war came in Europe.

Unfortunately these measures did not solve Britain's manpower problem. Shortfalls in recruitment continued into the 1970s and after 1973, when Britain's economic performance seriously deteriorated, this problem was exacerbated by the return of a cost constraint into defence management. The problem facing Britain in the early 1970s was that it was faced with a need to re-equip most of its conventional forces, while technological costs were rising above inflation levels. Furthermore rapidly escalating inflation in Britain not only undermined economic performance but also ensured rising demands for pay and welfare expenditure in the defence budget. Thus, ironically, it was becoming necessary to increase pay and conditions substantially merely to keep up recruitments to its inadequate level of the 1960s. This meant that the defence budget was and is squeezed from every direction in the 1970s and 1980s. Unfortunately, declining economic performance also imposed other problems. The deterioration in economic growth contributed to the costs of defence through the fall in the value of sterling relative to the strong German mark which increased the real cost of stationing troops in West Germany (see Table 8:2). This problem was compounded later by the unwillingness of the West German government to continue indefinitely its 'off-set' agreement to fund BAOR. Indeed after extensive and difficult negotiations in the 1970s it was decided that there would be no continuation of the 'off-set' agreement after 1980, which has imposed further burdens on the defence budget.[12] Governments, since the early 1970s, have been forced therefore to countenance further cuts in manpower requirements for front line and reserve units, in an attempt to pare defence spending. This has not always proved an easy or painless exercise. Inherent in everything that Labour and Conservative governments have done in the 1970s and 1980s has been an attempt to maintain NATO commitments with fewer resources. Unfortunately, while this was finally fully accepted in the 1975 Defence White Paper, the cost of maintaining this commitment in an era of declining economic performance and ever increasing costs has not been easy. Even in the 1970s Britain still maintained the second largest defence establishment in NATO despite the fact that it was far from the strongest European country. It is not surprising therefore that in so far as manpower, and in particular Britain's NATO commitments in BAOR are concerned, there was, and continues to be, an attempt to get 'a quart out of a pint pot'.

This policy of over-stretching and over-burdening an inadequate BAOR manpower force level was seen most clearly in the reforms of front-line troops and reserves and reinforcements which were introduced after the 1974 Defence Review. The basic aim of the post 1975 reorganisation of the front-line troops in BAOR was to reduce the size of the army by 15 600, while at the same time maintaining the combat efficiency of the regular troops on the Central Front. In other words this was an exercise in trimming the 'tail' (administrative and logistical support) to preserve the 'teeth'.[13] To this end then the Labour government tried to reduce the number of locally employed

TABLE 8.2 *Foreign exchange costs of UK forces in Germany (including Berlin), 1958/59–77/78*

	Foreign exchange costs £m	*Approximate sterling value of offsets £m* Direct payment	*Military purchases*	*Total*	*Net cost £m*
1958/59	55			12	43
1959/60	52			24	28
1960/61	58			12	46
1961/62	61			—	61
1962/63	68	} =		107	} = 33
1963/64	72				
1964/65	82			175	
1965/66	84	} =			} = 75
1966/67	84				
1967/68	89			50	39
1968/69	94			77	17
1969/70	110	} =		172[f]	} = 70
1970/71	132				
1971/72	172	12.5[c]	22.5	35	137
1972/73	206	13[c]	35	48	158
1973/74	283	17[c]	38	55	228
1974/75	340	21.5[c]	23.5	45	295
1975/76	403	23[c]	17[e]	40	363
1976/77	521[a]				
1977/78	544[b]	62.3[d]			

[a]=Forecast.
[b]=Estimate.
[c]=Approximate value in sterling of DM110 million.
[d]=Approximate value in sterling of DM250 million.
[e]=Includes military equipment purchases up to December 1975 only.
[f]=Including a government to government loan of US$125 million at an annual rate of interest of 3½ per cent and repayable after ten years.

SOURCE L. Freedman, 'Britain's Contributions to NATO; *International Affairs*, vol. 54 (January 1978) pp. 38.

civilians; to divert local consumer spending in BAOR to British goods; to cut down on supply and training resources (i.e. use of fuel oil on tank exercises); to reduce full re-equipment of all 'teeth' elements; and, the reorganisation of logistic support by giving the Royal Ordnance Corps cross-service responsibility for logistics and the Royal Corps of Transport responsibility for most vehicles.[14] The most important change however – and one which indicated the problem of trying to maintain existing commitments by organisational tinkering to save money – was the attempt to cut administrative costs in BAOR by completely abolishing one level of command at the brigade level.[15] Unfortunately, after field trials of the new structure it was discovered that the new divisional commander responsibilities were too complex and this reduced flexibility in the field. It was also realised there was a need for more rather thas less men, due to the new fighting equipment which was to be purchased to increase combat effectiveness. As a result the brigadier level was re-introduced (within a new level of command underneath the division commander level) known as a 'task force' command.[16]

This failure perhaps pinpoints the dilemma facing the BAOR and the government: if there is to be a commitment to an army then there is a level (of around 55 000) which it is difficult to reduce without making a nonsense of the original commitment to station troops on the Central Front. This dilemma has been witnessed in other measures introduced since 1975 which have attempted to reduce expenditure but which have proven problematic to implement. Related to the restructuring of the army in 1975 was a further reorganisation of TAVR which was aimed at reducing numbers while integrating the remaining units ever more firmly within BAOR units. This was achieved by earmarking all TAVR units to specific front-line units and dividing them into three echelon areas in Britain (Eastern, South-Eastern and South-Western) which were related respectively to NATO roles of BAOR reinforcement, SACEUR reinforcement and Home Defence. Unfortunately, if this integration was to be achieved it also required modern re-equipment of the TAVR so that it could fulfil its tasks if called upon to act in the field. This was expensive and required further reforms. In 1977/78, after the publication of the Shapland Report, the TAVR was further reformed; it was renamed the Territorial Army and was given more equipment and better pay and conditions in order to overcome the shortfall in skilled men and the high wastage rates then being experienced.[17] By 1977, despite these reorganisations, it was apparent that combat readiness in NATO was weak and that the shortfall in recruits was undermining Britain's commitment. To overcome these problems and to increase the number of men in the forces by 6 000, while improving pay, social welfare and other conditions within BAOR, the Labour government decided in 1977 to support a 3% increase in defence spending despite cutbacks in other domestic expenditure programmes.[18]

The Conservative governement which entered office in 1979 did not radically alter this programme. On the contrary it speeded up the increase in pay that the Labour government had promised and gave a commitment to the index-linking of service pay at a time when other pay levels in the public sector were being cut. But, even the Conservative governments maintenance of the 3% increase in defence spending and enhanced pay commitments could not escape the dilemma facing all post-war governments. At some point a choice has to be made between various defence commitments as economic performance deteriorates and defence costs rise. This choice was, indeed, made even more difficult because of the Thatcher government's parallel decision to purchase Trident nuclear weapons. The Conservative government had, therefore, to choose in 1981 to trim the naval and maritime side of British forces rather than its nuclear or BAOR roles.[19] This shows clearly that those critics of the 1970s who argued that Britain's weak economic performance would necessitate cuts and moves to specialisation in Britain's defence roles were absolutely correct. It seems clear also that the need to choose between roles will remain in the 1980s if Britain's economic performance does not improve.[20]

Given this brief overview of the major issues involved in the manpower question for Britain, it seems plain that these issues can be differentiated in terms of whether they are of policy importance, or whether they have a more efficiency or audit bias. Given the broad policy changes since 1945 it would seem that if a Parliamentary Committee were to be involved in influencing policy questions then it would have been interested in raising the following types of questions: should the armed forces be manned by all volunteer or conscript or a mix of the two?; are our allies doing enough in their burden sharing in NATO?; is the BAOR really necessary given the concept of 'massive-retaliation'?; are the threat perceptions of Soviet intentions adequate and do they imply the need for BAOR at its present levels?; can Britain afford a large army and all of the commitments it had overseas in the 1950s?; should the British have troops in Northern ireland given the need for them on the Central Front?; should Britain withdraw from the Central Front and specialise on the flanks of NATO or its maritime role?; can we afford BAOR at present force levels given our underlying weak economic performance?; and, is there a case for a New Model Army outside or within NATO? Furthermore, one might expect that a Parliamentary Committee involved in questioning existing policy commitments would be interested in taking up some of the alternative perspectives occasionally discussed in academic and informed circles over the manpower question.[21]

On the other hand there are a range of questions which a legislature might take up which are more centrally related to the efficiency of implementation of existing policy and which do not entail a fundamental questioning of the government's position. These more *managerial* and *audit* questions would include the following in relation to the manpower question: is the government doing enough to increase recruitment?; are the armed forces given the same pay and conditions as their civilian counterparts?; are the front-line and reserve forces adequately trained to do the job that was intended, given the threat which is perceived?; is there sufficient support for BAOR in logistics and men?; are there alternative ways in which the forces might be structured to ensure greater efficiency of readiness?; is transport efficient and adequate to meet all emergencies?; is there a case for trade unions to protect soldiers interests?; are the West Germans paying their share of British costs of maintaining an overseas garrison?; is there evidence of a failure by government to meet commitments entered into and of administrative 'red-tape' or corruption?

As we shall see, while DEASC certainly achieved more than the old Estimates Committee in scrutinising policy and influencing policy decisions, most of the work of these two committees fell within *managerial/audit* concerns. Once again this meant that DEASC failed to live up to the intentions of the more radical reformers who influenced the creation of the Select Committee on Expenditure.

A COMPARISON OF THE ROLE AND IMPACT OF THE ESTIMATES COMMITTEE AND DEASC ON THE MANPOWER QUESTION

Up to 1970 the interest of the British Parliament and its specialised Estimates Committee in the manpower question was almost non-existent. The major issues which Parliament might have raised during this period related to whether or not 'threat' perceptions were adequate; whether Britain should have forces on the Central Front; whether conscription or all-volunteer forces were the correct methods of recruiting for the armed forces; and, whether or not Britain should or should not consider a New Model Army outside NATO entanglements. While these issues were obviously touched upon in Parliamentary debates (particularly at times of ideological party political controversy such as over Korean rearmament and Suez)[22] the Estimates Committee completely failed to raise any of these key issues related to defence manpower. Rather the Estimates Committee concentrated on more *managerial* (value for money) topics such as: *British Expenditure in Germany* (8th Report, 1946/47); *Call-up, Posting and Movement of National Servicemen* (3rd Report, 1952/53); and *Military Expenditure Overseas* (10th Report, 1962/63 and 9th Report, 1963/64).[23]

These studies were unco-ordinated and dealt with such issues as: bottlenecks in conscription and accommodation; medical services; family welfare; and stores accounting issues in BAOR. The Estimates Committee did not consider such problems as the overall balance of forces between European and Colonial involvements; the role of reserves and reinforcements; logistic support, costs of pay and the problem of shortfall in recruitment. Indeed it was not until the Lacey Committee reported to Parliament in 1967 that the whole question of manpower was effectively debated in the legislature.[24] Generally, then, Parliament's scrutiny of the manpower question up to 1970 was piecemeal, ad-hoc and ineffective. It took the reform which created the Select Committee of Expenditure and the Defence and External Affairs Sub-Committee to bring this issue into the limelight for the first time. As we shall see, however, even DEASC eschewed strategic policy concerns, although it did undertake a much more effective and influential managerial and audit role than had been the case before 1970.

DEASC did not institute one or even a series of manpower related reports. Rather, DEASC's concern with the manpower question arose from the study of various related problems in the defence field. The major studies and reports which made conclusions and recommendations pertaining to manpower issues between 1971 and 1979 were then: *Defence* (HC 141, 1971/72); *Review of Previous Defence Recommendations* (HC 167, 1973/74); *Cumulative Effects of Cuts in Defence Expenditure* (HC 254, 1976/77); *British Forces Germany* (HC 472, 1974/75); *Defence* (155, 1975/76); *Reserves and Reinforcements* (HC 393, 1976/77); *Joint Training of Servicemen* (HC 86, 1977); and *British Forces Germany* (HC 563–1 and HC 563–11, 1977/78). Given Britain's shift to accept a mainly NATO–European role by the 1970s much of this work concentrated on British Forces in Germany and its reserves and reinforcements. It was supported by one committee visit to Norway in 1977 and three visits to BAOR in Germany in November 1971, April 1975 and April 1978.

It is clear,therefore, that DEASC was much more active in scrutinising manpower and related areas than the former Estimates Committee had ever been. It was the case, however, that in the same way as the Estimates Committee before it DEASC also chose to eschew any concern with major policy issues and when these issues were touched upon it was in an extremely cursory and tangential manner. Thus DEASC went so far as to argue that while it was unhappy with Reserve and Reinforcement policy in 1977 that:

> While we feel some apprehension about a strategy which is based upon (the assumption that there is adequate time to respond to a sudden Soviet attack and adequate) warning time we do not at this stage think it right to pass critical judgement on its validity without evidence of the sort which we have refrained from seeking in this enquiry.[25]

and,

> We have not thought it part of our brief to go behind the assumptions on which reinforcement plans are based in order to examine their merits; such an enquiry would involve questions of a more far-reaching political and military character than we believe it appropriate at present to raise.[26]

These statements were typical of DEASC's conception of its own role. The limited perspective which it adopted was also illuminated by the decision in 1978 to rely purely on MOD and Service perceptions of the Soviet 'threat' and Warsaw Pact capability. It is hardly surprising that some members returned from West Germany convinced that the Red Army would reach the Rhine within 48 hours of an attack![27] Nor is it surprising, therefore, that (as with other studies and reports) DEASC failed to live up to the expectations of the radical reformers of the late 1960s. They simply lacked any desire to question basic policy assumptions by the government and the Services as to threat perceptions, policy possibilities and future defence and foreign policy requirements. Indeed given this attitude on the part of most members of DEASC it is perhaps somewhat surprising that the committee actually did take issue with government policy over the reinforcement of the front-line. In the 1977 report on *Reserves and Reinforcements* the committee expressed concern that, because the government did not have a second-tier policy for mobilising conscription after the first wave of reserves and reinforcements had been sent to assist BAOR, the possibility of an early use of tactical nuclear weapons would be inevitable. This reliance on a 'trip-wire role' for BAOR was seen as undesirable. [28] Generally speaking for DEASC policy was not a major concern. This view was reinforced by the perceptions of the committee's specialist advisers about what it was possible for DEASC to achieve.[29] Their view was basically that the committee should be concerned with whether government policy could be implemented effectively and efficiently. In this way DEASC's activities on manpower tended to fall within two broad areas: DEASC assessed whether existing force levels and structures were able to fulfil the tasks that were allocated to them and within existing expenditure levels; and, secondly, DEASC concerned itself with the strains and stresses imposed upon overstretched manpower in the armed services from a social welfare perspective. As we concluded in Chapter 4 DEASC tended to have its most lasting impact on social welfare issues and this was particularly true in relation to manpower questions. Nevertheless, for a number of reasons (few of which were centrally related to its own specific competences as a committee) DEASC did record some limited success in reshaping government thinking of the restructuring of the Reserves and Reinforcement and also on increasing the manpower of the Central Front after 1977.

In general, however, DEASC was far superior in this field than the old Estimates Committee had been. DEASC was active throughout the period in indicating the problem of shortfalls in men for BAOR and the additional strains imposed on morale by regular tours of duty in Northern Ireland.[30] While it was not possible to end this practice, DEASC was instrumental in pressurising government and contributed to the demands from the Services which resulted in the Labour government partially reversing its 1975 cutbacks policy. In 1977/78 6 000 men were allowed to join the Services above original figures laid down[31] – a percentage of these were also specifically earmarked for BAOR duties.[32] DEASC also spent considerable time and effort indicating problems and inefficiencies in the restructuring of British Forces in Germany. In particular DEASC recommended action to locate Harrier 'jump-jets' at airfields closer to the front-line.[33] It called for the return to the army of the brigade level of command abolished after 1975;[34] and decried the over-reliance on the use of reserves and reinforcements.[35] Demands were also made to restore readiness and training by ending restrictions on the number of exercises and the use of fuel oil.[36]Further demands included the idea that the troops should receive MILAN anti-tank weapons from France and Weat Germany;[37] that the standardisation and interoperability of airfields should be enhanced;[38] that strengthening and hardening of existing airfields should continue;[39] that the replacement of civilian storemen by military personnel for security be speeded up whatever the cost;[40] and that low flying exercises in Canada should be increased to enhance readiness.[41] While DEASC did not achieve all that it wished in these areas it did see government accept a number of its recommendations. The most important successes being the decision to move Harrier jets closer to the front-line; the re-introduction of a brigade level of command; the re-equipment with MILAN anti-tank weapons; and the hardening and widening of Gutersloh airfield in West Germany.[42]

It would not be correct, however, to argue that all of these policy decisions were taken as a consequence of DEASC actions. On the contrary only in respect of the movement of Harriers and hardening of airfield defence was DEASC probably instrumental in influencing the government. On other policy decisions like the MILAN re-equipment and the increase in manpower the government was already under serious pressure from the Services and the MOD to act. What is more revealing perhaps is the fact that *most* of DEASC's recommendations were not accepted. This conclusion is particularly true also of recommendations which were made about cutting defence costs by encouraging moves to enhanced joint training of the Services. These recommendation and the report which DEASC called for were ignored by the MOD.[43] The reason for this ignominious failure was clearly because with this recommendation DEASC was acting on its own initiative and was actually recommending something which the individual Services did not really relish. The failure of DEASC in these circumstances was therefore wholly to be expected.

DEASC did however have one notable impact in this period on the issue of *Reserves and Reinforcements*. This unfortunately had little to do with MP initiative at all. The government did accept a number of DEASC recommendations. The most notable of these being the decisions to assign all reserves (and in particular RAF reservists) particular functions; to increase recruitment to transport roles in the reserves; to solve the icing problems of the Wessex helicopters on the Northern Flank; to improve regular contacts with the Post Office over call-up procedures; to ensure that TAVR units obtained training with up-to-date equipment which they would be called upon to use in the field; and to increase TAVR bounties to overcome shortfall and wastage rates.[44] Indeed the thoroughness of this study was seen in the impact it had in MOD where it led to the creation of an MOD study of these issues. The Shapland Report which resulted in implementing many of the recommendations put forward from DEASC and led to the closer integration of the Territorial Armty with the forces of BAOR in 1978.[45] Unfortunately, even this limited success was not really DEASC's. Without any doubt this study came about because of the specialist adviser – Brigadier Kenneth Hunt. He was an undoubted expert in this field and he felt that the MOD had not really thought the topic through.[46] If DEASC was not wholly responsible for this major success, it was mainly responsible for changes in social welfare provision for BAOR in the 1970s and 1980s. This was because the single most important characteristic which most members of DEASC shared was their support for the men in the field and a desire to do what they could for these men and women who were serving their country – often in difficult and dangerous conditions. This commitment was shared by both Conservative and Labour members on DEASC and this all-party support contributed to the ability of DEASC to influence MOD and government policy in these fields. The most notable successes for DEASC were the development (after some delay) of an English language television network in BAOR;[47] an improvement in pay, conditions and barracks and accommodation;[48] the rationalisation of voting registration;[49] the development of a standard appeals procedure for those suffering redundancy;[50] the provision of cheap loans for housing for servicemen;[51] an MOD review of shortfalls in nurses, general practitioners, social workers, transport facilities and community centres in BAOR;[52] and the encouragement of language training.[53]

Despite these successes DEASC was not always able to achieve all that it wanted and the MOD was occasionally reprimanded for obstructionism and delay in carrying through recommendations which it had fully accepted as necessary – barracks modernisation and television services were particular cases in point.[54] Clearly, it was not difficult for DEASC to achieve some success in these areas because it was 'pushing at an open door'. This is an important point when trying to draw conclusions about the efficacy of DEASC and whether it could have achieved more than it did. While it is true that DEASC's role was a success when compared with the earlier activities of the Estimates Committee in this area and that its activities certainly extended public and academic knowledge of defence, the limited successes of DEASC over manpower were hardly impressive.

In understanding this failure we must appreciate that DEASC itself chose to limit its own activities and to keep out of major policy issues, and this probably owes something to chairmanship of the committee. But it would not be fair to lay the blame for a lack of positive action only on a chairman coming to the end of his public life. The desire for a non-contentious role was supported by the vast majority of committee members who wanted to have a bipartisan approach to defence. This was made easier due to the fact that most of them were pro-defence, whichever side of the House of Commons they came from. Thus major policy questions which might have raised ideological temperatures in Parliament were eschewed in favour of more manageable and safe efficiency concerns. This indicates one major constraint against an effective policy role for DEASC, but it was not the major limitation on its role. The major limitation on the effectiveness, and one which was fully realised by the members of DEASC and their specialist advisers, remained the fact that the executive in Britain controls information and effective policy decision-making. For this reason DEASC eschewed strategic policy questions. Only on the issue of the Reserves and Reinforcements did Parliament attempt to make policy recommendations, but even here the weakness of parliament's role *vis-à-vis* the executive was indicated time and time again. The government only accepted those recommendations that it wanted to and these tended to be those which they were already bound to accept for other reasons (NATO commitments to increasing readiness and manpower in 1977 for example), or because they were in line with existing thinking.[55]

The manpower issue, therefore, further reinforces the general conclusion which has appeared throughout this study. Attempts at tinkering with existing Parliamentary institutions are unlikely to be effective unless two conditions are met. First of all there must be a willingness by MPs to put policy questions before party and personal ambition. Secondly there must be a fundamental restructuring of constitutional conventions which would allow the legislature in Britain to have a similar access to information as the executive, and an opportunity to use this information to develop an expertise to allow it to make or shape policy effectively. Without these changes legislative reform in Britain must be a limited exercise because Parliament is only able to play one of two roles: it can either raise slightly the veil of secrecy which shrouds executive decision-making; or act as an additional conduit for existing powerful interests within the executive branch of government. DEASC fulfilled both roles but this, unfortunately, was not a measure of its success but a measure of its failure to make the executive fully accountable in the defence field.

NOTES

1. Lawrence Freedman, 'Britain's Contribution to NATO', *International Affairs*, vol. 54 (January 1978) pp. 32–3; Kenneth Hunt, *The Alliance and Europe: Defence With Fewer Men* (London: Adelphi Paper No. 98, 1970) pp. 8–9; and P. J. Dietz and J. F. Stone, 'The British All-Volunteer Army', *Armed Forces and Society* (February 1975) pp. 168–9.
   Lawrence Martin, *British Defence Policy: the Long Recessional* (London: Adelphi Paper No. 61, 1969).
3. Ibid.
4. Dietz and Stone, op. cit., pp. 161–2.
5. Ibid., p. 161.
6. N. L. Dodd, 'Voluntary Recruitment in Great Britain', *Military Review*, vol. 53 (June 1973) pp. 77–9.
7. Discussed in Dietz and Stone, op. cit., pp. 168–9; and David White, 'Why Join the Army?', *New Society* (27 April 1972) pp. 172–5; and, C. B. Otley, 'The Social Origins of British Army Officers', *Sociological Review*, vol. 18 (July 1970) pp. 213–39.
8. 'Soldiering on, *The Economist*, vol. 228 (10 August 1968) p. 14.
9. T. A. Fabyanic , 'Manpower Trends in the British All-Volunteer Army', *Armed Forces and Society*, vol. 2 (August 1976) pp. 553–72.
10. Ibid., pp. 555–64; and, Hunt, op. cit., pp. 9–18.
11. N. L. Dodd, 'Britain's Most Important Investment for Defence', *Military Review* vol. 52 (July 1977) pp. 85–7; and, David Greenwood, *The United Kingdom's Current Defence Programme and Budget* (Aberdeen: ASIDES No. 17, Spring 1980) p. 27 and 44–6.
12. Freedman, op. cit., pp. 38–47; and, James Bellini, 'BAOR: the Next Test for NATO', *Royal United Services Institute journal* (June 1977) pp. 22–4.
13. Dodd (1977), op. cit., pp. 83–6; Freedman op. cit., pp. 39–40; Sir michael Carey, 'Britain's Armed Forces After the Defence Cuts', *Royal United Services Institute Journal* (March 1976) pp. 1–6; 'Britain's NATO Army', *NATO's 15 Nations*, vol. 22 (April–May 1977) pp. 82–3; and, Sir William Scotter, 'The British Army Today', *Royal United Services Institute Journal* (June 1976) pp. 16–23.
14. Dodd (1977), ibid., pp. 86–7; and, Freedman, ibid., pp. 39–41.
15. The basic changes made in 1974/75 to BAOR were from a situation in which BAOR had remained unchanged since the early 1950s. BAOR before 1975 had 3 armoured divisions, with their own support and logistic units and 2 artillery brigades. Reform was aimed at reducing the number of commands by scrapping the brigade level and creating four armed divisions to take pressure off divisional commanders. These four divisional commands would be assisted by a Field Force of one infantry brigade and an artillery division (the two artillery brigades amalgamated), with the normal logistic units in support.

16. 'As You Were', *The Economist*, vol. 265 (17 December 1977) pp. 24 and 26.
17. Greenwood, op. cit., pp. 44–6; and, P. C. Shapland, 'Reserve Forces', *Royal United Services Institute Journal* (September 1978) pp. 9–16.
18. Dodds (1977) op. cit., p. 89; and, 'Britain Does Its Bit, *The Economist*, vol. 268 (19 August 1978) pp. 24–6.
19. 'Defence Costs Put Under Radical Review', *Guardian* (16 April 1981) p. 1; and, 'Nott's Review Slims the Fleet', *Guardian* (26 June 1981) p. 1.
20. The need for specialization has been discussed by Greenwood and also by Freedman, op. cit., *passim*.
21. For these types of discussion see: Hunt, op. cit., pp. 25–40; Freedman, op. cit., pp. 44–6; M. Mushkat, 'Military Manpower Procurement: From Conscription to Volunteer Service', *Political Science*, vol. 31, no. 2 (December 1979) pp. 108–16; Greenwood, op. cit., p. 27; G. Pattie and James Bellini, *A New World Role For the Medium Power: the British Opportunity* (London: RUSI, 1977); and, W. J. Money, 'Do We Need a New model Army?', *Sociological Review*, vol. 23 (August 1975) pp. 577–605.
22. William P. Snyder, *The Politics of British Defense Policy* (Ohio State University Press, 1964) pp. 66–72.
23. *HC 147–148* (1946/47; *HC 133* (1952/53; *HC 282* (1962/63); and, *HC 302* (1963/64).
24. Fabyanic, op. cit., pp. 557–8.
25. *HC 393* (1977) pp. x–xi.
26. Ibid., p. ix.
27. HC 563–*1* (1978) p. xii.
28. *HC 393* (1977) pp. xv–xvi.
29. The authors must thank Rear-Admiral Gueritz and Brigadier Kenneth Hunt, two of the specialist advisers to DEASC for the interviews and correspondence on which this particular piece of interpretation is based.
30. *HC 259* (1976/77), p. xii.
31. *Cmnd 7399* (1978), p. 5.
32. *Hansard (Commons Debates)*, vol. 950, no. 120, Col. 177 6.
33. *HC 563–1* (1977), p. xv; and, *HC 472* (1974/75), pp. viii–xi.
34. *HC 472* (1974/75), p. x.
35. ibid., p. xi.
36. Ibid., p. xi
37. ibid., p. xi.
38. *HC 141* (1971/72).
39. *HC 563–1* (1977) pp. xx–xxi.
40. ibid., p. xvi.
41. Ibid., p. xvi.
42. On the government's responses see: *Cmnd 7399* (1978); *HC 563–1*(1977); and, *Cmnd 6285* (1975).
43. *HC 86* (1977/78) p. xiii; and, *Cmnd 7147* (1978).
44. Details from *HC 393* (1977) *passim*; and, *Cmnd 7011* (1977) *passim*.
45. Shapland, op. cit., *passim*.
46. Correspondence and discussions with Brigadier Kenneth Hunt were again important in the development of this argument.

47. *HC 141* (1971/72); *HC 167* (1973/74) p. ix; *HC 472* (1974/75) p. xiv; and, *HC 563–1* (1978) p. xxxi
48. *HC 254* (1976/77) p. xv.
49. *HC 472* (1974/75) p. xiv.
50. *HC 155* (1975/76) pp. xliii; and, *Cmnd 6489* (1976) pp. 14–15.
51. *HC 563–1* (1978) p. xix.
52. Ibid., p. xix.
53. Ibid., p. xix.
54. *Cmnd 7399* (1978) p. 8; and, ibid., p. xxxi.
55. *HC 563–1* (1978) pp. 57–9.

Part V
Conclusions

9 Defence Accountability and Legislative Reform in the 1980s

We commenced our discussion with a note on recent revelations concerning leaks from the British Ministry of Defence and how this raises questions about defence accountability to Parliament. Similar questions were also raised about American defence accountability in the light of the Watergate scandal and recent insights into the behaviour of the American defence establishment during the Vietnam War. We argued, however, that these developments – while clearly questioning the accountability of defence – were merely the most sensational aspects of a much more fundamental problem. Hopefully, after completing this book, the general dilemma facing the American Congress and British Parliament should now be apparent. Neither legislature is in a position to scrutinise or control defence spending and policy-making effectively. We would argue that this is so despite the reforming movements in the 1970s and 1980s. In general we would contend that, while the reforms did have some impact, they fell far short of the intentions set for them by many of the reformers who had hoped to make defence more accountable. One way of reinforcing this conclusion is by summarising the broad findings of our study.

DEFENCE ACCOUNTABILITY IN BRITAIN AND AMERICA PRIOR TO REFORM

In Chapter 1 we argued that public accountability through legislatures can be delineated in three fundamental ways. First of all, a legislature can have a strategic role for policy accountability. This involves the legislature in taking decisions in relation to overall defence policy and expenditure *vis-à-vis* decisions taken in other spending areas of the whole budget; or it can involve the legislature in ensuring that the executive branch is made to justify publicly its decisions. A second area of accountability might involve a managerial role for programme accountability. This role would involve the legislature in scrutinising the process by which the executive sets priorities and fulfils commitments within the overall expenditure and policy framework laid down strategically. A third area might involve a legal role for financial accountability. Under this function the legislature would be involved in auditing the value for money and probity of the financial allocations made within the defence programme. Prior to the reforms of the 1970s, if for different reasons, neither the British Parliament nor the American Congress was able to fulfil all three roles effectively. While each legislature was able to discharge some of these roles reasonably successfully, neither was in a position to render defence spending or policy fully accountable to the public.

In the United States Congress and the executive branch share theoretical responsibility for all three roles. In practice either the executives was able to dominate the process or Congress fulfilled aspects of the three roles but in a largely irresponsible manner. This apparently contradictory state of affairs existed because, nothwithstanding the 1974 Freedom of Information Act, both the Department of Defence (DOD) and the executive were often able to control information of crucial importance to public oversight. This was achieved either by claiming that national security was imperilled or that sensitive information might infringe 'executive privilege'. Furthermore, the structure of Congress – with its specialist legislative committees being able to change and add-on to executive budget requests – militated against any co-ordinated Congressional view of overall budgetary allocations. Decisions taken about defence versus welfare issues were never taken together because specialist committees (like Armed Services and Appropriation for defence) tended to have in-built pro-defence or pro-welfare majorities. This ensured that, whatever overall view was taken of strategic budget decisions by the President and the Office of Management and Budget, Congress was always in a position to tinker with executive priorities.

While this power might appear to provide Congress with a dominant role, in practice it did not. In reality Congress suffered from information overload and the 'politics of the pork barrel'. What this meant was that Congress traditionally had all three roles but failed to discharge them responsibly. Both welfare and defence committees would use their powers to add-on programmes and commitments to the budget to favour those special interests lobbying successfully for favours, without taking an overall view of the total budget commitment and tax consequences which might ensue. Congress could always blame the President if taxes were raised or if he used his impoundment and veto powers to hinder their financially profligate and irresponsible behaviour. In the defence field this problem was glaringly apparent, particularly during the Vietnam period when the Services were able to lobby Congress for additional expenditure. As a result Congress failed to co-ordinate the myriad of individual decisions being taken by committees and this undermined the search for a co-ordinated and responsible strategic role. On the managerial and audit sides, however, Congress has traditionally been better served.

Due to the extensive research and auditing services enshrined in the activities of the General Accounting Office (GAO), Congressional Research Service (CRS) and Office of Technology Assessment (OTA) – plus the creation in 1969 of the continuous review of procurement known as the Selected Acquisition Reporting System – Congress has extensive facilities to scrutinise defence programmes and audit financial allocation decisions. Indeed, information on defence matters has always been widely available in general because defence contractors, independent research institutes, the Services and the DOD are constantly in the public eye debating the relative worth of specific programmes and weapon systems before the Congressional defence committees. Despite this both the GAO and Congressional committees have uncovered evidence of continuous problems with time and cost over-runs in weapons procurement. This reinforced the view, either that the executive was not adequately discharging its own responsibilities for making defence programmes and procurement accountable, and/or that Congress ought to reform itself to deal with the problems more effectively.

It was out of these twin concerns over strategic policy irresponsibility and lack of control over procurement that Congress moved to reform itself. The situation was, however, very different in Britain prior to reform. Although Parliament is formally responsible for policy in Britain in practice its role is largely confined to managerial and audit functions. While Parliament might debate strategic policy issues on the floor of the House of Commons, the inbuilt majority of the executive ensures that the government of the day sets defence versus welfare and intra-defence budget priorities.

Prior to the 1970s, therefore, the executive determined the strategic decisions over defence and other policy areas. Parliament's role was largely confined to the scrutiny of detailed programmes and policies in the Estimates Committee or other *ad-hoc* specialist committees. The audit role was fulfilled mainly by the Comptroller and Auditor-General and the Public Accounts Committee. As we saw, while the Estimates Committee did spend more time scrutinising defence related rather than other issues, its role was largely after the fact and confined to non-sensitive issues.

Despite this the PAC was reasonably successful in discharging it limited scrutiny role. In the 1950s and 1960s the PAC was instrumental in revealing maladministration and inefficiency in a range of defence procurement contracts. Nevertheless, taken as a whole, Parliament was not able to question executive dominance of policy-making. One key reason for this failure to discharge an effective scrutiny or managerial role was the lack of information available to Parliament. The secretiveness of the British system in relation to all areas of government activity is assisted by the omnibus provisions of the 1911 Official Secrets Act. Section 2 of this Act makes disclosure of any government information regarded as confidential a criminal act which threatens national security. When applied to the defence field the Act can and has been used, as we saw, to withhold information on such issues as contracting costs and performance, foreign arms sales totals, aircraft accident rates and the number of foreign soldiers on British soil. It has been argued that such information is hardly a threat to national security because much of it is readily available in NATO publications. It is further argued that this type of information is freely disseminated to American legislators without any acute threat being posed to national security. Whatever the merits of these arguments there is little doubt that this Act has reinforced security in the MoD and ensured that both sensitive national security as well as potentially embarrassing political and administrative information has been denied to Parliament and the people.

It is against this background that reformers in Britain and America attempted to innovate in their respective legislatures. Of course, the problems of defence accountability were not the only reasons for reform but they were symptomatic of a more general malaise in executive–legislative relationships. The problem with defence, however, is that unlike all other areas of government activity it is a highly sensitive area in which calls of national security and executive privilege can be used. Perhaps this is the key to why the subsequent reforms of the 1970s and 1980s failed to achieve all that had been intended in the defence field. If this is the case then we can terminate our conclusions here and argue that defence accountability is an insurmountable problem. But, as our study has shown, there are other reasons why it is difficult to make defence more accountable than the paucity of information. Indeed, and somewhat ironically, in the United States the problem of information overload can be just as important a restraint as the lack of information. By summarising the major findings of our study of the reform movement in the defence field it should be possible for us to better understand why defence is difficult to make more accountable and why it is that the provision of more information will not on its own make defence more publicly accountable.

THE IMPACT OF REFORM IN THE 1970s AND 1980s

In 1974 Congress moved towards reform with the object of regaining control of the budgetary process from the executive. This involved Congress in attempting to take control of functional budgeting as well as the setting of overall budgetary priorities (defence versus welfare). The Congressional Budget Office and the House and Senate Budget Committees were the chosen instruments of this policy. These new institutions were to provide a more responsible and centrally co-ordinated budget process for Congress. This was to be achieved by undoing the dominance of the executive in setting budget totals and undoing the intensely political and fiscally irresponsible behaviour of specialist committees for appropriation and authorisation in the raising of revenue and allocation of expenditure.

Despite these innovations the reforms have not been as successful as intended. There are a number of reasons for this. First of all, the new committees have limited constitutional powers *vis-à-vis* the established legislative committees. To win acceptance at all the Budget committees have had to tread warily and behave very generously in recognising existing committee jurisdictions and special interests. This is compounded by the problem of timetabling which leaves the budget committees little time to oversee the rectitude of the details of the decisions taken by the legislative committees. As a result the new committees have concentrated largely on broad budgetary totals and the mismatch between budget requests and revenue availability.

While this is a desireable innovation, because it does allow Congress to look at the overall consequences of the multitude of individual committee actions, in practice overall budget totals have still been dominated by Presidential requests. In defence specifically the oversight of defence totals and programmes is still the preserve of the DoD, President and Armed Services and Appropriations Committees. The latter committees have continued to add on to and substract from Presidential and DoD requests in the light of their perception of public opinion and special interest lobbying. Thus, while one might have expected the new budget committees to have taken issue with some of the questionable assumptions used by the executive and legislative committees to justify massively enhanced defence expenditure in the wake of the Iranian and Aghanistanian crises, in practice the new system has not been able to willing to halt this pro-defence bandwagon. This has taken place despite the fact that Congress has always had an abundance of information and the CBO was created to extend the capacity of Congress to arrive at impartial analysis of problems. The fact that such an alternative view has not emerged to any great extent in Congress indicates that the provision of information alone is not sufficient to ensure the creation of a questioning or alternative priority setting role.

There are a number of reasons for this. Perhaps the most important is the fact that the new system is a compromise which seeks that which is not achievable. Congress was to be given the capacity to set budget priorities, but without undermining the traditional authority of the spending committees – the actions of which had always made priority setting impossible. Unfortunately these spending committees have jealously defended their 'turf' and excluded the budget committees from detailed scrutiny of the 'line-items' which make up the overall defence budget. This means that the tendency of these pro-defence committees to continue to support special interest lobbying from the defence establishment has not been undone. Indeed, under the Reagan administration the combination of special interest pressure and strong public support for an increased defence role allowed Reagan in his first two years of office to steamroller through Congress a massive shift in public spending away from welfare towards defence. Even in his second two years of office Reagan was able to counteract the small cuts in defence requests made by Congress by submitting highly inflated defence budgets. This ensured that defence continued to grow throughout Reagan's first term despite the opposition of welfare groups and the growing realisation in Congress that the burgeoning budget deficit was fuelled by defence spending.

Unfortunately, for reformers, it was this dilemma which the new system was supposed to overcome. The fact that it has not been able to do so is due in part to the success of the New Right and Reagan in mobilising public opinion behind the enhancement of defence. It is also, however, reinforced by the attitudes and behaviour of legislators in the traditional spending committees and the technical problems which face any concerted attempt by Congress to question executive control of defence budgeting. This problems include the fact that defence budgeting involves weapons procurement decisions and forward costings over at least a ten year period; while Congress is involved in taking decisions on an annual budgetary basis. It is not surprising that Congress often finds decisions were made many years before the consequences of those decisions are felt in annual budget requests. Relatedly the Budget Committees have found it difficult to find the time to fit even their general co-ordinating activities into the annual legislative timetable, never mind approach the more time consuming problem of assessing 'line-items' within the defence budget itself. An additional problem has been that the extensive research staffs of the traditional spending committees have normally used information available to Congress for the purposes of advocacy rather than impartial analysis of Policy or programme choices. It is not surprising, therefore, that the CBO – with its fledgeling staff and lack of experienced experts – has been unable to provide clear alternative priority and programme choices to question the traditional executive and legislative committee dominance of the defence field.

Despite the fact that Congress did move to cutback defence spending in early 1985 in an attempt to reduce the burgeoning American federal deficit it is fair to say that as yet the new budget system has not achieved all that was intended for it. True, it has provided Congress with the capacity to look at the overall consequences of its individual committee actions, but these actions are still all too often based on partisan and fiscally irresponsible behaviour. The failure of the new system to fundamentally challenge Reagan's massive increase in defence spending in the 1980s is ample testimony to the failure of reform. The Congress may tinker with totals sent too it from the President and the budget system may provide a more rational framework for this, but the legislature is still working with, and contrained by, figures sent to it by the President.

In Britain the success or failure of the reform movement is slightly more difficult to assess because the goals of reformers were less clear cut than in the USA and there have been two reforms in the 1970s and 1980s. We saw that historically Parliament's role has been largely confined to a legal/audit role. The managerial function for programme accountability was limited to the activities of the Estimates Committee and other *ad-hoc* specialist committee reports and studies. These activities might provide details on the behaviour of the executive but always after the event and with little direct impact on government policy. Against this background reformers in Britain wanted to achieve different things. At a minimum the majority of reformers agreed that Parliament's ability to scrutinise government activity should be enhanced. This implied that Parliament ought to be able to do more than audit the books on a regular basis; rather the *ad-hoc* studies of the past by the Estimates Committee were to become the basis of an extended and continuous review of executive decisions and administration. At a maximum, however, a smaller number of reformers wanted to provide Parliament with the facilities to allow it to share power with the government and set alternative strategic budgetary priorities.

The 1971 reform was therefore something of a compromise between these two broad views. The Estimates Committee was replaced by the Select Committee on Expenditure (SCOE) with a range of sub-committees dealing with all aspects of government policy. In theory this provided Parliament with the mechanism to co-ordinate its scrutiny of government and the capacity to set alternative priorities. In practice this goal was not achieved. The goal of setting priorities was eschewed in favour of fulfilling the managerial/scrutiny role more effectively. There were a number of reasons for this. Parliament is normally dominated by the executive through its majority in the House of Commons. While backbenchers do occasionally indulge in revolts these are rarely a fundamental threat to the authority of the government and its ability to control legislative decision-making and agenda setting. The situation after the 1971 reforms was no different because the committees created always retained government majorities. Thus, although radical reformers could point to the existence of the institutional structures they had desired these could only be made to work if backbenches from the governing party behaved in a non-partisan manner when confronted with pressure not to question the actions of their own party in government.

It is not surprising, therefore, that SCOE did not achieve all that radical reformers had intended that it should. To be able to operate at all the new committees had to avoid conflict and pursue non-contentious, bipartisan problems. This made their actions somewhat anodine and biased towards scrutiny of what the government had done, rather than challenging government policy priorities through a co-ordinated perusal of government activities. This lack of a co-ordinated priority setting approach was compounded by the fact that the sub-committees jealously guarded their own areas of responsibility from one another and the co-ordinating role was lost by default. Nevertheless, it would not be fair to argue that the reform was a complete failure. In reality the new system did allow Parliament to fulfil its managerial role for programme accountability more effectively than had been the case in the past. This fact is testified to by the activities of the sub-committee for Defence and External Affairs (DEASC), which substantially improved on the scrutiny performance of the old Estimates Committee.

DEASC achieved more than the old Estimates Committee because it maintained a continuous review of defence expenditure policy and followed up its own recommendations. This kept the MOD on its metal. There was also a more consistent use made of outside experts, which encouraged the development of expertise amongst staff and committee members. Relatedly the committee had far more staff assistance clerically and administratively – especially from the Comptroller's office – than had been the case in the past. The committtee was also able to make overseas and domestic fact finding visits to extend its expertise and knowledge. Nevertheless this was still a limited role. DEASC tended to adopt a bipartisan approach to minimise conflict and even when it did question government policy – as in the case of the MRCA – its advice was ignored. DEASC confined the bulk of its activities, therefore, to value for money considerations (mirroring in a more detailed way the traditional function of the Public Accounts Committee). At no time did DEASC (or SCOE) achieve what radical reformers had intended and question government assumptions about defence and its relationship with social expenditure.

It should be fairly clear by now why it was that DEASC found its role circumscribed. By and large most members selected for DEASC were pro-defence in their attitudes whichever political party they came from. This meeting of minds was not just due to the unwillingness of anti-defence MPs to sit on the committee; it was also assisted by collusion between the Whips Office, the MoD, the Cabinet Office and the chairmen of the committee. Even if anti-defence MPs had chosen to sit on the committee, instead of condemning defence spending out of hand, it is doubtful whether either the first chairman, James Boyden (Labour), or his replacement, Sir Harwood Harrison (Conservative), would have supported their applications. James Boyden was concerned to keep 'dangerous men' from his own party off the committee.[1] Harwood Harrison was prone to similar views about men of 'unusual' political views.[2] Secondly while it might be true that staff resources had been substantially improved, when compared with the facilities available in Congress, they were totally inadequate to allow DEASC or SCOE to fulfil the tasks with which they had been charged. This problem was compounded by the fact that all of the outside experts used by the committee shared the same general pro-defence outlook as the committee. There was, and is an acute paucity of independent research and advisory institutes in the British system. As a result the role and activities of DEASC were limited.

It is arguable, however, whether these factors were the major cause of this circumscribed role. It would appear that there are two further factors which are of crucial importance in this regard. Firstly, British MPs tend to have a very myopic view of their own role. As a result one might argue that the 1971 reform was 'conceived by radicals and implemented by conservatives'.[3] The reason for this conclusion is that the men who are instrumental in demanding reform in the 1960s were not the men who created the institutional structure of the 1970s. Thus, while they had desired departmental committees reporting to a co-ordinating and alternative priority setting general committee to match Whitehall's PESC system, what was created was very different. Instead of departmental committees subject or area committees were created and the co-ordinating committee was given only weak general powers to control and order sub-committee work. This meant that the desirable committee structure was not created. This failing was, however, compounded by the activities of MPs as legislators.

The major reason why MPs rejected the co-ordinating and priority setting role lies deep within the part-time attitude many MPs bring to their job. This tends to militate against the creation of that quasi-bureaucratic/specialist function which the SCOE and DEASC reforms inherently required. Instead of time-consuming and laborious scrutiny of a subject area and the development of detailed expertise British legislators tend to prefer the role of the political magpie. By this we mean that they prefer to be free to jump from one issue to another as it enters the political agenda and win popular and peer support by appearing to be all things to all men. There is, then, a tendency for MPs to favour political influence without responsibility. They want to be free to look at issues which appear in the public limelight and score debating points from their colleagues and the government, without being prepared to look in detail at the difficult choices which those in government often have to make. The problem with the SCOE and DEASC reforms was that it required that MPs should become specialists and be prepared to spend long and often politically and publicly unrewarding hours scrutinising policy areas and co-ordinating these to set overall priorities. It is not surprising that – while some MPs took up this challenge with relish – the majority did not, and even those who did become involved tended to be single issue/subject specialists and eschewed consideration of co-ordinated priorities.

It is not, however, only the attitude of MPs to their role which delimits the impact of institutional reforms in Britain. Even with all the will in the world the scrutiny and policy role of the legislature is effectively circumscribed by the tendency to two party politics and government majorities in the House of Commons. Both of these factors tend to ensure that the executive in Britain can effectively veto Parliament's actions. This negative veto over Parliament was seen throughout the life of DEASC in the 1970s as governments of both ideological persuasion refused to allow the committee to see relevant papers on grounds that national security would be threatened.[4] This effectively delimited the role which Parliament – through DEASC – could fulfil. This creates a particularly acute problem in Britain. Whereas Congress may be able to behave irresponsibly because of information overload and special interest lobbying, in Britain the legislature is bound to behave in a relatively irresponsible manner because of the paucity of information. When all actions of the government are shrouded in secrecy then when backbenchers rebel they do so out of pique or the defence of special interests. Whichever of these is the major cause it is normally brought about by an ignorance of the difficult choices governments have to make and implies that, without a constitutional role in shaping all resource allocation decisions, individual defeats for governments in Parliament must tend to be politically irresponsible, however noble the particular cause.

This conclusion is important in respect of the subsequent reform of the SCOE system which took place in 1979 under the first Thatcher administration. SCOE and its subject sub-committees was abolished and replaced by fourteen independent department related committees. It might on the surface appear that this has been an extension of the 1970s reforms because one of the major demands in the 1960s was to allow for department based committees. These were not granted in 1971 and there is a school of thought which argues that this is a definite advantage in the new system.[5] While this may be true the Thatcher government gave with one hand and took away with another. Reformers of the 1960s had always argued that departmentally based committees ought to feed into an overall co-ordinating committee to parallel the role of the Treasury and PESC system in Whitehall. The 1979 reforms did not provide for a co-ordinating committee and this has led to fears that the 1979 reforms were in fact a retrograde step. This arises because Parliament is now without any facility to co-ordinate and this reinforces the tendency to politically irresponsible behaviour. A tendency which was reinforced by the failure of the government to allow Parliament any of the extra powers to force Ministers to give up papers which Parliament was demanding.

The new department based committees have, therefore, tended to continue as limited *post-hoc* scrutinisers and auditors of government actions which was the role of SCOE and its sub-committees prior to 1979. Indeed in the 1980s the Select Committee on Defence has tended to replicate the activities of DEASC which it replaced. It has tended to concentrate on single issues but it does not now have the advantage of being able to look at defence issues in relation to foreign policy considerations. These are now the responsibility of a Select Committee on Foreign Affairs. This implies that SCOD is not in a position to fundamentally appraise defence policy and that the problem of paucity of information remains. This was confirmed in the 1980s when there was a Parliamentary furore over the alleged censoring of the committees own first report on ammunition storage sites in Germany.[6] It has been underlined as well by the failure of SCOD to raise any of the crucial issues involved in the Belgrano affair– these being left, ironically, to the Foreign Affairs Committee and leaks from disgruntled civil servants.

This fact may actually indicate what is a potentially worrying tendency in the new committee structure which further erodes the independence of Parliament from the executive. In the past the Estimates Committee and DEASC did not spend all of their time scrutinising defence issues, and this may have kept them from becoming the creatures of the Departments which they were called upon to oversee. Nevertheless, there was, as we saw, a tendency for DEASC to become something of an additional conduit by which the demands and fears of the Services and MoD were publiscised. This implies that there may well be a tendency for departmentally based committees to become the instruments of the very individuals they seek to control and check. It was for this reason – amongst others – that politicians of such diverse ideological presuppositions as Michael Foot and Enoch Powell chose to resist the move to reform in 1979. They argued that, if civil servants were clearly not worried by these new developments, then they must have decided that they could be used to their advantage.[7]

One must conclude, therefore, that the further reform experienced by Parliament in the 1980s has not really taken the legislature much further than the reforms of the 1970s. This is so even though there is no doubt tht Parliament is much better informed that it ever has been – in particular in relation to defence. Yet it is still the case that policy-making and agenda setting is still the preserve of the executive. This is true in defence despite the prodigious efforts of SCOD to discover what the basis of government policy-making is in such diverse areas as procurement, nuclear weapons and the Falklands (for a full listing of SCOD reports to 1984 see Table 9.1). As the Belgrano affair and the decision in 1985 by the Secretary of State for Defence to refuse SCOD access to an internal report alleging gross incompetence in defence stocks practices reveal,[8] the government can still ignore Parliamentary requests and ensure that its defence committee does not ask difficult questions.

Finally, while it may be the case that SCOD has a limited role, confined largely to public information and piecemeal scrutiny of executive actions, there is some doubt about the capacity of the committee fulfilling this role effectively. We argued at the conclusion of chapter one that, whatever institutional reforms are made in either the British or American legislatures, they can only be made to work for public accountability if the executive branch itself is holding the Services and defence contractors accountable.[9] Recent evidence seems to indicate that this problem is indeed a real one. Clive Ponting has argued that the Services are able to eschew the implementation of government policies when they do not agree with them.[10] In America the recent revelations over the activities of General Dynamics and Boeing, who have been able to pass on political campaign

TABLE 9.1 *Reports from the Select Committee on Defence (1979–84)*

1979/80	HC 556: Ammunition Storage Sites for British Forces Germany.
	HC 571: Statement on Defence Estimates, 1980.
	HC 773: The D Notice System.
1980/81	HC 53: RAF Pilot Training.
	HC 218: The Sting Ray Lightweight Torpedo.
	HC 266: Strategic Nuclear Weapons Policy.
	HC 302: Statement on Defence Estimates, 1981.
1981/82	HC 22: Ministry of Defence Organization and Procurement.
	HC 93: Allied Forces in Germany.
1982/83:	HC 17: The Handling of the Press and Public Information during the Falklands Conflict.
	HC 55: Previous Recommendation of the Committee.
	HC 154: The Future Defence of the Falklands Islands.
	HC 176: British Forces Hong Kong.
	HC 242: Positive Vetting Procedures in HM Services and the Ministry of Defence.
1983/84:	HC 397: The Physical Security of Military Installations in the UK.
	HC 436: Statement on Defence Estimates, 1984.
	HC 584: Ministry of Defence Reorganisation.

contributions, lobbying and entertainment expenses in their bills to the government for defence contracts,[11] seems to indicate that there is an acute problem of scrutiny and oversight within the respective legislative branches.

The point here is that, despite almost fifteen years of extended legislative scrutiny of defence, these insights were only made public from leaks from disgruntled civil servants and participants in the defence establishment. Thus while the revelations of the Belgrano and Watergate type hit the headlines they are, arguably, hardly the most worrying aspects of defence accountability. There seems to be sufficient evidence from our study to conclude that defence policy-making and expenditure is becoming more rather than less accountable to the public. This would appear to be so despite the legislative innovations of the 1970s and 1980s and the diligence of legislators. This is a measure of the failure of the reforms and a cause for public concern.

IS IT POSSIBLE TO MAKE DEFENCE ACCOUNTABLE?

We commenced this study with the intention of discovering whether legislative reforms in the 1970s and 1980s were able to make defence more publicly accountable in Britain and America. Our general conclusion is that despite the provision of more information to legislatures – particularly in Britain – these reforms have not radically improved the accountability of defence to the public. One broad conclusion flows from this: it is not the quantity of information which is crucial to legislative oversight but its quality and the use that the legislature makes of such information that is available. Further conclusions flow from this insight. As the American case reveals, simply having masses of information does not make defence accountable unless the legislative institutions which process it are capable of dispassionate, non-partisan and rational analysis. But, when the traditionally responsible legislative committees are staffed by legislators who have a vested interest in supporting defence then impartial analysis is improbable. Such committees historically have used (and continue to do so) information to provide advocacy for the special interests which lobby them.

In Britain this dilemma recurs. Despite the creation of new oversight committees in the 1970s and 1980s MPs serving on these bodies have also tended to have pro-defence attitudes. This, we would contend, has militated against the raising of embarrassing questions and undermined any attempt at either discovering the underlying rationale of defence commitments or the setting of alternative priorities. In this way, as in America, while the quantity of information has been increased by reform, quality information – which provides real insights into defence policy – has been at a minimum. In Britain this problem is exacerbated by the omnibus provisions of section 2 of the 1911 Official Secrets Act which, as we saw, has been used to refuse information to Parliament even when national security has not been threatened. While one cannot deny that defence matters do require protection under national security clauses the worrying factor here is that the blanket of national security can and is used to hide incompetence, protect vested interests and to overturn the search for a sensible and reasonably open debate about defence priorities. Indeed this problem is unlikely to go away in the future because the defence establishment faces acute problems in the late 1980s and 1990s.

The major problems facing defence are that even within existing commitments, due to the continually escalating costs of new technology, merely maintaining existing commitments can involve governments in massively increasing defence costs. The cost of sophisticated technology for new 'state of the art' weapons systems is so far in advance of general inflation rates that there is a continuous upward pressure on defence spending. The problem this leads to is all too readily apparent in the time and cost over-runs witnessed in major weapons programmes like the Trident nuclear submarine, the MX missile and the MRCA. Thus, at a time when economic growth is in relative decline and pressure is increasingly being exerted on welfare spending, it is not surprising that the public in liberal democracies should be concerned about whether governments have achieved the correct balance between defence and welfare programmes and priorities. This is surely one of the major factors involved in the growth of anti-nuclear movements like CND.

Unforunately, while such scepticism is wholly understandable it is all too easy for the defence establishment and pro-defence governments (like Reagan and Thatcher) to react in a paranoid manner whenever defence policy and commitments are challenged. Instead of recognising that the cost of defence is a real problem such governments can all to easily fall into the trap of seeing such criticism and desire for accountability either as a conspiracy or merely self-motivated propaganda on behalf of those threatened by cuts in social spending. The irony here is that such governments may well, then, become the prisoners of vested interests in the defence field (and their legislative supporters), whose perceptions of reality are as much conditioned by a desire to protect their own self-interests as by any real external 'threat' to the state. This leads to a denial of democracy because groups like CND may become polarised into an unhealthy antipathy to defence as a whole and the defence establishment becomes entrenched in a bunker mentality of hindering the dissemination of any and all defence related information – even that which is not a threat to national security.

Since we believe that recent trends seem to be taking Britain and America down this road we conclude our discussion by outlining a number of reforms which might, on the one hand, ensure that the public and legislatures have access to quality information to foster genuine public debate and, on the other, provide clear guidelines so as to protect national security. In making these suggestions – which affect legal rights to information and institutional reforms in Congress and Parliament – we recognise that to suggest them is easy; to implement them is far more difficult because they threaten powerful vested interests in legislatures, executives and society. Proposals for reform fall into two broad categories: those which ensure that information is freely available to the public when national security is not at issue; and (since information on its own is not sufficient) legislative reforms to provide the institutional structures in legislatures to allow information to be used to foster rational and non-partisan debate.

On the basis of our study we would argue that the system for accountability created in the Congressional Budget committees offers the best way forward to make defence accountable. These committees, with their research agency the CBO, operate within a legislative framework which legally protects the citizens rights to information. There seems little justification for Britain to maintain the omnibus provisions of the 1911 Official Secrets Act. Since section 2 of this Act has been used to withhold information which has little direct bearing on the defence of the realm or the security of the state it should be abolished immediately and replaced by a similar Freedom of Information Act as obtains in the USA. By this means both the quantity and quality of information available to the British citizen could immediately be improved. National security considerations could be protected as they are in the American Act by the creation of clearly defined limits and parameters. This, we believe, would immediately transform Britain from being one of the more secretive liberal democracies into one of the more open.

On its own, however, there is no guarantee that the provision of information will ensure accountability in defence. As the American experience amply reveals the legislature has to use information in such a way as to ensure and support rational and non-partisan debate. Thus, while the Budget Committees in Congress offer the basis for legislative reform, they face intense opposition within the American legislature and cannot easily be transposed to the British Parliament. Before looking at the British case in more detail it is necessary first to outline the ways in which the opposition to the Budget system might be overcome in Congress.

Congress has always shared responsibility for budgeting with the executive under the American constitution. The major difficulty for Congress in practice has been the unwillingness to co-ordinate its internal committee activities – particularly those for spending and revenue raising. As a result Congress has only been able to see the global effects of its spending legislation when the last of its thirteen spending bills are enacted. Under these conditions it has always been impossible for Congress to consider budget priorities or set alternatives. As we saw this dilemma has been exacerbated by the tendency of the traditional legislative committees to defend their jurisdictions, to the point were co-operation between committees was the exception rather than the rule. On the floor of the House and Senate members voted to support their committee bill and gave scant attention to the global budget of which it was part. This neglect of the global budget reflects the fact that the President dominates the budget; not only because he announces the budget before Congress begins its work but also because he is responsible for the formulation of an integrated budget which contains revenue and spending assumptions. Thus, even when th legislative committees meet to consider their part of the federal budget expectations about programme content have already been set. If the committees want to challenge these commitments they can sometimes change priorities but in general the President is much more able to mobilise support for his budget than are the Congressional party leaders. No more graphic demonstration was given of this than during the first two budgets of President Reagan.

The overall conclusion might be, therefore, that the budget committees and the CBO have achieved little and are merely a gloss on the traditional power of Congressional committee structures which do not question executive dominance of the budget process. At one level this is certainly true. At another level the budget committee structure does provide a mechanism by which Congress can be made aware of the global consequences of its actions. This is clearly a desirable development and one which can only encourage a questioning of parochial and partisan approaches to Congressional budgeting. Nevertheless, an effective reform can only be achieved if there is a redefinition of the powers of the traditional legislative committees and the development of a new relationship between them and the budget committees. But even this will not be adequate unless Congressmen apply national and impartial criteria to the scrutiny of the executive instead of the partial and parochical criteria of the past.

Ironically, while expecting Senators and Congressmen to behave differently may be like waiting for the proverbial 'leopard to change its spots', the conditions for a move in this direction may have been laid by the Budget system. The profligate spending on defence under the Reagan Presidency has fuelled a major increase in federal deficits; this has not been reduced despite large cuts in welfare programmes because the increase in defence spending has been so large. In the future his problem of uncontrolled expenditure and inadequate revenue may create horrendous problems for the dollar and inflation rates in the United States. In such circumstances – and in the continuing absence of Presidential parsimony in defence spending – Congress and its traditional legislative committees may be forced to turn to the budget committees in the search for more responsibility in fiscal and budgetary affairs. The budget committees are ideally suited to fulfil this role if the occasion arises. At the moment, however, they merely offer the opportunity for this to be achieved because Congressmen and Senators persist in behaving in a parochial and partisan fashion.

Future reform in Britain is somewhat more difficult to achieve because Parliament has rarely had the ability to make policy and priority decisions. The provision of more information under a Freedom of Information Act suggested earlier would not on its own, therefore, make Parliament more effective in holding the executive accountable. Nor does it seem practical to suggest that the Congressional system can be transposed wholesale in Parliament. Under certain circumstances it might, however, be possible to extend Parliament's ability to share responsibility for policy and priority setting with the executive to provide more accountable government. To understand what might be possible, via a radical reform of Parliament in the spirit of creating a Congressional style budgeting system, it is first necessary to understand the various schools of thought on the issues of Parliamentary reform which have been current since the 1960s.

Basically there are three broad views on the possibility of legislative reform in Britain. Each of these can be differentiated in terms of the degree to which proponents wish to extend the role of the legislature *vis-à-vis* the executive. The first view of reform can be called a minimalist approach. Writers in this school argue that it is not a good thing for Parliament to have a detailed policy role, but that the legislature can fulfil a more effective scrutiny role if only MPs would use the powers which are already available to them. This view assumes that commonsense or a flash of insight by MPs is all that it takes to encourage legislators to change the behaviour they have traditionally indulged in.[12] The second view may be termed internal reform. Writers in this school disagree about the need for Parliament to have either a scrutiny or policy role. What they do agree on is that to expect MPs to behave differently and fulfil either of these roles in the absence of institutional reforms within Parliament is naive. Finally, there are radical reformers who argue that Parliament should have a more effective scrutiny and policy role. Such writers argue that while this must involve internal legislative reforms power sharing with the executive is impossible without a fundamental reform of political representation first. This involves the demand for proportional representation to destroy the unrepresentative two party system and the tendency to elective dictatorship enshrined in executive majorities in the House of Commons. By creating coalition governments in Parliament it is argued the executive would be forced to share more information and decision-making with the legislature.[14]

On the basis of our research into the problems of defence accountability it would appear that only the latter view is likely to offer – with a Freedom of Information Act – an effective means by which the legislature can hold the executive accountable in a responsible manner. We can more fully comprehend this fact if we look at the weaknesses of the other schools of reform. Taking the minimalist view first it can be argued that to rely solely on the independent actions of MPs to create an effective scrutiny or policy role is naive. More worrying perhaps is the fact that it also consigns Parliament to a relatively irresponsible political role. The reasons for this conclusion are clear. MPs have many roles to fulfil and of these sitting on select committees is for many the least desirable aspect of their job. Furthermore, there is little compelling reason in an unreformed Parliament for MPs to involve themselves in the detailed scrutiny of the minutiae of government business – especially when their actions rarely influence government policy directly. MPs prefer, therefore, to play the role of the political magpie and pursue issues which provide them with the opportunity to make a media or debating impact in the hope of preferment by their political leaders. This means that when MPs do act to scrutinise government policy they tend to so for the worst possible reasons – to enhance their political reputations or to protect special interests – without any concern for the broad balance of competing interests in society.

We would contend, therefore, that proponents of the view that MPs should be encouraged in these actions are consigning Parliament to an irresponsible and fiscally profligate role. The weakness of this view derives from the failure of its proponents to differentiate between irresponsible backbench action and an informed and responsible legislative role based upon the impartial assessment of the appropriateness of policy and the proper management of programmes measured against national needs. Such a responsible role is only achievable through the institutional restructuring of parliament and a new balance in the relationship between executive and legislature. This is so whether one believes that Parliament should merely scrutinise government behaviour or assist in the formulation of policy and priority setting.

The question remains, however, how are the two goals of scrutiny and power sharing to be achieved? It would seem clear from our analysis of the failure of internal reforms in the 1970s and 1980s that while this approach is laudable – particularly in legislatures like Congress which have a history of power sharing – creating new committees in Parliament without transforming the relationship between executive and legislature is an exercise in futility. While more information has been generated by the new select committees it is neither of the quality not available at the correct time to allow the legislature to challenge executive priorities.[14] Thus, it seems reasonable to conclude that under the present electoral system, which encourages government majorities in the House of Commons within an adversarial political system, no executive will willingly provide information to the legislature or its committees which might limit its own room for manoeuvre or provide the opposition with potentially embarrassing political and administrative insights. This means that, as Walkland has argued for a number of years, effective scrutiny and power sharing is contingent on reforms external to Parliament coming first.[15]

The logical conclusion from this is that adequate accountability can only be achieved through the development of proportional representation in Britain. Under such an electoral system coalition governments would have to be formed and this would immediately ensure that Parliament was more actively involved in decision-making than it has been since the nineteenth century. This conclusion follows from the assumption that coalition governments – operating under a new Freedom of Information Act – would be forced to act with Parliamentary committees to develop a co-ordinated and consistent view of government policy. If coalitions were fluid it might well be that the departmentally based committees which exist might come to be the repositories of expertise and knowledge which the coalition government of the day might require. In this way such departmental committees might come gradually to take on the role of formulating and enacting departmental policy. It would be important, however, to ensure that the departmental committees did not ape the activities of the Congressional legislative committees. This might lead to the same problem of the departmental committees becoming the prisoners of special interests and, therefore, irresponsible. Since Parliament does not have the tradition of powerful legislative committees – which the budget committees have experienced difficulty in overcoming in Congress – it should be possible to create a general committee (perhaps along the lines of SCOE or the general committee of co-ordination suggested in the 1968 Procedure Committee report) to ensure the impartial and co-ordinated budgeting takes place.

In conclusion then we would argue that the intentions of the reformers of the 1960s and 1970s in Britain and America have not been fulfilled. Congress and Parliament are no more able to determine fundamental defence priorities than they ever have been in the post-war period. While there has been some increase in the ability of other legislatures to scrutinise executive behaviour, overall this has been a fairly limited development. A great deal of important and high quality information is still denied to the legislature, and this failing is compounded by the continuance of irresponsible budgeting behaviour by many legislators in both countries. This is worrying because policy responsibility in the legislature and executive was the basic goal of those who brought pressure for legislative reform in the 1960s and 1970s. While this goal has not been achieved yet it is likely that there will be a pressing need for it in the constrained economic circumstances of the late 1980s and 1990s. Although we are not optimistic about defence accountability being achieved in the future, due to the parochial and partisan attitudes of legislators and those whose control the executive branch of government, there is always the possibility of circumstances conspiring to create the opportunity for a forward looking legislature to create a more effective role for itself. If those conditions arise in the manner we have suggested here then both the American Congress and the British parliament already possess the embryos of more responsible budgetary systems.

NOTES

1. This information was based on a personal interview with James Boyden at the LSE in 1979.
2. Again this information was based on a number of interviews with clerks to the committee and members of DEASC but it is not possible to substantiate it in any definite or definitive way.
3. This view was derived from an interview with R. S. Lankester, chief clerk to the House of Commons in 1980.

4. For details of the power of information and civil service autonomy see: K. P. Pooke, 'The Power of Select Committees of the House of Commons to Send for Persons, Papers and Records', (*Parliamentary Affairs*, vol. 33 (Winter 1980) pp. 67–78.
5. P. Norton, *The Commons in Perspective* (Oxford: Martin Robertson, 1981) pp. 133–7 takes this view. But see also the views expressed in Dermot Englefield (ed.) *Commons Select Committees: Catalysts for Progress* (London: Longman, 1984) *passim*.
6. Richard Norton Taylor, 'Row Over Censored Commons Defence Report', *Guardian* (6 June 1980) p. 4.
7. Norton, op. cit., pp. 217–18.
8. Cabinet–Commons Struggle over defence spending *The Times* (March 1985) p. 1.
9. See Chapter 1, p. 000.
10. Clive Ponting, *The Right to Know* (London : Sphere Books, 1985) *passim*.
11. Similar problems were discovered in relation to defence contracting in Britain in 1985.
12. This is associated with the Norton view of how Parliament should be reformed, but also includes people like George Cunningham (MP) and Jorgen Rasmusen, see: Norton, ibid., pp. 219–35.
13. Ibid., pp. 208–9.
14. Ibid., pp. 209–12.
15. Poole, op. cit., *passim*.
16. S. A. Walkland, 'Wither the Commons?', in Walkland, (ed.), *The Commons in the Seventies* (London: Fontana, 1977) pp. 238–56.

Index